SOCIAL ORDERS AND SOCIAL CLASSES IN EUROPE SINCE 1500

Social Orders and Social Classes in Europe since 1500:

Studies in Social Stratification

Edited by M.L. Bush

LONGMAN
London and New York

Longman Group UK Limited
Longman House, Burnt Mill, Harlow,
Essex CM20 2JE, England
and Associated Companies throughout the world.

*Published in the United States of America
by Longman Inc., New York*

First published 1992

British Library Cataloguing in Publication Data
Social orders and social classes in Europe since
1500: Studies in social stratification.
  I. Bush, M.L.
  305.5094

ISBN 0-582-08344-3
ISBN 0-582-08343-5 pbk

Library of Congress Cataloguing-in-Publication Data
Social orders and social classes in Europe since 1500: studies in
  social stratification/edited by M. L. Bush.
      p.   cm.
    Papers from a conference held in Manchester, Sept. 19–21, 1988,
  and organized by the History Dept. of Manchester University
    Includes bibliographical references and index.
    ISBN 0-582-08344-3 (csd). – ISBN 0-582-08343-5 (ppr)
    1. Social classes – Europe – History – Congresses.   2. Social
  structure – Europe – History – Congresses.   I. Bush, M.L.
  II. University of Manchester. History Dept.
  HN380.Z9S6466   1991
  305.5'094 – dc20   91-2404 CIP

Set in Linotron 202 10/12 Bembo

Produced by Longman Singapore Publishers (Pte) Ltd.
Printed in Singapore

Contents

Contents

Preface

The origins of this book lie in a conference held in Manchester 19–21 September 1988, and organised by the History Department of Manchester University. The purpose of the conference was to take another look at the concepts of order and class and to reconsider their usefulness for stratifying societies and explaining social relationships in early and late modern Europe. Through the medium of such a subject, it was intended to bring together specialists of different periods and countries so that they could participate in the same discussion; and this is what happened. It was left to the speakers to decide how to approach their subject. The outcome was a variety of studies, some comparative, some focused upon a single society. However, because of the way in which the conference was structured, the majority of speakers were obliged to concentrate upon one basic social group: nobility, clergy, the middle classes, the peasantry, the proletariat, the poor. To avoid creating a book which was merely a compilation of conference papers, the speakers were given a year in which to transform their talks into properly referenced, carefully expressed and interrelated chapters.

Thanks are due not only to the conference speakers but also to the following conference participants whose comments on the papers bore influence as the latter came to be reworked into the contents of this book: J.V. Beckett, John Breuilly, Andrew Charlesworth, John Garrard, Peter Gatrell, Sharon Gewirtz, Ralph Gibson, Robbie Gray, Don Hartley, Joanna Innes, Pat Johnson, R. Keys, A.J. Kidd, Keith McClelland, Peter McMylor, D. Nichols, Frank O'Gorman, J.P. Osmond, Vivienne Parrott, Margaret Pelling, Maureen Perrie, Colin Phillips, Iori Prothero, Brian Pullan, David Rheubottom, Patrick Riley, Michael Rose, Valerie Saunders, Timothy Scott, Virginia Smith, David Sturdy, P. Summerfield, Amanda Vickery, James Vernon, Richard Wall, John Walter and Roger Wells.

M.L. Bush
Manchester, June 1990

CHAPTER ONE
The language of orders in early modern Europe

Peter Burke

University of Cambridge

> Une hiérarchie sociale, après tout, est-elle jamais autre chose qu'un
> système de représentations collectives, par nature mobiles? (Marc Bloch)

It was in 1966 and 1967 that two rival conferences on the subject of
social stratification were held in Paris and Saint-Cloud, organised
respectively by Roland Mousnier and Ernest Labrousse. Labrousse
concentrated on orders and classes, Mousnier included castes as well.[1]
However, as in the case of industrialisation, coming later has its
advantages. Today, a discussion on the subject of orders can make
use of some first-rate studies published since 1967, notably Georges
Duby's well-known book *Les Trois Ordres*, particularly interesting on
the political context in which the idea was formulated, and an
important (if less celebrated) study of 'priests warriors and peasants'
by Ottavia Niccoli.[2]

More important still, we can take advantage of a shift in the theory
of social stratification over the last generation, a linguistic turn which
involves taking the creativity of language and metaphor more
seriously than used to be the case. Instead of viewing language as a
mere 'reflection' of social reality, recent sociological and anthropological theory stresses the role of images, models (or 'collective
representations', as Durkheim called them) in constituting the social
order they purport to describe. It is for this reason that any critique
of the concept of 'order' needs to be introduced by some reflections

---

[1] R. Mousnier (ed.) *Problèmes de stratification sociale* (Paris, 1968); E. Labrousse (ed.)
Ordres et classes (Paris, 1973).

[2] G.Duby, *Les Trois Ordres ou l'imaginaire du féodalisme* (Paris, 1978: English trans.,
The Three Orders: Feudal Society Imagined (Chicago, 1980); O. Niccoli, *I sacerdoti, i
guerrieri, i contadini: storia di un'immagine della società* (Turin, 1979).

1

on the history of the concept, and on the intellectual package of which it forms a part.

It may be useful to tell this story backwards. One might begin with a book recently published by Ernest Gellner, *Plough, Sword and Book*, a brilliant discussion of the structure of world history, in terms of the division of labour between production, coercion and cognition. However, like the celebrated Indo-Europeanist the late Georges Dumézil, Gellner is concerned more with the three functions than with the particular social groups who perform them.[3]

Hence a more useful point at which to start may be the work of Roland Mousnier, who has devoted so much of his life to arguing that the old regime in general and France in particular must be seen as a 'society of orders', as distinct from one of classes or castes.[4] This chapter makes a number of criticisms of Mousnier. Today he is in danger of becoming a historiographical villain or, at any rate, an Aunt Sally, so it may be worth saying, before going any further, that Mousnier's argument about orders has had the great virtue of forcing us all to clarify our ideas about old regime society.

Mousnier has two main sources of inspiration: seventeenth-century lawyers, notably Charles Loyseau, and twentieth-century sociologists, notably Bernard Barber (whose study, *Social Stratification*, had itself drawn on Mousnier's work in its brief discussion of 'Estate Society'), but going back behind him to the functionalist school of Talcott Parsons and behind Parsons to Emile Durkheim.[5]

Parsons and his followers accepted the essential contrast between two types of social structure, class society and estate society (*Ständische Gesellschaft*), offered by German sociologists, notably Max Weber and Ferdinand Tönnies, in the years around 1900. In class society, so the theory goes, social opportunities are determined by the market; that is status and power follow wealth. In estate society, on the other hand, wealth and power follow status; social opportunities are

---

[3] E. Gellner, *Plough, Sword and Book* (London, 1988).

[4] The fullest and most explicit discussion is in R. Mousnier, *Les Hiérarchies sociales de 1450 à nos jours* (Paris, 1969: English trans., *Social Hierarchies: 1450 to the Present*, London, 1973).

[5] C. Loyseau, *Traité des Ordres* (Paris, 1610); B. Barber, *Social Stratification* (New York, 1957). The reference to Mousnier's *Vénalité des offices* is on p. 56. Mousnier's debt to Barber is discussed and perhaps over-emphasised in A. Arriaza, 'Mousnier, Barber and the "Society of Orders"', *Past and Present* 89 (1980): 39–57. I would only add that Barber is a declared disciple of Parsons (see *Social Stratification*, p. 16), and that Mousnier makes use of other sociologists such as T.H. Marshall and K. Davis. See R. Mousnier, J.-P. Labatut and Y. Durand (eds) *Deux cahiers de la noblesse* (Paris, 1965), p. 15n.

determined by style of life, social estimation or 'status honour' (*Ständische Ehre*).[6] Unlike classes, *Stände* are communities with legal definitions and legal privileges. Here as elsewhere in Weber's work (the debate over protestantism and capitalism, for example) we can see him reacting to – and to some extent against – the ideas of Marx, in this case not so much turning them on their head as limiting the area in which they apply.

In the German-speaking world, historians such as Otto Hintze and Otto Brunner drew on this sociological theory of estate society decades before Mousnier. Hintze, for example, neatly defined estate society as a society based on the principle of inequality before the law.[7] This domestication of sociology by German historians was all the easier because the sociologists concerned had themselves drawn on an earlier generation of legal and administrative historians. Max Weber was a man of an extraordinarily wide historical culture, concealed by his antipathy towards footnotes. Particularly important for him was the German tradition of legal history, although he adapted this tradition to his own purposes. A name which recurs in Weber's *Economy and Society* is that of Gierke.

It was Otto von Gierke who coined the phrase 'estates constitution' (*Ständische Verfassung*). He thought of estates and corporations in organic terms as moral or legal personalities with their own *Ständesgeist*, in other words *esprit de corps*.[8] Gierke was a leading member of the so-called 'historical school of law', a group whose 'organic' view of society and the state was formulated in conscious reaction against the 'mechanical' and rationalist views which they associated with the Enlightenment, individualism, utilitarianism, political economy and capitalism.[9]

---

[6] M. Weber, *Wirtschaft und Gesellschaft* (Tübingen, 1922: new edn, Tübingen, 1956), pp. 631–40 (English trans., *Economy and Society*, New York, 1968); F. Tönnies, 'Stände und Klassen' (1931) trans. in R. Bendix and S. M. Lipset (eds) *Class, Status and Power* (London, 1954), pp. 49–63.

[7] O. Hintze, 'Typologie der ständische Verfassung' (1930: reprinted in his *Staat und Verfassung* (Göttingen, 1962), pp. 120–39, a discussion clearly indebted to Max Weber. O. Brunner, *Land und Herrschaft* (Baden bei Wien, 1939) uses the term *Ständestaat*, which was also employed at this point by Brunner's fellow-Austrian Dollfuss to characterise his regime. But the term was used in a less value-laden context by Max Weber (e.g. *Economy and Society*, pp. 1,086f).

[8] Gierke's major work was his *Genossenschaftsrecht* (4 vols, 1868–), partially translated as *Natural Law and the Theory of the State* (Cambridge, 1934).

[9] R.M. Berdahl, 'The *Stände* and the origins of conservatism in Prussia', *Eighteenth Century Studies* 6 (1972–3): 298–321, stresses the aristocratic reaction in early-nineteenth-century Prussia as background to the critique of political economy and of capitalism by F.A.L. von Marwitz and Adam Müller. Also see Berdahl, *The Politics of the Prussian Nobility* (Princeton, 1988). On Stein, see W. Isenburg, *Das Staatsdenken des*

In their reaction against these tendencies, the conservatives revived (or better, appropriated and transformed) the social vocabulary of the old regime, notably the idea that society is divided into 'orders' or 'estates' each of which performs a necessary function. A key figure in this reaction was the Prussian Freiherr von Stein. Stein stressed the division of the German people into 'corporations' including the three estates of nobility, citizens and peasants, and argued that 'each estate has its own sense of honour' (*Jeder Stand hatte seine Ehre*).[10]

In early modern Europe, as is well known, the traditional tripartite image of society continued to be employed, despite the fact that the nobility did less and less fighting, while the protestants, from Luther onwards, denied that the clergy formed a separate estate. At the beginning of the period, Dudley's *Tree of Commonwealth*, written *c.*1509, divided the commonwealth into 'clergy, chivalry and commonalty'.[11] At the end of the period, in the year of the French Revolution, the abbé Sieyès devoted a polemical pamphlet to a vindication of the third estate and a critique of the other two.[12] The model was employed in eastern as well as in western Europe. The *Kronika polska* of Stryjkowski (published in 1582) explained the origin of the three estates in terms of division of labour among the sons of Noah. The descendants of Sem pray, the descendants of Japhet fight, and the descendants of Ham work.[13] The image took visual as well as literary forms, such as the early-sixteenth-century German woodcut showing the tree of the estates, peasants at the bottom, pope and kings at the top; or the prints published at the beginning of the French Revolution showing the first and second estates riding on the back of the third.[14]

In the Middle Ages, from the time of King Alfred onwards, it became increasingly common to divide society into those who prayed, fought or worked the land – *orant, pugnant, laborant*.[15] Georges

---

Freiherrs vom Stein (Bonn, 1968), esp. pp. 11f, 17f, 82f. For the wider background, see R.A. Nisbet, *The Sociological Tradition* (New York, 1966), pp. 47f, 174f.

[10] Stein, letter to Arndt, 1818, in his *Briefe*, 5, ed. M. Botzenhart (Stuttgart, 1964), p. 698.

[11] E. Dudley, *Tree of Commonwealth* (Cambridge, 1948), p. 48.

[12] E. Sieyès, *Qu'est-ce que le tiers état?* (1789: ed. R. Zapperi, Geneva, 1970).

[13] Quoted in C. Backvis, 'Individu et société dans la Pologne de la Renaissance', *Individu et société à la Renaissance* (Brussels, 1967), p. 120. See the use of the model by the Polish preacher Piotr Skarga, quoted in S. Ossowski, *Class Structure in the Social Consciousness* (1957: English trans., London, 1963), pp. 58–9.

[14] Hans Weiditz II, *c.*1530: see the forty-six illustrations to Niccoli.

[15] Duby, *The Three Orders*; see E.A.R. Brown, 'Georges Duby and the Three Orders', *Viator* 17 (1986). Earlier studies include R. Mohl, *The Three Estates in Medieval and Renaissance Literature* (New York, 1933).

Duby has described in detail the political and social context of this model, introduced into France in the eleventh century by bishop Adalberon and others. However, the idea that society is divided into three main groups goes back much further in European or even Indo-European history.

In Rome, the term *ordo* meant something like 'social group' and was used to refer to senators, equestrians and plebs. Incidentally, Charles Loyseau was well aware of this fact and his treatise on orders discusses ancient Rome in detail as well as modern France. Behind Rome, we find the Greeks. Plato distinguished philosophers, soldiers and workmen, arguing that each of these groups corresponded to one of our three faculties – reason, anger and appetite. Behind Plato, we find ancient India. In the ancient Indian Laws of Manu, those who pray, the Brahmins, are placed first; those who fight, the Kshatriyas, come next; then come the Vaisyas and Sudras, who engage in trade and husbandry respectively. Four groups (or *varna*) instead of three, but the parallel is clear.[16] We should not forget what the Greeks owed to the culture of ancient India.[17]

We must be careful not to make the tripartite image appear more clear or sharp in the minds of contemporaries than it actually was.

In the first place, the model was normative rather than purely descriptive, at least for some of its users. It was recognised that actual social groupings might conflict with this model, but these anomalies were condemned on occasion: witness the fourteenth-century English sermon in which the preacher declared that 'God made the clergy, knights and labourers, but the devil made the burghers and usurers'.[18] The quotation illustrates not only the hostility to moneylending common among the friars, but also Mary Douglas's well-known generalisation that we perceive whatever does not fit our categories as both dangerous and impure, dirty and diabolical.[19]

In the second place, some Europeans as well as Indians thought in fours. The Swedish *riksdag*, for example, was divided into four estates, with representatives of the peasants as well as the townsmen sitting alongside the two privileged orders. The phrase 'fourth estate' is no

---

[16] See Mousnier, *Hiérarchies*, p. 19, omitting the Sudras.

[17] It is of course the late G. Dumézil who insisted most on this parallel and on the tripartite image generally, passing over the inconvenient division into four groups.

[18] Quoted in G.R. Owst, *Preaching in Medieval England* (Cambridge, 1933), p. 553.

[19] M. Douglas, *Purity and Danger* (London, 1966). Here and elsewhere I must express my dissent from the views of L. Dumont, *Homo hierarchicus* (1966; English trans., London, 1972), who identifies the contrast between hierarchical and egalitarian societies with that between east and west.

recent coinage. The idea of the workers as a fourth estate goes back to Lassalle in the mid-nineteenth century; the idea of the press as a fourth estate to the end of the eighteenth century, to Edmund Burke.[20] However, the phrase was not infrequently used about the *noblesse de robe* in France in the later sixteenth century (by Montaigne among others).[21]

Lawyers appear as a fourth estate in the French woodcut of the eighteenth century, the *Quatre verités*, which represents a priest, a soldier, a peasant and a lawyer. The priest says, 'je prie pour vous tous'. The soldier (not a knight), 'je vous défends tous'. The peasant, 'je vous nourris tous'. The lawyer, 'je vous mange tous'.[22] We should probably read the image in two complementary ways (like the medieval sermon already quoted). Not only is it an expression of popular hostility to lawyers, but also it suggests that the attempt to adapt the image of the three estates in this way is illegitimate. In a similar manner, Fielding mocked the 'mob' as the fourth estate of the realm.

In the third place, some writers blurred the clarity of the three estates by introducing subdivisions. To take two seventeenth-century French examples. Loyseau notes that the third estate (*tiers état*) has its own 'ordres ou degrez' from *gens de lettres* and *advocats* down to *marchands* and *artisans*.[23] In similar fashion his contemporary, the political economist Antoine de Montchrestien, described the third estate (*tiers ordre*) as 'composé de trois sorts d'hommes, Laboureurs, Artisans et Marchands' and went on to relate these three groups (and not, like Plato, the workmen, soldiers and philosophers) to three kinds of soul, vegetative, sensitive and intellectual.[24] Later in the century another political economist, Johann Joachim Becher, would describe the entire three estates in similar terms as the *Bauernstand, Handwerkstand* and *Kaufmannstand*.[25] By the early eighteenth century, we can find a division into *Adelstand, Burgerstand* and *Bauerstand* (the language later used by Stein).[26]

---

[20] *OED*, E, p. 300.

[21] Montaigne, *Essais* 1. 23; also see J. Russell Major, *Representative Institutions in Renaissance France* (Madison, 1960), pp. 136f, 144f.

[22] Niccoli, *Sacerdoti*, pp. 125f.

[23] C. Loyseau, *Traité des ordres et simples dignitez* (1610; Paris, 1613 edn), pp. 93f.

[24] A. Montchrestien, *Oeconomie Politique* (Paris, 1615), pp. 12f. The distinction into three kinds of soul is of course taken from Aristotle. The title of the treatise is an early example (if not the first) of the phrase 'political economy'.

[25] J.J. Becher, *Politische Discurs* (Frankfurt, 1668) part 2, ch. 1.

[26] *Gedanken von dem Ursprung und Unterscheid des Adelichen, Burger und Bauer-Standes in Deutschland* (Cologne, 1710).

Finally, some medieval and early modern writers employed models of society completely different from that of the traditional three orders. Some of them used the term 'estate' (in Latin, *status*) to refer to a multiplicity of different social roles, including different crafts and professions and even married and single people.[27] Others, especially in the cities of northern Italy, abandoned the language of orders altogether and divided society into two or three groups according to their wealth, contrasting *popolo grasso* and *popolo minuto*, or using terms such as *ricchi, grandi, mediocri*, and *infimi* or *plebe*.[28] In similar fashion Sancho Panza's grandmother divided society with brutal simplicity into two groups, the haves and the have-nots, *el tener y el no tener*.

In the Dutch Republic in the seventeenth century, since many of the nobility had emigrated and the Calvinist preachers, unlike Catholic priests, were not considered to be a separate estate, the way was clear for a classification of society essentially according to wealth, in tax classes.[29] Spinoza, incidentally, used the term 'class' to refer to a social group, and Sir William Temple divided 'the People of Holland' into five 'classes' (peasants, seamen, merchants, rentiers and gentlemen).[30] The French adopted the system of fiscal classes in 1695 and this administrative change affected social thought in the eighteenth century.[31] In all these cases the parallels with the nineteenth- and twentieth-century language of class, ordinary language rather than Marxist analysis, will be obvious enough.

I turn at last to a discussion of the utility of the concept or model of the three orders for historians today when studying the society of early modern Europe. I shall not be talking about a 'crisis' in the concept of orders, as Professor Reddy has done in the case of classes. I shall not be pleading for its abolition. What I propose to do is to discuss its intellectual costs and benefits, prefacing this discussion with a few remarks on historical method in the form of an attack on three idols of the tribe of historians.

[27] S. de Arevalo, *Speculum vitae humanae* (Rome, 1948); J. Ammann and H. Sachs, *Eigentliche Beschreibung aller Stände auf Erden* (1568; English trans., New York, 1973).

[28] On Florence, F. Gilbert, *Machiavelli and Guicciardini* (Princeton, 1965), pp. 23f. Also see S.K. Cohn, *The Labouring Classes in Renaissance Florence* (New York, 1978), and J. Delumeau, 'Mobilité sociale: riches et pauvres à l'époque de la Renaissance' in Labrousse, pp. 125–34.

[29] I. Schöffer, in *Problèmes* (1968), p. 121. Also see P. Burke, *Venice and Amsterdam* (London, 1974), pp. 19f.

[30] Ossowski, *Class Structure*, p. 122; W. Temple, *Observations upon the United Provinces of the Netherlands* (1673; ed. G.N. Clark, Cambridge, 1932), p. 97.

[31] J.-C. Perrot, 'Rapports sociaux et villes au 18e siècle', in Labrousse, pp. 141–63.

7

The first is the idol of empiricism. In a debate in *Past and Present* a few years ago about models of the social structure of early modern England, one contributor suggested that we give up models altogether.[32] However, it is impossible to talk or think about social structures without models and metaphors. The very phrase 'social structure' is a metaphor. It is virtually impossible to do without spatial metaphors when talking about society; about 'social mobility' or 'social climbing', looking 'up' to some people and 'down' on others. We use this sort of language all the time in our own society; early modern people did the same in theirs. More generally, we should recognise that models are not something exotic invented by so-called 'social scientists'. We all use models, just as we speak prose, whether we are aware of this or not. The question at issue is therefore not whether to use models, but which models to use.

The second idol might be called the 'idol of legalism', in other words, assuming (as Mousnier too often does) that people in early modern Europe behaved in the way that the laws and the treatises on the social order (generally written by lawyers) declared that they should behave. To say this is not to deny that law (and other kinds of theory) have social consequences (making nobles a tax-free group, allowing them a virtual monopoly of offices in the army, and so on). It is to assert that social behaviour cannot be explained by the law alone.

The third idol is the idol of synchronism, by which I mean the argument or assumption that in order to avoid anachronism, historians have to accept, take over and incorporate into their account of a given society the model of it offered by contemporaries, the 'folk model' as it is sometimes called (actually I would prefer the term 'insiders' model).[33] This is the basic argument employed by Mousnier against Porchnev, Mandrou and others who talk about 'classes' in early modern Europe.[34] Since I have been stressing the point that language creates the social reality it purports to describe, you may think that for consistency's sake I should agree with Mousnier. However, I reject this argument for a number of reasons.

[32] W. Speck, 'Social status in late Stuart England', *Past and Present* 34 (1966): 127–9 (replying to L. Stone's article in the previous issue).

[33] L. Holy and M. Stuchlik (eds) *The Structure of Folk Models* (London, 1981), esp. the editors' introduction.

[34] B. Porchnev, *Les Soulèvements populaires en France de 1623 à 1648* (1948; French trans., Paris, 1963); R. Mandrou, *Classes et luttes des classes en France au début du 17e siècle* (Messina and Florence, 1965); D. Parker, 'Class, clientage and personal rule in Absolutist France', *Seventeenth-Century French Studies* 9 (1986): 192–213.

One reason is that contemporaries disagree with one another. Early modern writers did not agree over the number of orders. Those who thought there were three orders sometimes identified them differently, excluding the clergy, dividing the third estate and so on, while others used a totally different language, much closer to the language of class. Phrases like 'classes of estates' can be found in eighteenth-century writers from Moser to Marat. The ambiguity of the German term *Stände* in particular, which means (according to context) 'assembly', 'orders' or 'status groups', makes it a dangerous weapon in the hands of modern historians.

In any case, we need to remind ourselves that contemporaries were not describing their social structure for the benefit of future historians but for their own purposes, which were not infrequently political. The idea of the three orders is part of an intellectual package, which is in turn part of a political tradition. This is clear enough in Mousnier himself; his conservative critique of the modern world goes with a nostalgia for the early modern period which he sees as a time of social harmony. A similar point might be made about the Freiherr von Stein, *c.*1800, who was fighting on two fronts against what he believed to be the twin evils of absolutism and democracy, the two great levellers.

Stein had probably studied Montesquieu at the university of Göttingen.[35] In any case, the ideas of the two men are similar in a crucial respect, their concern with orders as intermediary powers between the ruler and the people.[36] When he was preparing his book on law, Montesquieu studied the work of his fellow-magistrate Charles Loyseau.[37] As for Loyseau, he was not simply describing French society in his time, as Mousnier seems to think. He saw that society from the standpoint of a member of the *noblesse de robe*, and he was concerned to present its social position as an elevated one. In addition, as was recently pointed out, Loyseau has a political theory of his own.[38]

In the course of time, the model of the three orders has become associated with the idea of the *Ständestaat*: with the argument of Montesquieu, Tocqueville and others that liberty and equality are incompatible, that privilege sustains freedom, and that democracy is

[35] Isenburg, p. 86, noting that Stein went to the lectures of Schlözer who was interested in Montesquieu.
[36] Montesquieu, *Esprit des lois* (Paris, 1744), esp. 2.4, 5.11.
[37] E. Shackleton, *Montesquieu* (Oxford, 1961), p. 241.
[38] H.A. Lloyd, 'The political theory of Charles Loyseau', *European Studies Review* 11 (1981): 53–76.

close to despotism.[39] It has also become associated with two binary oppositions. The first opposition contrasts the west and the rest, occidental liberty with oriental despotism, drawing attention to the importance of legal corporations in European history (towns, guilds, and representative assemblies made up of the three estates) and claiming that thanks to these corporations 'we' have enjoyed a liberty which 'they' have lacked.[40] The second opposition or contrast is that between the 'classes' of industrial society and the social 'orders' which existed before the French and industrial revolutions.

The orders model has become associated with a view of society as essentially harmonious, minimising conflict; the 'Durkheimian' model it is often called. The class model has become associated with a view of society as essentially conflictual, minimising solidarity: the Marxian model. There are important insights embodied in both models, but the danger of oversimplification is obvious.

Of course we do not have to accept these intellectual packages. We can use the term 'orders' for our convenience, elaborating it into an analytical model of a kind rather different from the folk model employed by contemporaries. However, we have to be on our guard not to accept more than we intended. We have to look out for what might be called the 'false friend'. It is at once a strength and a weakness of the analytical models of orders and classes that they use the language of insiders; we are using traditional terms but giving them modern meanings. The weakness is that we tend to forget that such terms as 'humanism' and 'absolutism' did not exist in the Renaissance or the age of Louis XIV, while the words *humanista* and *absolu* had rather more limited meanings. Even concepts like 'religion' and 'magic' have changed their meaning over the centuries.[41] This is also the case for 'order' and 'class'.

These reflections have been rather negative. To conclude, I shall try to be more constructive. I imagine that we all agree that a central task for social historians is to describe and analyse both social solidarities and social conflicts in the past. To do this we have to reconstruct social identities. In order to reconstruct these identities, historians

---

[39] A. de Tocqueville, *L'Ancien régime et la révolution* (1856: new edn, Paris, 1952), esp. Book 2, ch. 10.

[40] Along Weberian lines, O. Hintze emphasised the uniqueness of the western system of representative assemblies in his *Historical Essays* (ed. F. Gilbert, New York, 1975), p. 308.

[41] The dangers of false friends are underlined in a review of Keith Thomas's *Religion and the Decline of Magic* by the anthropologist Hildred Geertz in *Journal of Interdisciplinary History* 6 (1975): 71–89.

need to make a careful study of what is sometimes called the 'social vocabulary' of a given society, including the language of class and the language of orders.[42] This has to be done in order to recover the insiders' models of society, the 'blueprints' without which their actions will remain unintelligible.[43]

When we examine the social vocabulary in detail, we need to remember that we are not (*pace* Mousnier) reading objective accounts of the social hierarchy. This hierarchy looks very different according to one's place in it. We tend to think of Brahmins as the summit of the social hierarchy of traditional India. This was a claim they made, and it has tended to be accepted because it was the Brahmins who produced the best-known texts describing the social order. However, research on a specific region and period, Nepal in the eighteenth century, has shown that kings and ascetics also claimed to be at the social summit.[44] Again, the duc de Saint-Simon has sometimes been criticised for describing Colbert and other robe ministers of Louis XIV as 'bourgeois'. From a legal point of view he was of course inaccurate and he may have been deliberately malicious into the bargain. However, we should also consider the possibility that from a duke's point of view, the difference between a bourgeois and a *robin* may not have been all that important. Similarly, the differences between marquesses and dukes probably meant little to craftsmen and peasants.

A close analysis of social vocabulary is necessary but not sufficient to the understanding of a given social hierarchy. We need to reconstruct collective identities, forms of social consciousness. Historians of class have written a great deal about the problem of consciousness; historians of orders, rather too little. It would be interesting to see a study of clerical consciousness in the old regime or the Middle Ages; some medieval chronicles seem to express anti-lay attitudes, the inverse of the better known anticlericalism of modern times.

Noble consciousness has been rather better studied, including what it might be useful to call noble 'racism', the myth of a specially pure noble 'blood', or of noble descent from a different ethnic group from ordinary people, the Franks rather than the Gauls, or the sons of

---

[42] J. Batany, P. Contamine, B. Guénée and J. Le Goff, 'Plan pour l'étude historique du vocabulaire social de l'Occident médiéval', in Labrousse, pp. 87–92; W.H. Sewell, 'Etat, corps and ordre: some notes on the social vocabulary of the French old regime', in H.-U. Wehler (ed.) *Sozialgeschichte Heute* (Göttingen, 1974), pp. 49–66.

[43] Holy and Stuchlik, *Structure of Folk Models*.

[44] R. Burghart, 'Hierarchical models of the Hindu social system', *Man* 13 (1978): 519–36.

Japhet rather than the sons of Ham.[45] All the same, it is far from clear what noble consciousness meant in practice, the extent to which great magnates (in Poland, for example) felt solidarity with the numerous and poor *szlachta*, as well as the other way round. As for the third estate, their consciousness is the most problematic of all, like the class consciousness of the peasantry, described by Teodor Shanin in a famous phrase as 'a social entity of comparatively low "classness"'.[46]

We also need to be able to compare and contrast social hierarchies, and to describe changes over the long term. In order to do this we need to employ analytical models. Since insiders were not normally concerned with these contrasts and changes, we need outsiders' models, of which the best known are those of orders and classes in their different varieties. We should not expect too much from these models. They are simplifications by definition. They can never be 'correct', in the sense of corresponding to objective social reality, because there is no objective social reality to describe; the social world is constructed by social actors who see it differently. Models cannot aspire to be more than useful. Different models may have their uses for the analysis of the same society, and it is worth looking at early modern Europe both as a system of classes and as a system of orders.

If, finally, I have to choose, I would say that the orders model is probably the least misleading, provided we can liberate the model from its intellectual packaging. Like democracy, it seems despite all its faults to be the least dangerous solution to our problems. It is always possible to throw away both models and find a third. If a third model is offered, however, we must be careful not to expect too much from it. It will necessarily simplify, it will reveal some aspects of society at the price of obscuring others. The problems I have been discussing are inherent in the enterprise of writing social history.

[45] See e.g. A. Devyver, *Le Sang épuré* (Brussels, 1973), and A. Jouanna, *Ordre social* (Paris, 1977).

[46] T. Shanin (ed.) *Peasants and Peasant Societies* (London, 1984), p. 253.

CHAPTER TWO
The concept of class

William M. Reddy
Duke University

The concept of class has never been used with great precision by
historians, and for good reason: most historians have recognised that
it is impossible to be precise about class boundaries or class membership without violating the complexities and subtleties of social
relationships. The concept of class is in this respect no different from
other elements of the common vocabulary of social description. It
would be futile to attempt to define with precision the boundaries of,
say, German 'society' in 1848, as it would be to delimit exactly a
bureaucratic 'stratum' in the bewildering edifice of French government under the old regime, or to say exactly who was or was not a
member of 'Grub Street' in early-nineteenth-century London. None
the less, that these and other imprecise terms of social analysis – class
among them – still refer to something real seems indisputable. To
raise the question, therefore, whether the concept of class has outlived
its usefulness, might seem at first glance to be an act of folly. Just
because of its imprecision, its inherently approximate character, and
the ease with which it has long lent itself to innumerable uses in a
wide variety of arguments, it seems unassailable. To attack the
concept of class would appear to be roughly like trying to hit the
wind with a stick. This has been a common reaction to the argument
which I made in my *Money and Liberty in Modern Europe* that the
concept of class was indeed in crisis and that it was time to replace it
with something better.[1]

We use the word class and its subordinate terminology (e.g.

[1] W.M. Reddy, *Money and Liberty in Modern Europe: A Critique of Historical
Understanding* (New York, 1987).

peasantry, working class, bourgeoisie, aristocracy, *petite bourgeoisie*, and so on) because they offer us bundles of associations. Each term has a history of attempted definitions and applications, a literature of specialist studies, and an essential role to play in the conveniently simplified paradigms of long-term social change. In any given context of analysis, their use seems unambiguous and straightforward for large numbers of historical individuals. At the same time, among the bundles of associations evoked by these terms subsist long-standing tensions and potential contradictions which can shift or grow over time.

J.C.D. Clark, in his recent iconoclastic synthesis, *Revolution and Rebellion*, for example, echoes a complaint made by J.H. Hexter over thirty years ago. In 'A new framework for social history', Hexter decried the received canons of interpretation of social change as follows:

> The gratuitous assumption is that the total history of all the major processes of change – economic, social, political, religious, intellectual – for the whole millenium [1000 AD to the present] can be explained in terms of the ceaseless conflict of the two classes, the landed class and the business class, a conflict marked by the gradual, irregular, but uninterrupted decline of the former, and the contrapuntal, uninterrupted, irregular, but gradual rise of the latter.[2]

Clark, at the beginning of his 1986 essay, cites a long passage from Lawrence Stone's *The Causes of the English Revolution, 1529–1642*, but in Clark's citation all clues to the identity of the century in question have been removed. The passage speaks of 'a growing body of men of substance, rich property owners, professionals and merchants'. The citation continues:

> These men were the leading figures among the county squirearchy, the successful London lawyers, the more eminent [word deleted by Clark] divines, and the urban patriciates that dominated the cities [and they] were steadily enlarging their numbers, their social and economic weight, and their political influence.[3]

Clark's objection to this passage, that the language could as easily be applied to the eighteenth as to the seventeenth centuries (or indeed, with only minor alterations, to the nineteenth), is making essentially the same point as Hexter's. In spite of all the increased knowledge,

---

[2] Reprinted in *Reappraisals in History: New Views on History and Society in Early Modern Europe* (2nd edn, Chicago, 1979), this quote from pp. 15–16.

[3] Quoted by J.C.D. Clark, *Revolution and Rebellion: State and Society in England in the Seventeenth and Eighteenth Centuries* (Cambridge, 1986), p. 24.

and the greater sophistication of the language with which conclusions are hedged about, there is a continuity in the underlying class concept that is being deployed. There is also, I would contend, an increasing unease about this concept, and Clark's essay is a symptom of it. Whether this unease warrants the use of the term 'crisis' may be disputed. But there can be little doubt that the gradually accumulating body of social historical research has contributed to the rise of this unease.

An even sharper sense of disquiet over the received vocabulary of class has arisen among researchers working on the origins of the French Revolution. When William Doyle published in 1980 his sweeping overview of thirty years of post-war research, *Origins of the French Revolution*, he painted a picture of the gradual but inexorable decline of a reigning paradigm that had achieved a pinnacle of clarity and vigour in Georges Lefebvre's *The Coming of the French Revolution*, first published in 1939.[4] Where Lefebvre had convinced a whole generation of historians to see a stalwart, self-conscious bourgeoisie marching forward to overthrow feudalism, subsequent research had found that the bourgeoisie was all but indistinguishable from the nobility, aspiring to the same way of life, enjoying the same types (if not the whole range) of privileges, managing the same forms of wealth in the same conservative manner. What capitalists there were played no role in the Revolution; the overthrow of 'feudalism' such as it was, was forced on a reluctant National Assembly by peasant uprisings.[5] The whole edifice of Lefebvre's synthesis was in shambles. Doyle himself pointed out the many happenstances involved in the Revolution's outbreak and, when it came to identifying the 'classes' who took part in it, Doyle did so only with the greatest circumspection. They were, he suggested, coalitions of the moment, called into existence by the astonishing power vacuum created by the collapse of monarchical government.

Eight years later, on issuing a second edition of this overview, Doyle states that he has found no need to make major revisions in his exposition; eight years of continued, vigorous research and discussion have yielded little progress in the strategies for conceptualising social classes in the old regime. The revisionist critique has achieved wider acceptance (as well as efforts to integrate its findings into a new

[4] G. Lefebvre, *Quatre-vingt-neuf* (London, 1939), trans. R.R. Palmer as *The Coming of the French Revolution* (London, 1974); W. Doyle, *Origins of the French Revolution* (Oxford, 1980; 2nd edn, 1988). References are to the 2nd edn.

[5] Doyle, *Origins*, pp. 202–3.

Marxist view of the Revolution).[6] But wider acceptance seems like a very small result in view of the fact that the revisionists have no explanation for the outbreak of the French Revolution. Or rather, they have too many explanations, which amounts to the same thing. The crisis of the class concept seems in this field of research to be lengthening in a manner reminiscent of the course of the Revolution itself: from virtuous Terror fading into fence-sitting Thermidor, and from Thermidor to drifting Directory, without any of the fundamental problems being solved.

One way of exploring some of the ongoing tensions tugging at the bundle of associations historians link to the term class, is to admit, for purposes of argument, E.P. Thompson's insistence that class be seen, not as a group of individuals, but as a relationship. Let us accept that class is essentially a relationship, that classes do not exist by themselves, but come into existence only when human beings enter into vital relationships with each other to produce and distribute resources and to control the application of coercion.

This is a classic definition with a long history. Marx used the term class in this way, for he saw class as fundamentally a relation to the means of production (that is to other persons). But this is not the only way he used the term. In Marx's political narratives, such as the *Eighteenth Brumaire*, class is not treated as a precise, analysable relation to the means of production, instead classes appear as collective actors who exist on their own and struggle for dominance on the stage of history. But the effect of recent research has been to sharpen and refine our awareness of class as relationship to such an extent that we must put into question the notion that classes can be neatly identified with national-level political factions or movements. This is precisely how the revisionist research into the origins of the French Revolution has proceeded, for example. Lefebvre's whole synthesis rested on a convenient elision of the differences between class and order, first of all, and second on an equation of order and political faction that he borrowed uncritically from the polemicists of the time. (Pamphleteers first raised the banner of the Third Estate in the autumn of 1788, calling for a righteous struggle against the pretensions of the other two. Lefebvre's narrative strategy consisted of substituting the word 'bourgeoisie' for 'Third Estate' and replicating the pamphleteers' analysis of the situation with only minor alterations.) Revisionists ironically have outdone the Marxists in their attentiveness to relations

[6] See G.C. Comninel, *Rethinking the French Revolution: Marxism and the Revisionist Challenge* (London, 1987).

to the means of production, and have thereby been able to cast doubt on the validity of equating the patriot party with the 'bourgeoisie' or the Assembly of Notables with the 'nobility'. By emphasising that non-nobles enjoyed extensive privileges, that many nobles were impoverished, that noble and commoner alike depended overwhelmingly on land and venal office, revisionists have shown that distinctions between the first, second, and third estates no longer corresponded (if they ever did) to significant differences in the relation to the means of production. To say nothing of their efforts to problematise the relation between class and order, the revisionists have thus forced us to recognise that class as relationship and class as faction may be two incommensurable notions.

A rough catalogue of the difficulties that the notion of 'class as relationship' has posed for thinking in terms of 'class as faction' is as follows.

First, classes cannot rise or fall. The moment a class significantly increases its power, for example, this increase constitutes a fundamental change in its relationships. It is therefore a new class. Classes might grow or decrease in number, to a limited degree, without becoming a new class, but even mere increase or decrease in size will, sooner or later, result in the alteration of the defining relationship. This is the kind of problem presented by, for example, the Prussian Junker class, many of whom, in the course of the eighteenth century, benefited directly from the rising price of grain on the international market. At mid-century, the government offered them a system of mortgage guarantees, a speculative boom in land prices resulted. The Junkers fundamentally altered their relationships to creditors, to serfs, to grain merchants, to the state. These changes were a necessary prelude to the liberation of the serfs after 1807: that is; these subtle changes cumulatively made the Junkers prepared to acquiesce in the complete transformation of the serf class into a free class of mostly landless labourers.[7] A conventional approach to this story might be to say that the Junker class was rising in power and wealth up until Prussia's defeat at the hands of Napoleon, when political conditions forced them to relinquish extensive powers over the serfs. But in terms of changes in relationships, these developments represent a smooth evolution that was in the end transforming. The question might be asked: are Junkers without serfs the 'same' class as Junkers with serfs?

[7] A good introduction to the literature is H. Schissler, *Preussische Agrargesellschaft im Wandel: Wirtschaftliche, gesellschaftliche und politische Transformationsprozesse von 1763 bis 1847* (Göttingen, 1978).

Second, no individual can be assigned definitively to a single class. Because relationships are not necessarily exclusive and permanent, indeed, because class relationships often turn on the way (legal or illegal) in which they can be terminated or occur only seasonally or affect people only from certain age groups, it is impossible to say that such-and-such an individual is 'in' or 'of' such-and-such a class. Individuals are not relationships, nor are they merely parts of relationships. Not only may an individual's class relationships change over time, but also they may be such as to put the individual in more than one class at a time. Patrick Joyce gives evidence, for example, that many Lancashire mill-owners of the nineteenth century found their origins in or had important links to the lesser gentry. Certainly there were some we would want to call gentry and industrial capitalist at once.[8] Jacques Rancière, in his important essay, 'The myth of the artisan', forcefully argued that many key figures in the French labour movement of the 1830s and 1840s, who preached the dignity of work and the ennobling character of skill, were part-time journalists, would-be secretaries, novelists, even landlords, with one foot in the world of the artisan and another, however hopefully or tentatively, in that of a *petite bourgeoisie* or, if one prefers, an intellectual lumpenproletariat.[9] Olwen Hufton has described with compelling detail the 'economy of makeshift' of the eighteenth-century poor, who sought to make ends meet by an endless variety of means.[10] Smallholders in marginal areas spent many months each year migrating to engage in wage labour in cities or richer agricultural areas – were they workers or peasants? Individual women might in the course of a single week work as market gardeners, stall operators and peddlers (self-employed *'petit commerce'* activities), as spinners (wage labour), and as principal caretakers of the family plot (peasant self-exploitation). Class as a relationship is not a label that can sum up the social identity of an individual.

Third, class may generate community but cannot include community. In so far as a number of people share a common position within a class relationship (as miners, for example, who are all wage labourers for a group of mining firms), they may seek each other out

---

[8] P. Joyce, *Work, Society, and Politics: The Culture of the Factory in Later Victorian England* (Brighton, 1980), p. 20.

[9] J. Rancière, 'The myth of the artisan: critical reflections on a category of social history', in S.L. Kaplan and C.J. Koepp (eds) *Work in France: Representations, Meaning, Organization, and Practice* (Ithaca, 1986), pp. 317–34.

[10] O. Hufton, *The Poor in Eighteenth-Century France, 1750–1789* (Oxford, 1974), pp. 69–127.

and form relationships among themselves. But these new mutual relationships may easily take on a character similar to class relationships, may become class relationships. When Zola, in *Germinal* for example, depicted the principal leader of the miners as a barkeeper, he was transmitting only what he had seen and heard on his own visit to the Anzin mining region, where the strike which inspired the novel occurred in 1884. In most European countries in the nineteenth century, leaders of working-class resistance were unable to remain employed after their role became known. Not only was barkeeping a common expedient that kept them close to their comrades, but also it created a new kind of commercial relationship with them. My own work on the Lille region has shown that labourers who were out of work for whatever reason frequently resorted to providing their former co-workers with commercial services. These services were in fact essential to the working-class community's way of life and its ongoing sense of identity.[11] As working-class communities grew in size and self-consciousness in the nineteenth century, they necessarily also grew in complexity, generating institutions such as unions and union halls, singing clubs, newspapers, political parties, national union federations – each staffed by people who were no longer wage labourers and whose relationships to wage labourers constituted their 'relation to the means of production'. Class, as relationship, can give rise to community. But if a class community achieves significant size or complexity it will inevitably begin to generate class relationships within it, which become essential to its organisation and its survival.[12]

Fourthly, it is difficult to distinguish class relationships from other kinds of relationships. This problem has been most conspicuous recently in the discussions of the connection (or lack thereof) between class and gender. At one extreme, there is G.E.M. de Ste Croix, who would put all women of the ancient world into a class by themselves (he does the same for slaves) – with evident impatience for those who might object that this is too peremptory a manner of applying the

[11] W.M. Reddy, *The Rise of Market Culture: The Textile Trade and French Society, 1750–1900* (New York, 1984), esp. pp. 253–325.

[12] This is not far from the point which Craig Calhoun was attempting to explore in *The Question of Class Struggle: Social Foundations of Popular Radicalism during the Industrial Revolution* (Chicago, 1982). Although his distinction between the communities formed by artisans in traditional trades and those formed by factory workers seems unacceptable, none the less he is at least concerned to raise the issue whether kinds of relationships that held working people together and made protest possible were not so diverse as to force us to reject a single class label for them all.

term.[13] At the other extreme lies a theorist like Carole Pateman, whose critique of the Lockean social-contract tradition is based on the contention that prior to any arrangement for the establishment of civil society there exists a social contract between the sexes that implicitly ratifies men's leading role in civil society.[14] Thus gender difference is prior to all the relationships associated with modern social classes. Joan Scott would appear to be holding a middle ground, insisting that class cannot be understood apart from gender, and vice versa.[15] While gender is an obvious difficulty in the definition of class relationships, difficulties arise elsewhere as well. If class is a relationship, not all relationships can be class relationships. Yet, however one defines the scope of specifically class relationships, it will be possible to find important instances of relationships which both do and do not belong. A noteworthy example is John Foster's willingness to cite Lancashire spinners' use of their own children as piecers in the late nineteenth century as an element of workplace stratification that lifted the spinners into a labour aristocracy.[16] Here the class relation becomes an intra-family affair, as it does in two recent studies of German villages in the early modern era, where research shows that marriage and inheritance practices made possible consolidation of holdings in a period of demographic expansion. Some children and grandchildren fell away into a marginal status as landless or near landless labourers, others of the same family inherited the farm and its security.[17]

Fifth, class is not a good instrument for identifying the underlying motivations of national-level political factions, parties or movements. The difficulties researchers have had trying to identify the class origins of the Puritan Rebellion or the French Revolution or the Nazi party are remarkably similar in nature. Rebellions, parties and movements on a grand scale cannot exist without organisers and organised, communicators and listeners, leaders and followers. These

---

[13] G.E.M. de Ste Croix, *Class Struggle in the Ancient Greek World from the Archaic Age to the Arab Conquests* (Ithaca, 1981), pp. 98–103.

[14] C. Pateman, *The Sexual Contract* (Stanford, 1988).

[15] J.W. Scott, *Gender and the Politics of History* (New York, 1988), especially chs 2 and 3.

[16] J. Foster, *Class Struggle and the Industrial Revolution: Early Industrial Capitalism in Three English Towns* (London, 1974); Joyce offers a critique of Foster's interpretation in *Work, Society, and Politics*, pp. 50–89.

[17] D. Sabean, *Property, Production and Family in Neckarhausen, 1700–1870* (Cambridge, 1991); T. Robisheaux, *Rural Society and the Search for Order in Early Modern Germany* (Cambridge, 1989). See also H. Rebel, *Peasant Classes: the Bureaucratization of Property and Family Relations Under Early Habsburg Absolutism, 1511–1636* (Princeton, 1983).

relationships alter the social identities of the vanguard group; it is hardly appropriate to think of the Hitler of 1933 as an impoverished artist, or the Robespierre of 1793 as a struggling provincial lawyer. Moreover such movements cannot exist unless they bind together a network of communities. Even if the communities bound together in a specific movement were all of one class, which historically has been the exception rather than the rule, the mere organisation of a coherent movement will bring with it the beginnings of class distinctions within these communities. Even those who claim that some twentieth-century revolutions have been carried out by genuine class movements, must admit that the subsequent histories of countries like Russia and China confirm the importance of the germination of new class relationships within class communities or class movements.

Furthermore, national movements seldom depend on a single class for the simple reason that single classes are small. Whenever one looks closely at a large group, such as the Russian peasantry in 1860 or London artisans in 1820, one discovers bewildering diversity. If one defines the class relationship with even a modicum of precision, it quickly falls out that such groups must be subdivided. Any one class is only a small minority of society. But if one defines class loosely, then it appears that, not specific grievances, but only a generalized contention over world views, fundamental values, or transcendent issues can engage the loyalties and enthusiasm of such diverse constituencies. Only the loosest of definitions of 'bourgeoisie', for example, can encompass all the revolutionary forces that combined to produce the Declaration of Rights of Man and Citizen in 1789, just as only the loosest definition of 'working class' can hold together all those who fought for Chartism between 1838 and 1848. By the same token the goals which these forces combined to fight for were couched in the most abstract terms, and promised definite material advantages to no one. Necessarily, many must have been moved by idealistic and altruistic allegiances that only loosely derived from their specific current life experiences. If the future promises a simplifying trend in social structures that will some day make the organisation of class-based movements easier and neater, there is to date no sign of this on the horizon. Quite the opposite. If one were to take simply a strict definition of 'proletariat' and look across the globe today, one would find an awesome diversity of fates summed up in that word.

What these five disturbing consequences of treating class as a relationship add up to is that class as relationship can be a useful, even vital instrument of analysis. However, a strict construction of the notion of class as relationship has a damaging effect on the standard subsidiary vocabulary of class. Moreover, since they offer of themselves no precise information about the class relationships in question, the usual class labels must be considered blunt instruments, bulls in the china shops of our research findings.

To say that a bourgeoisie existed at such-and-such a time is not objectionable. This bourgeoisie can easily be defined by means of a bundle of attributes (that is, of relationships) that characterise a cluster of individuals or families. Jean-Pierre Chaline makes an excellent job of this kind of analysis in his recent work *Les Bourgeois de Rouen*, in which a large cluster of families, identified by statistical means, were found to possess similar levels of income and kinds of wealth, to have residences with similar floor plans, and to engage in similar styles of consumption and sociability.[18] But a great distance exists between defining a bourgeoisie in a manner consistent with evidence from a number of different sources, as Chaline has done, and making some such statement as 'the bourgeoisie defended its interests'. It would appear that classes cannot be collective actors. They therefore cannot be brought on to the stage as protagonists of a political narrative. Individuals who have in common a similar relationship to some other group of individuals (but who cannot be defined by this relationship, as we noted above) will not act collectively to defend interests which they share as such, unless they in turn build a set of new relationships that somehow link them together. This building process, the historical record shows, is a potent transformative force, as likely to create new groups, even new ruling classes when it goes far enough, as is any other development of a new type of relationship. Therefore, the standard class labels that we all find indispensable (at least from time to time) are *faux amis* when used to explain social change or social conflict. They are too imprecise when it comes to distinguishing the vital elements of specific class relationships; and when used to name the supporters of factions or movements they oversimplify. They may easily misrepresent the broad, altruistic appeals that are usually necessary to motivate a significant number of followers, and obscure the all-important internal articulation of relationships that makes collective action possible. But if we abandon these subsidiary terms, as I think we must, as devices to explain conflict and change, what is left of the concept of class as it was developed in classic socio-political narratives such as the work of Lefebvre for France, or those of

---

[18] J.-P. Chaline, *Les Bourgeois de Rouen: une élite urbaine au XIXe siècle* (Paris, 1982).

Christopher Hill for England, or Rudolf Stadelmann for Germany?[19] The inadequacies of these works is old news, but are we equally agreed as to the inadequacies of their very social vocabulary and the approach to social existence that it implies?

These difficulties are clearly reflected in research on early-nineteenth-century English working-class history, as represented by the works of E.P. Thompson, John Foster and Gareth Stedman Jones.[20] These historians have offered starkly different answers to the question of the popular origins of Chartism. Thompson examines in admirable detail a myriad of disparate relationships between labouring people and owners of capital. He devotes long chapters to field-hands, weavers, skilled urban artisans, croppers and stockingers, but remains elusive when it comes to documenting the ground and reality of their common perception of shared interests. Foster marshals a strict Leninist definition of class consciousness, based on a restrictive notion of who is, genuinely, working-class (so that, for example, the enfranchised shopkeepers and barkeepers of Oldham are kept strictly separate in his conceptual scheme from the mill operatives), and he discovers that only a handful of workers achieved this consciousness for a fleeting moment. All of the conceptual rigour missing in Thompson's optimistic vision is here present, but the results seem equally dissatisfying, because they reduce the possibility of the desired outcome (a true working-class movement) to next to nil for almost all times and places. Gareth Stedman Jones argues that the Chartist movement, in so far as its explicit ideology and vision were concerned, cannot be considered a working-class movement. Its basic terms and aims derived from eighteenth-century radicalism, a phenomenon which included a significant middle-class component and which aimed only at greater equality of citizenship rights. No analysis of the special economics of wage labour in industrial capitalism was offered, nor any programme to protect or ameliorate the wage labourer's plight. But Stedman Jones, who is highly critical of Foster, shares more with Foster than he seems willing to admit. Like Foster, he has a restrictive and demanding notion of what working-class consciousness should look like. Like Foster, he finds that people, by and large, do not have such a consciousness. But when it comes

---

[19] C. Hill, *The Century of Revolution, 1603–1714* (Edinburgh, 1961); R. Stadelmann, *Soziale und politische Geschichte von 1848* (Munich, 1948).

[20] E.P. Thompson, *The Making of the English Working Class* (London, 1963); J. Foster, *Class Struggle and the Industrial Revolution* (London, 1974); G. Stedman Jones, *Languages of Class: Studies in English Working-Class History, 1832–1982* (Cambridge, 1983).

to saying why they do not, he demures. At least Foster attempted an explanation for what he saw as the cooption of the self-conscious worker by maturing Lancashire capitalism (but one which Joyce has rightly set aside as unworkable). Stedman Jones insists on political conjuncture and on the independent momentum which language imparts to historical events. These are important issues, but in his essay, as in Foster's study, there is an implied assumption that there was a working class at that time and that it ought to have seen its situation more clearly.

All three historians share a preoccupation with the omnibus term 'working class' that gets in the way of their understanding of the period. The term either appears to have too broad a definition, or else, if given a narrow focus, offers little help in explaining the developments of the time.

Let us therefore not reject the notion of class as relationship, and let us continue to use the word with renewed confidence, but let us avoid using its subsidiary terminology, proletariat, working class, *petite bourgeoisie*, peasantry, bourgeoisie, aristocracy, gentry, Junker class, in all sentences in which these terms appear as subjects of action verbs like perceive, resist, seek, struggle, think, rule, demand, and so on. We have, of course, or many of us do, a significant emotional investment in making these dubious statements. Many of the political aims which such statements have been made to serve are both worthy and uplifting; many of them remain to be achieved. At the same time, if we cannot entertain doubts about their cognitive validity, or about the validity of any part of our habitual analytical vocabulary, then our claim to know what has happened in the past and what we must do in the future is questionable.

In recent years the trend in historical research has been away from language of this kind, and toward appreciation of the complex internal structure of political movements and conflicts. It is no longer acceptable to examine the socio-economic position and experiences of a given group and from there to leap to consciousness and ideology. An all-important and intermediary step consists of examining how, why, and by whom the necessary communication is established to make political action possible. This trend can be seen in the study of the French Revolution over the last decade. While there has been little progress in conceptualising class in this field, there has been a flood of new studies examining what underlies the creation of public opinion. Since it is no longer tenable to associate the rise of public opinion, as both institution and symbol, with the rise of a bourgeois class, the precise parameters of the development of the 'public sphere' have attracted great interest. The press, journalism, aristocratic salons, street life and popular rumour have been the subjects of creative research.[21] This new interest has been closely associated with the attempt to place gender issues at the centre of our understanding of eighteenth-century social change.[22] Even if we wish to retain the notion of class in some form, which is unobjectionable, a very significant revision is necessary in received practices. That notion of class which was widely held at the time Georges Lefebvre wrote his stirring synthesis on the origins of the French Revolution must be set aside. Class as relationship has undermined class as faction.

[21] Representative titles include: R. Darnton, *The Business of Enlightenment: A Publishing History of the Encyclopédie, 1775–1800* (Cambridge, Mass., 1979); idem, *The Literary Underground of the Old Regime* (Cambridge, Mass., 1982); idem, *The Great Cat Massacre and Other Episodes in French Cultural History* (New York, 1985); C. Labrosse, *Lire au XVIIIe siècle: La Nouvelle Héloïse et ses lecteurs* (Lyon, 1985); C. Labrosse and P. Rétat, *Naissance du journal révolutionnaire: 1789* (Lyon, 1989); R. Chartier (ed.) *Les Usages de l'imprimé (XVe–XIXe siècle)* (Paris, 1987); idem, *Lectures et lecteurs dans la France d'ancien régime* (Paris, 1987); J.D. Popkin, *Press and Politics in Pre-Revolutionary France* (Berkeley, Calif., 1987); idem, 'Pamphlet journalism at the end of the old regime', *Eighteenth-Century Studies* 22 (1989): 351–67; A. Farge, *La Vie fragile: violence, pouvoirs et solidarités à Paris au XVIIIe siècle* (Paris, 1986); A. Farge and J. Revel, *Logiques de la foule: L'affaire des enlèvements d'enfants, Paris 1750* (Paris, 1988); D. Roche and R. Darnton (eds) *Revolution in Print: The Press in France, 1775–1800* (Berkeley, 1989).

[22] See e.g. J. Landes, *Women and the Public Sphere in the Age of the French Revolution* (Ithaca, 1988); N.R. Gelbart, *Feminine and Opposition Journalism in Old Regime France: Le Journal des Dames* (Berkeley, 1987); D. Goodman, 'Enlightenment salons: the convergence of female and philosophic ambitions', *Eighteenth-Century Studies* 22 (1989): 329–50.

CHAPTER THREE
An anatomy of nobility

M.L. Bush
University of Manchester

The nobility was inclined to see itself as a race. Some historians follow suit, calling it a caste. Neither term is appropriate since membership of the nobility was not simply a birthright. In fact, nobilities continually admitted new families, partly through entitlement of the royal kin and partly through the immigration of foreign nobles, but chiefly through the ennoblement of commoners.[1] Ennoblement was not only a reward for service but also a perquisite of wealth since entry could often be gained by purchasing a noble estate, an ennobling patent or an ennobling office. Commoners attained nobility in three basic ways: by royal grant (the award of a patent, the conferment of knighthood, the acquisition of office); by assumption, the result of living nobly or claiming nobility for a requisite number of generations; or by royal confirmation of an undocumented claim. For this reason, a record of royal grants is no adequate measure of the rate of ennoblement; and ennoblement could be prolific even at times when the number of royal elevations was limited, as in early modern Castile and Poland.[2]

---

[1] See M.L. Bush, *Rich Noble, Poor Noble* (Manchester, 1988), ch. IV (a).

[2] Castile: M.-C. Gerbet, 'Les guerres et l'accès à la noblesse en Espagne de 1465 à 1592', *Mélanges de la casa de Valasquez* 10 (1972): 295–326; I.A.A. Thompson, 'The purchase of nobility in Castile, 1552–1700', *Journal of European Economic History* 8 (1979) 313–60; J. Fayard and M.-C. Gerbet, 'Fermeture de la noblesse et pureté de sang en Castille à travers les procès de hidalguía au XVIe siècle', *Histoire, économie et sociale*, 1982: 52–75; A. Dominguez Ortiz, *Las clases privilegiadas en la España del antiguo régimen* (Madrid, 1973), pp. 39–40. Also see Bush, op. cit., pp. 19–21. Poland: W. Dworzaczek, 'Perméabilité des barrières sociales dans la Pologne du XVI siècle', *Acta Poloniae Historica* 24 (1971): 22–50, and his 'La mobilité sociale de la noblesse polonaise aux XVIe et XVIIe siècles', *Acta Poloniae Historica* 36 (1977): 147–61. Also see Bush, op. cit., pp. 17–18.

Royal governments generated new nobles by granting ennoblement and by tolerating its assumption. The emergence of the noble grant as a fruitful source of ennoblement stemmed from the Crown's appreciation of it as a cheap form of patronage. By the modern period it had ceased to entail a grant of land and was therefore an economical device for securing and rewarding service.[3] In the early modern period royal governments also promoted ennoblement by enlarging the state apparatus, thus increasing the possibilities of securing noble status through the tenure of office, and by regarding noble status as a commodity which could be extensively sold to raise revenue. Their toleration of assumed nobility stemmed from an unwillingness to question undocumented, or prescriptive, nobility, a willingness to admit ennoblement by an informal process of aggregation, and the failure to keep comprehensive registers of the noble membership.[4]

Ennoblement was also encouraged by noble tolerance and commoner aspiration. In the modern period nobles no longer possessed the capacity to ennoble by patent, but could still promote commoners into the nobility by selling them land and by warranting, rather than disputing, their claims to noble status. Thus in Poland and Hungary nobles assisted the process of ennoblement by supporting in courts of law false claims to nobility, largely in the interest of creating clientage.[5] An equivalent ennobling device, practised in Poland and by the patrician nobility of Genoa, was admission to a noble clan.[6] Finally, ennoblement came of the commoner's capacity to serve the Crown, a consequence of growth in the bureaucracy and army and the creation of more offices than the existing nobility could fill, or to purchase noble status outright or, at least, to acquire the trappings of nobility, thus preparing the way for ennoblement by assumption. The requisite trappings were the possession of a manorial estate and the pursuit of an appropriate occupation. Much depended upon the liveliness of the land market: quickened by the Reformation, which gave Catholic and Protestant monarchs the chance to annex Church lands, and their need to sell them to raise revenue. Also stimulating the land market was a succession of economic crises – occurring

---

[3] Ibid., ch. IV (a/ii).
[4] Ibid., ch. IV (a/v).
[5] Poland: K. Górsky, 'Les structures sociales de la noblesse polonaise au moyen âge', *Le Moyen âge*, 1967. Hungary: E. Fugedi, 'Some characteristics of the medieval Hungarian noble family', *Journal of Family History* 7 (1982): 27–39.
[6] Genoa: J. Heers, *Gênes au XVe siècle* (Paris, 1961), pp. 553, 564–76 and 610. Poland: Górsky, op. cit., pp. 73ff.

notably in the late Middle Ages, between 1650 and 1750 and from the late nineteenth century – which obliged failing nobles to sell their estates.

In the early modern period commoners surged into the nobility; and the rate of ennoblement was normally sufficient both to counter the effect of family extinction upon the noble order and to syphon into it the wealth of the commonalty. Accompanying ennoblement was denoblement.[7] Not only did men born as commoners frequently die as nobles, but also men born as nobles occasionally died as commoners. Governments had considerable, if underused, powers of denoblement. Local communities, moreover, had a strong incentive to question claims to nobility when the government, as it frequently did, placed its tax burden upon the local community rather than upon the taxpayers, causing any increase in numbers of the fiscally exempt to enlarge the individual contributions of the fiscally liable. Nobles, moreover, could abdicate in order to escape service obligations or to avoid the humiliation of being tried for ignobility. But before the nineteenth century the process of denoblement was much less strong than that of ennoblement. It had profound effect only when a government ordered mass demotion or when a rebellious nobility was subdued or driven into exile – both, rare events – or when a nobility was inclined to shed the members incapable of abiding by the noble code, a phenomenon confined before the nineteenth century to England.[8] None the less, over the centuries handfuls of noble families were dropped into the commonalty for practising ignoble occupations, for committing a major crime or for failing to fulfil their obligation of service to the Crown, while others quietly and voluntarily gave up all claim to nobility in order to reap the advantages of commoner status or to avoid the shame of failing to subscribe to the noble ethos.

Since noble status and its attendant privileges were normally held by hereditary right, the blood was clearly an important feature of nobility. Yet it fails to account for the total membership. If the terms caste or race will not do for the nobility, what suffices? In finding an adequate term, a basic problem is to accommodate the diversity of occupation and disparity of interest evident in any one noble order. Heterogeneity was an integral feature of nobility, springing directly from three of its basic characteristics: the inheritance of noble status; the attachment to landownership; and the belief that, apart from

---

[7] Bush, op. cit., ch. IV (b and c).
[8] For spectacular denoblements, see ibid., pp. 26 and 84–5.

exercising lordship, the proper occupation for nobles was to serve the Crown.

By the modern period nobility was usually transmitted to all the offspring of a nobleman (that is by gavelkind). Moreover, nobles had a strong incentive to claim their noble status because of the privileges it conferred. Likewise, commoners found in the privileges a good reason for seeking noble status. The gavelkind inheritance of noble status, the ability of wealth to secure ennoblement, and the inducement offered by privilege for the retention or attainment of nobility, ensured that the noble order should contain the noble-born poor as well as the commoner- and noble-born rich.[9]

It was most unusual for the privileges of a nobility to be uniformly enjoyed by its members. As well as those imparted by noble status – that is the corporate privileges – there tended to be additional privileges, confined to nobles with special qualifications such as landownership, lineage and entitlement. Privilege, for this reason, not only defined nobility but also stratified it into a 'mere nobility' and an upper nobility.[10] The privileges of nobility awarded a variety of benefits. Some were simply honorific – acting as the badge of either status or rank.[11] But several awarded political and material advantages. Some granted rights of political participation (for example parliamentary membership or access to offices legally reserved for the nobility); others conferred political immunities such as exemption from conscription and billeting.[12] Of the privileges with material benefits, the outstanding one was fiscal exemption.[13] The value of the privileges can be easily exaggerated, especially as, in the course of the modern period, governments were bent on devaluing them, either by seeking to rule without parliament or by relying upon general taxes. But to dismiss them as unimportant prior to 1800 makes nonsense of the appreciation of noble status shown by those who clung on to it, even when humiliated by an inability to subscribe to the noble ethos, and by the rich commoners who went to the expensive lengths of attaining it. It also makes nonsense of the revolutions of 1789–1848 and their fervent belief in *égalité*. With the corporate privileges removed, nobility crumbled away, leaving little more than a peerage.

In contrast to hereditary privilege, a primary feature of nobility

---

[9] See ibid. chs IV (a) and V (b).

[10] See M.L. Bush, *Noble Privilege* (Manchester, 1983), ch. I.

[11] See ibid., ch. V.

[12] See ibid., chs III and IV.

[13] See ibid., ch. II.

since, in its corporate form, it inevitably went with noble status, landownership was a secondary characteristic. The existence of landless nobles and landed commoners meant that nobility and landowning, while closely associated, were not inextricably linked. Landowning, none the less, was of tremendous importance to the nobility, forming the basis of the noble ethos. Nobilities were moved by a belief in true nobility. True nobility resided not simply in a genuine claim to noble status but also in subscribing to a certain lifestyle. Landownership was the mark of the true noble, providing the ideal source of income and power. A landed income drawn either from rents or demesne farming enabled the noble to escape the ignoble need to sell his labour or service and conferred upon him the financial independence necessary for living the noble life. Moreover, central to the concept of true nobility was the belief that ideally a noble should have the means to serve his prince in a non-professional capacity. Land made this possible in conferring upon its owner manorial rights which were not only sources of income but also exercises in political authority. The point was made by Tentetnikov in Gogol's *Dead Souls*. Having resigned from the civil service he declared to his uncle: 'Please don't forget that I'm a landowner, a calling not without duties' since 'a landowner is at one and the same time a judge, a manager and a guardian of law and order'. Because landownership was appreciated by the nobility as a source of lordship, it had to take a certain form. To fulfil its expected purposes a noble estate had to be tenanted and manorial.[14]

However, the possession and maintenance of a tenanted estate required considerable wealth. As a result, many nobles failed to attain true nobility. This could amount to a majority in the populous nobilities of Poland, Hungary and Castile and a substantial minority in the other noble orders.[15] Many nobles were landless; many held estates which were too small to contain a tenantry. There were three potent causes of noble landlessness. The most fruitful was the conjunction of primogeniture in the inheritance of property with gavelkind in the transmission of status. Younger sons were a constant

[14] See Bush, *Rich Noble, Poor Noble*, ch. V (a).

[15] Hungary: B.K. Király, *Hungary in the Late Eighteenth Century: the Decline of Enlightened Despotism* (New York and London, 1969), pp. 34–5. Poland: A. Zajaczkowski, 'En Pologne: cadres structurels de la noblesse', *Annales d'histoire E.S.* 18 (1963): 90–1, and N. Davies, *God's Playground: a History of Poland* (Oxford, 1981), I, pp. 228–9. Castile: M.-C. Gerbet, 'La population noble dans le royaume de Castille vers 1500', *Anales de historia antigua y medievale*, 1977–9: 83–93, and A. Dominguez Ortiz, *La sociedad española en el siglo XVIII* (Madrid, 1955), pp. 104–5. Also see Bush, *Rich Noble, Poor Noble*, ch. V (b/ii).

and productive source of landless nobles. So was the impoverishment of noble families and the inclination of absolute monarchy to reward its commoner officials with noble status but not with the means to purchase an estate. Tenantless estates came of the conjunction of partible inheritance with the gavelkind transmission of status. The outcome was a generational subdivision of the estate which eventually converted a collection of farms held by a tenantry into one farm worked by its noble proprietor.

The lack of a tenantry did not deprive nobles totally of an appropriate way of life. Some avoided ignobility by securing service with the king or fellow nobles; others did so by obtaining pensions, thereby avoiding the need to work. But, in most societies, and profusely in regions of high noble density, tenantless nobles had to follow commoner occupations: working as artisans, traders, servants, labourers, farmers, peasants and professional men. For them, subscribing to the noble ethos was no more than an unrealistic aspiration.[16] Laws often existed to safeguard the nobility from such debasement, but they failed in their purpose.[17] Their enforcement was notably limited; countering the handful of nobles stripped of nobility for following commoner pursuits was the continual spawning of nobles who had no option but to break the law and live by trade and manual work. The ineffectiveness of the derogation laws, both in evicting commoner nobles and in persuading them to abdicate their nobility, the remorseless operation of the laws of inheritance, the continual willingness of governments to grant nobility to subjects who were unable to subscribe to the noble code, created and preserved within nobilities a breathtaking variety of life-style and occupation. On the other hand, the diversity evident was not, for the most part, a matter of choice. Nobles with sufficient resources consistently used them to acquire or keep manorial estates. Only poor nobles completely forsook the noble code; they did so out of necessity rather than disbelief.

The noble ethos entailed a ruling function. Besides exercising lordship as landowners, nobles were expected to serve the Crown as officers and officials. Throughout the modern period state service and nobility were closely connected. This was due not only to the ennoblement of state servitors but also to the aspirations of the noblemen-born to hold royal office. As landless younger sons, some sought in this way to avoid ignobility. But nobles as a group were

---

[16] Ibid., ch. V (b).
[17] Ibid., ch. IV (b).

strongly inclined to royal service because of the power and patronage flowing from it, and also out of respect for the society of orders. The theory of orders made a formal differentiation between political and economic functions. In so doing, it presented the nobility as a ruling elite whose task was to aid the king in defending the realm, enforcing the law and maintaining order. In contrast, the commonalty was conceived as the means by which wealth was generated. Ideally, then, nobles were meant to have a political rather than an economic task. This expectation strongly influenced their behaviour as a group, although the prospect of easy profits continually lured nobles into entrepreneurial ventures. Needless to say, subscription to this ideal ensured diversity rather than uniformity within the noble order since many poor nobles lacked the means to secure office; if unable to live off the charity of the state or their relatives, they had no choice but to offend the basic principle of the society of orders by pursuing a commoner occupation. Moreover, rich as well as poor nobles participated in economic activities: as farmers, traders, industrialists, bankers. But the rich noble saved face by exercising his commercialism within an aristocratic framework – that is through the medium of landed and manorial rights and with the aim of display and consumption rather than of increased production – and by ensuring through office-holding, as well as by the exercise of manorial rights, that his family was complying with the expectations of the society of orders.[18] A world of difference separated the poor Polish noble working a smallholding with hired or family labour for a commercial or subsistence purpose, from the rich Polish noble who was also involved in farming but operated through the obligatory labour services of his tenants and, as a seigneur, parliamentarian and possibly official, had a vital part to play in the running of the state.[19] The nobility's keen subscription to the ideal of political service was catered for in the absolute monarchies by the expansion of the military and bureaucratic apparatus and in constitutional monarchies by the development of representative assemblies.

The membership of a nobility was often not only diverse but also divided. Division could take the form of conflicts between individuals, families or parties, but it sometimes expressed a structural rift

[18] Ibid., ch. V (c).

[19] A. Wyczański, 'En Pologne: l'économie du domaine nobiliaire moyen', *Annales d'histoire E.S.* 18 (1963): 86; A. Kaminski, 'Neo-serfdom in Poland and Lithuania', *Slavic Review* 34 (1975): 257–60; A. Mączak, 'The social distribution of landed property in Poland from the sixteenth to the eighteenth century', *Third International Conference of Economic History* (Munich, 1965), I, pp. 463–5.

between different types of nobility, pitting, for example, country against court nobles, seigneurs against noble bureaucrats and old noble families against parvenus. Inducing such conflicts was either the monopolisation of royal patronage and policy by a self-seeking magnate oligarchy or a process of bureaucratic centralisation. The noble opposition tended to be a provincial lesser nobility objecting to nobles who were branded as undeserving courtiers or oppressive officials. The arena of conflict was often parliament, notably the assembly in which the higher and lesser nobility were represented in separate chambers (as in England, Hungary or Poland) or when parliament was dominated by the lesser nobility while the Council was the preserve of magnates and bureaucrats as in Sweden. Yet structural conflicts within nobilities were not confined to parliamentary systems. They were to be found in absolutist as well as constitutional regimes. In the former they sprang from the bureaucratic development of the state and featured the hostility of aristocratic nobles, whose political function essentially stemmed from landownership, to professional nobles, whose political function stemmed from public office. Frequently, the structural conflicts within nobilities involved poor nobles against rich nobles; but the source of conflict tended to be political rather than economic – a struggle for political influence rather than a redistribution of wealth. Accounting for the absence of class conflict within nobilities was the nature of the noble opposition which was inclined to be not simply a movement of the poverty-stricken but of the wide spectrum of wealth found within the lesser nobility.[20]

[20] See Bush, *Rich Noble, Poor Noble*, ch. III (c). Poland: H.E. Dembkowski, *The Union of Lublin* (New York, 1982), pp. 40–1. Sweden: K. Ågren, 'Rise and decline of an aristocracy: the Swedish social and political elite in the seventeenth century', *Scandinavian Journal of History* I (1976): 56–7 and 79–80; M. Roberts 'Sweden' in A. Goodwin (ed.) *The European Nobility in the Eighteenth Century* (London, 1953), pp. 139–40 and Roberts, *The Age of Liberty: Sweden 1719–1772*, pp. 111–15. Hungary: A. Kubinyi, 'The road to defeat: Hungarian politics and defense in the Jagiellonian period' in J.M. Bak and B.K. Király (eds.) *From Hunyadi to Rákóczi* (New York, 1982), ch. 9; F. Szakaly, 'The Hungarian–Croatian border defense system and its collapse', ibid., ch. 8; L. Makkai, 'La noblesse de la Hongrie historique à l'époque du féodalisme tardif (1516–1760)', in B. Kopeczi and E.H. Balazs (eds) *Noblesse française, noblesse hongroise* (Budapest/Paris, 1981), pp. 166–7; Király, op. cit., pp. 25–34. France: A.N. Hamscher, *The Parlement of Paris after the Fronde* (Pittsburg, 1976), pp. 32–6; J. Dewald, *The Formation of a Provincial Nobility: the Magistrates of the Parlement of Rouen, 1499–1610* (Princeton, 1980), pp. 69–70 and 111–12, and J.H.M. Salmon, 'Storm over the noblesse', *Journal of Modern History* 53 (1981): 242–57. Russia: R.O. Crummey, *Aristocrats and Servitors: the Boyar Elite in Russia, 1612–1689* (Princeton, 1983), pp. 21–2 and 32–3; B. Meehan-Waters, *Autocracy and Aristocracy: the Russian Service Elite of 1730* (New Brunswick, 1982), pp. 5–8 and 12–22; R. Hellie, *Enserfment and Military Change in Muscovy* (Chicago, 1971), chs 2, 3 and 14.

Nobilities were constantly, almost naturally, prone to tension and conflict. Much of it was family feuding and party conflicts but often it featured serious rifts between greater and lesser landowners or between professional and aristocratic nobles. None the less, in spite of these divisions and in spite of the diversity of occupation, wealth and life-style within the membership, noble orders, in practice, possessed a durable cohesiveness. This was founded on the privileges imparted by noble status. Before the nineteenth century these corporate privileges were usually not outweighed by the special privileges. Privilege therefore united rather than divided the noble membership. Another source of unity was the power and wealth of magnates. Countering the divisive effect of disparate privileges and inequalities of wealth was the clientism used by magnates to retain the fidelity of other nobles upon whom their power was ultimately founded. Also uniting higher and lesser nobles were family ties. Since titles tended to be transmitted by primogeniture, the lesser nobility was continually recruiting new members from the younger sons of the higher nobility. Furthermore, the strata of nobility were rarely endogamous. Through descent and matrimony, then, kinship knitted together the landless and landed, the small and large landowners, the titled and the mere nobility. Shared values and aspirations contributed to the cohesion. Nobles of all hues held the same belief in landownership as the ideal source of wealth and power and in state service as the ideal occupation. A further bond was social mobility. By means of it *anoblis* became *noblesse de race*, and *hidalguía de privilegio* became *hidalguía de sangre*, simply with the passage of time.[21] Moreoever, binding higher and lesser nobility was not only the demotion of the younger sons of titled nobles but also the entitlement of lesser nobles since the bulk of titles was normally reserved for men who had already attained noble status.[22]

Finally, holding the noble membership together was a sense of being different from the commonalty. This derived from an elemental belief in the theory of orders. Sustaining this sense of difference were not only the distinction juridically evident in the noble privileges and socially evident in the noble ethos – in subscribing to which nobles were considered to behave properly and commoners, improperly – but also the nobility's fear of the many-headed monster: that, if left

---

[21] France: three generations altered to four in 1583 (R. Mousnier, *The Institutions of France under Absolute Monarchy* (Chicago, 1979), I, pp. 122–4 and 127. Spain: Dominguez Ortiz, *Las clases privilegiadas en la España del antiguo régimen*, pp. 30–1.

[22] Bush, *Rich Noble, Poor Noble*, p. 57.

unled and unchecked, the people would demolish the divinely ordained social hierarchy.

The social superiority of nobility, assumed by nobles and kings, accepted by the clergy and commonalty, and reiterated in contemporary accounts of the society of orders, rested, in practice, upon the power the political system and the social structure allowed the noble order to exercise. This power, however, did not simply lie in controlling the means of production; nor was it achieved by brute force; nor was it simply a consequence of noble privilege or the values that the nobility and commonalty shared. Much of it depended upon a permissiveness that derived from the advantages both kings and commoners espied in maintaining the traditional social hierarchy.

The essence of noble power was the capacity of nobles to direct the government and to dominate society. By nature it was a compound of authority and contrivance. Thus, the nobility drew considerable legitimate authority from its inheritable privileges and manorial rights, but the social and political effectiveness of nobles often extended beyond what was conferred upon it by juridical right. Privilege could impart rights of parliamentary membership and the exclusive tenure of office; but a nobility's control over the machinery of state often came of its ability to monopolise offices which the commonalty was not barred from holding, and to dominate parliaments in which the majority of seats or estates were not reserved for nobles and where control therefore lay in persuading commons and clergy to accept the nobility's lead.[23] Likewise, the control that nobles exercised over their tenantry was not the simple outcome of manorial lordship but stemmed from an ability to encourage compliance by paternalism or intimidation, and to quell protest by concession or force. Only when the law reserved all offices of state and the majority of parliamentary seats for nobles, and forbad commoners from becoming lords of the manor, was a close correlation established between noble power and the principles of the society of orders: a familiar situation in early modern eastern Europe (e.g. in Prussia, Bohemia, Austria, Hungary and Russia) but absent in western Europe and the Scandinavian and Italian peninsulas.[24] Moreover, the capacity of nobles to achieve a political and social supremacy that was independent of privilege became evident in the nineteenth century when their power in the countryside and over the machinery of state

[23] Bush, *Noble Privilege*, ch. IV.
[24] For office-holding: ibid., ch. IV (1). For parliamentary membership: ibid., ch. IV (2). For landownership: ibid., ch. VII.

often outlived the demolitions of noble privilege and manorial right that occurred between 1789 and 1861.

Noble power in the modern period had four bases: landownership; parliamentary membership; the tenure of public office; and the force of arms (that is the possession of arsenals, fortresses and troops). It was a mixture of the privately owned and the publicly conferred. Private ownership could even apply to public office: by 1700 most public offices in France were proprietorial, their possessors holding them by hereditary right as a result of an act of purchase and enjoying over them, in the manner of property, a right of sale.[25] The relative importance of these power bases was determined by the nature of the state but all four tended to be operational within the same political system, no matter how primitive or sophisticated the polity. Thus, in absolutist France and Prussia, as in the constitutional monarchies of Poland and Hungary, nobles held power and influence not simply as officials but also as manorial lords and members of parliament.

Landownership was an important source of noble power because the nobility held most of the land, either by outright ownership or by leasing it from the Crown or the Church, and because their tenantry included the bulk of the population. Landownership, in fact, often awarded the nobility lordship over most of the people. Under the old regime these powers were formalised in a range of manorial rights. Then, with the removal of the manorial system, the noble's powers of tenant control endured, often in an intensified form, in the landlord's right to determine the rent and the duration of the lease.[26] Landlordship served both as a source of following and a means of subjection. Landownership could also confer parliamentary membership, a legacy of feudalism when tenants-in-chief were obliged to provide advice to their suzerain as well as military assistance. Thus in pre-revolutionary France membership of the noble estate in provincial assemblies often depended not upon noble status but upon the possession of a fief; in the Prussian and Austrian monarchies the nobility's privilege of parliamentary membership was confined to the owners of noble estates (*Herren-* or *Rittergüter*).[27] Landownership also

---

[25] F.L. Ford, *Robe and Sword* (Harvard, 1953), ch. 6.

[26] Bush, *Noble Privilege*, ch. VI.

[27] France: J. Russell Major, *Representative Government in Early Modern France* (New Haven and London, 1980), chs 3–6. Austria: J. Blum, *Landowners and Agriculture in Austria, 1815–1848* (Baltimore, 1948), p. 23. Prussia: H. Rosenberg, *Bureaucracy, Aristocracy and Autocracy* (Harvard, 1958), p. 32; F.L. Carsten, *A History of the Prussian Junkers* (Aldershot, 1989), p. 92.

allowed nobles to represent their tenants in parliament since it was frequently accepted in estates assemblies that the peasantry should have the right only of indirect representation: that is through their landlords and therefore in the noble estate. This was even the case in parliaments with peasant estates, since the latter confined their representation to Crown tenants and freeholders.[28] Moreover, as democratic parliamentary systems developed in agrarian societies, nobles as landlords were able to direct the electoral process in such a way as to ensure the success of their own candidates. Finally, landownership could impart power through qualifying nobles for public office. Thus, during most of the modern period, landownership enabled the English gentry to hold the offices of justice of the peace, sheriff and deputy lieutenant.[29]

The power the nobility derived from landownership in an agrarian society depended upon the capacity of nobles to retain most of it in their possession and upon the government's willingness to accept the landlord as a vital intermediary between itself and the population. Maintaining the nobility's retention of much of the land was its continued appreciation of the landed estate as a vital ingredient in the noble ethos and the regular absorption of commoner landlords into the nobility. Maintaining the reliance of governments upon the landlord were the logistic problems of ruling a population scattered in the countryside. The most obvious and convenient solution was to operate through the landlord. Royal absolutism extended bureaucratic control into the localities and even sought in France, Prussia and Russia to divorce some office-holding from landownership by barring leading provincial officials from holding office in the regions where their estates were located. But until the revolutionary era it inclined to retain the seigneur as an instrument of government, giving him basic administrative powers over his tenantry. These included the right to administer civil and criminal jurisdiction in the manorial court, the right to determine how much in state taxation each of his tenants should pay and the right to decide which of them should be conscripted.[30] Where the seigneur's powers were minimal, the landlord found compensation in holding the public offices which developed in their stead. As lord and official the noble landowner retained power under the old regime, irrespective of whether or not it became a royal absolutism. In fact, seriously eroding this power

[28] Bush, *Noble Privilege*, pp. 116–17.
[29] M.L. Bush, *The English Aristocracy* (Manchester, 1984), ch. 4.
[30] Bush, *Noble Privilege*, ch. VI (f and i).

base was not so much political centralisation as the emergence of the commoner landowner and the spread of industrial or agrarian capitalism. Modernising changes in the nature of the state, whether they be centralising, through the extension of bureaucracy, or representational, through parliamentary reform, tended in themselves only to curtail, not to abolish, the political effectiveness of noble landownership. Much more damaging were social changes which left the majority of society independent of the noble landlord. The special value of landownership to the nobility is evident in the coincidental reduction in their landed possessions and political power during the nineteenth and twentieth centuries. Some of this decline was due to the emergence of a non-noble landed elite, the result of a slowdown in the rate at which nobility was granted; some of it was due to the termination of the manorial system, especially where the terms of emancipation converted tenants into freeholders. In addition, agrarian capitalism proletarianised the peasantry though encouraging the development of the large farm. When this was accompanied by the nobility's stolid refusal to abandon its rentier position, the outcome, as in England, was the release of large sections of the community from direct dependence upon it.[31] Similarly, the nobility's aversion to direct involvement with industry meant that the development of industrial capitalism, especially in connection with steam power, removed much of the population from the direct sway of the landlords by converting it into an urban proletariat.[32] The property rights possessed by noble landlords in industrial towns lacked the capacity for tenant control which they had exercised over pre-industrial towns and rural communities. On the other hand, both industrial and agrarian capitalism were belated developments. Especially where society remained predominantly peasant, nineteenth-century nobles continued as landlords to wield enormous local influence.

The nobility's control of parliamentary assemblies rested upon privilege and manipulation. Thus, in the English parliament the peers enjoyed membership by hereditary right whilst the lesser nobility, the gentry, could gain entry only by a process of election to the House of Commons. Until the late nineteenth century landowners and their relatives were naturally inclined to become MPs and found admission to the Commons far from difficult. The outcome was that both parliamentary chambers were dominated, if in a different

---

[31] Bush, *The English Aristocracy*, ch. 10.
[32] Ibid., ch. 11 and p. 146.

manner, by men from the same social background.[33] In a number of states nobles could control parliament by means of their privileges. But, apart from the kingdom of Naples, all the known examples are confined to eastern Europe (that is Poland, Hungary, Bohemia and Austria). Elsewhere noble control was secured by enlisting the support of the other estates.[34]

A nobility's control of parliament did not necessarily confer upon it a great deal of political power. Much depended upon the extent of the royal authority. In constitutional polities the nobility's parliamentary power was considerable, allowing, for example in England and Poland, not only tax-granting and legislative powers but also some management of government policy and even the ability to shape the development of the state in the noble interest through resisting the Crown's attempts to enlarge its prerogative and to equip itself with a large standing army and an extensive professional bureaucracy. Although much less important for the nobility than landownership and office-holding, representative assemblies remained a basis of noble power in the absolute monarchies. Until the French Revolution two-fifths of France possessed regular provincial diets. In them the noble chamber needed to persuade the clerical and third estates if it aspired to control parliamentary business. These assemblies had comparatively limited powers – they mainly concerned granting and collecting the taille – but acted, along with the provincial *parlements*, as guardians of provincial liberties and estates privileges against the encroaching state.[35] Until revived in the 1820s, the provincial assemblies of the Prussian monarchy withered away, but earlier, from the fifteenth to the seventeenth centuries, they had acquired some control of government policy through a right to grant, collect and allocate taxes. Dominated by the noble order, they awarded the nobility considerable power in relation to the ruler.[36] The nobility's parliamentary power was not completely extinguished by royal absolutism because, besides the provincial diets, there developed local assemblies (*Kriestage*) empowered to grant the land tax in rural areas and to appoint the *Landrat*, a leading local official. These assemblies had a predominantly Junker membership and their powers remained intact,

---

[33] W.L. Cuttsman, *The British Political Elite* (London, 1963), p. 82.

[34] Bush, *Noble Privilege*, ch. IV (2b)

[35] M. Wolfe, *The Fiscal System in Renaissance France* (New Haven, 1972), p. 47; Russell Major, op. cit., pp. 138–59 and 630–52.

[36] O. Hintze, 'The Hohenzollern and the nobility', in F. Gilbert (ed.) *The Historical Essays of Otto Hintze* (Oxford, 1975), pp. 41–3, and F.L. Carsten, *The Origins of Prussia* (Oxford, 1954), ch. 12.

with one brief intermission between 1849 and 1853, until the local government reforms of 1872.[37] In fact, royal absolutism not only reduced the authority of representative assemblies, but also ensured that those retaining some potency should consist overwhelmingly of noblemen, or at least landowners. Thus, in Bohemia and in the Austrian Territories, the estates assemblies were organised in such a way as to ensure that a majority of the membership were from the noble order.[38] The same was true not only of the Hohenzollern *Kreistage* but also, from the late eighteenth century, of the provincial and district assemblies of the Romanovs.[39] Moreover, in eighteenth-century France, the *parlements* (sovereign law courts representative of the bureaucracy) had become predominantly noble assemblies, the result of the ennobling capacity of the more important offices and the aspiration of nobles to become *conseilleurs*.[40] Thanks to the preservation of representative assemblies and lordship of the manor, the power enjoyed by nobles under royal absolutism was not simply the perquisite of being professional civil servants and army officers. Royal absolutism smashed the independent power of the magnates, not the independent power of nobles. This nobles continued to exercise as an order through representative assemblies, and as an aristocracy through the medium of landownership.

Traditionally, European nobilities were service elites. In this respect, much of their power derived from the tenure of military and civil offices. Under the old regime nobles held a wide range of office. Municipal offices gave them control over autonomous or semi-autonomous townships; household or estate offices in the service of magnates allowed minor nobles to exercise the delegated authority of their masters; offices elected by representative assemblies could confer upon nobles considerable power in central and local government. A range of official functions, then, were performed by nobles apart from the service they provided by government appointment. As

---

[37] Carsten, *The Origins of Prussia*, p. 199; H. Rosenberg, *Bureaucracy, Aristocracy, Autocracy: The Prussian Experience, 1660–1815* (Cambridge, Mass., 1958), pp. 166–7; L.W. Muncy, *The Junker in the Prussian Administration under William II, 1888–1914* (New York, 1970), pp. 175–7, and R.M. Berdahl, 'Conservative politics and aristocratic landholders in Bismarkian Germany', *Journal of Modern History* 44 (1972): 7–9; idem, *The Politics of the Prussian Nobility* (Princeton, 1988), pp. 91–2.

[38] Bush, *Noble Privilege*, pp. 115–16; Blum, *Noble Landowners and Agriculture in Austria*, pp. 25–8.

[39] Seymour Becker, *Nobility and Privilege in Late Imperial Russia* (Dekalb, Ill., 1985), pp. 136–44.

[40] Ford, *Robe and Sword*, pp. 63–4, and Mousnier, *The Institutions of France under Absolute Monarchy*, I, pp. 102–3.

sources of political power, however, these official functions were minor when measured against the rewards accruing to royal office. The machinery and effectiveness of royal government upheld not only the power of the Crown but also that of its leading officials who were almost invariably nobles, if not clerics, some of them ennobled in reward for their official services to the Crown, but many, noblemen by birth.

Most states in the modern period reserved certain offices for noblemen; but rarely were all offices, or even a majority of offices, closed in this way to commoners.[41] Rather than by means of their privileges, nobles controlled the political system by virtue of the Crown's conviction that, on the whole, nobles were better equipped than commoners to hold public office. This royal preference for noble servitors was not simply an admission of the power nobles already possessed as landlords. The Crown's preference was not based upon rationality but upon an ingrained belief in the political efficacy of nobility, a belief to which it was naturally prejudiced since to question the nobility's birthright to rule implicitly questioned its own inherited authority. The nobility's enduring ascendancy in the service of the state meant that the enlargement of the latter's authority modified rather than diminished the former's political powers: curtailing the nobility's authority as an order through devaluing its privileges and limiting the lord of the manor's political importance, while elevating the authority of the nobles prepared to serve as state functionaries. In this respect, a strengthening of the state reduced the nobility's power in relation to the Crown, but increased its control over the rest of society.

Finally, the force of arms remained a source of noble power well into the modern period. This was evident, for example, in noble rebellions against the Crown and the crushing of peasant revolts by noble armies. Sustaining the noble as warlord was the government's dependence upon his private military resources for waging its own wars. However, decisively eroding this source of noble power, which prior to 1500 had been undermined by the vulnerability of fortresses to cannon and mining and the susceptibility of armoured knights to arrows and pike, was the emergence in the seventeenth and eighteenth centuries of national armies composed not of noble retinues but professional troops raised either by hire, impressment or conscription. Adapting to the changing political situation brought about by this development, the wealthier nobles chose to operate through the

---

[41] See Bush, *Noble Privilege*, ch. IV (1).

Court and within the system of royal government, rather than simply by means of their own resources and within an enclave of power from which the Crown and its officials were excluded. This was not the case, however, in parts of eastern Europe, notably in Poland and Hungary, where strongholds and private armies remained a source of noble power well into the eighteenth century.[42] Moreover, while nobles in the west lost the military capacity to challenge the state in the course of the seventeenth century, they retained the capacity to terrorise society through maintaining extensive entourages of flunkeys.

Stemming from these four bases, the power of the nobility, and its survival, owed much to certain political and social preconditions. Crucial to the degree of power that nobles enjoyed *vis-à-vis* the state was the nature of the monarchy. The terms nobles could exact of an elected king as a condition of his election awarded them a greater opportunity to extend the power of the noble order and to formalise it in privilege. Essentially the principle of election allowed the nobility to preserve its independence of state control by limiting the powers of the Crown and also to extend its domination of the peasantry by ensuring that the rights of the peasantry were reduced to a minimum in the law. Elective monarchy was outlived by hereditary monarchy. In fact, when Poland was partitioned in the late eighteenth century elective monarchy had been obliterated throughout Europe, although in 1500 it was found in Sweden, Denmark, Hungary and Bohemia as well. In the early modern period hereditary monarchy easily led to absolutism, but it could also create constitutional and imperial forms of monarchy which respected the nobility's traditional powers in so far as they were marked by a freedom from government interference. Furthermore, the imposition of state control under royal absolutism modified rather than removed the nobility's political functions. Absolute monarchy also maintained continuity with the past by retaining a political role for the manorial system. A major source of noble power had been the government's traditional reliance upon the capital resources of the nobles. This was evident in the dependence of governments upon unpaid offices, privately maintained fortresses, the privately furnished military equipment associated with knighthood and the lordship associated with the private ownership of land or serfs. In the course of the modern period, a state apparatus developed directly and comprehensively financed by government, but the trans-

---

[42] O. Subtelny, *Domination of Eastern Europe* (Gloucester, 1986), pp. 125–30 and 145ff.

ference from a 'feudal' to a 'patrimonial' system was a slow process. On the other hand, the extension of bureaucracy and the creation of huge standing armies under royal absolutism, coupled with the limited resources available for rewarding the loyalty of its servitors, spawned nobles whose wealth and power, in stemming only from office, were of a purely professional character.[43]

A second basic precondition of noble power lay in the subservience of the commonalty. The openness of nobility played a part in maintaining the commonalty's respect for nobility. The rich were continually bought off by admission to its membership. But ennoblement helped to pacify the bourgeoisie, not the peasantry. The latter was kept in check partly by the landlord's capacity to quell disobedience and partly by the proprietary rights awarded the holders of manorial tenures. Ennoblement and tenant right ensured that within the commonalty was an influential element of collaborators who had much to gain from preserving the system. Generally, the acceptance of noble privilege was encouraged by the fact that differential privileges or rights infiltrated most parts of society. Matching tenant right in the countryside were the freeman rights of the towns.

The power of a nobility clearly owed much to its great wealth. Upholding the latter was the high economic value of land in advanced agrarian societies and the nobility's absorption of commercial wealth through the mechanism of ennoblement. However, no matter how powerful a nobility, no matter how generous its privileges in awarding political advantages over the commonalty, the poor noble tended to be powerless, expecially if he were too poor to own a tenanted estate or to afford the education necessary for obtaining office. Such nobles were as impotent as ordinary commoners.

A fourth pre-condition lay in the nature of urbanisation and capitalism. Until industrialisation created Coke towns, cities were noble habitats. For this reason, in moving from countryside to town, people remained in the noble presence. Moreover, prior to the nineteenth century, capitalism typically developed in such a way as to preserve the power of landlordship. Predominantly in early modern Europe, it took the form of merchant capitalism. The mode of production, both agricultural and industrial, remained that of the peasant or the rural cottager. Consequently, the sway that nobles held over much of the population simply through landownership endured, although limited by the intrusion of the state and by the land purchased by commoners. It lasted until capitalist farming and

[43] Bush, *Rich Noble, Poor Noble*, ch. V (b/ii).

industry caused the great migration from the European countryside to worlds which were alien to, or indifferent of, nobility: that is settlements overseas or the industrial towns of nineteenth- and twentieth-century Europe.

The existence of nobility resident in privilege, and of 'true nobility' resident in subscription to the noble code, and the failure of the two to coincide, created two contradictory sources of social status. One rested upon recognition in the law and therefore by the state. Essentially it granted a special social position to everyone privileged to be noble-born or properly ennobled. The other rested upon recognition by the various components of society, the nobility, clergy and commonalty. This recognition took into account not only the juridical fact of nobility but also the capacity of nobles to live in a manner and occupation befitting their status. For nobles unable to fulfil this condition, they gained nothing from nobility apart from the privileges automatically conferred by their right to it. In practice, then, the status of a noble related to wealth and occupation as well as blood, and derived from the power individual families were able to secure through land, office and entourage.

The concepts of orders and class have been effective ideologies, the one in maintaining the old regime, the other in destroying it. But how useful are they for purposes of social stratification or for explaining the social distinction accruing to nobility? The concept of orders was principally a political statement, laying down the ideal relationship between society and the state, not a device to explain social relationships. As a means of social stratification its weakness lay in creating one largely undifferentiated group, the commonalty, and in failing to account for social conflict. It also failed to do justice to the complexity of relationships within the nobility, tending to present it as a coherent group bonded together by its privileges and political functions. Furthermore, it failed to identify basic sources of social differentiation, notably the distinctions perceived in the village between the landed and the landless, and the distinction generally perceived between rich and poor. On the other hand, the concept created an influential ideal. Moreover, it persistently proposed that wealth and social status were not coequal, that the basic source of superior status was the political function, and that the basic source of inferior status was a full-time participation in economic activity. That this squared with the reality of the time is evident in the nobility's enduring association with political authority through its appreciation of lordship and office, and also in the rich commoner's ambition to acquire noble status and to sever his connection with trade. The concept of the society of orders, however, oversimplifies reality in presenting a clear-cut distinction between nobility and commonalty. Complicating the picture, commoners held office and exercised lordship; many nobles had no part to play in the political system; the ennobled frequently had difficulty in forgoing trade; nobles were caught up in the commercial world through their estate management, their noble privileges and their manorial rights.[44] The meaningfulness of the society of orders could perhaps be tested by an examination of society's comparative regard for the commoner official and for the noble whose poverty denied him political authority. Moreover, a feature of societies of orders was not simply the capacity of rich commoners to attain noble status but also the tendency of the resourceful commoner to attain the trappings of nobility, principally through the acquisition of land, offices and some of the noble privileges. Thus whereas many of the noble ideals stemmed from the attempts of nobles to distinguish their way of life from the wealthier commoner, they were continually upstaged and deprived of social distinction by the imitativeness of the bourgeoisie.

Although deficient, the concept of the nobility as an order is more satisfactory than its conception as a class. To refer to the nobility as a class is arguably as misleading as to designate it a caste. The existence of noble status as a juridical fact and its automatic transmission from one generation to the next ensured that the noble membership as a whole could not be defined in terms of its wealth and its relationship to the means of production. Poor nobles could be weeded out but, before the nineteenth century, not to the extent of ensuring a coincidence of noble status and noble life-style. Quite exceptional was the English aristocracy whose homogeneity was maintained by primogeniture in the transmission of titles and estates, the inclination of the landless products of aristocratic families to sink into the commonalty, having next to no corporate privileges to sustain their nobility, and by the fact that landownership was the basic means whereby commoners gained aristocratic status. On the other hand, thanks to ennoblement and its own capital assets, nobility stood to represent wealth in an agrarian society. But to present the relationship between noble and commoner as resting upon class would misrepresent the nobility's relationship both with the bourgeoisie and the peasantry. The former relationship was harmonised by the process of ennoblement and disturbed by political rather than economic considerations; the latter was harmonised by tenant rights and disturbed

[44] Ibid., 131–2.

by their attempted infringement. Conflict was not generated by the clash of interest thought to be naturally present in the relationship between feudalism and capitalism or between capital and labour.

Central to the nobility's social superiority was its political power and the special role that political theory awarded the noble in ruling and defending the realm. Yet equally misleading is the term 'political elite' since by the modern period noble membership was not determined by function and many nobles had nothing to do with politics. At the heart of nobility is the contradiction between the importance attached to occupation and the importance attached to birthright. The need to accommodate both characteristics strongly suggests that the nobility is best regarded as an order.

CHAPTER FOUR

Between estate and profession: the clergy in Imperial Russia

Gregory L. Freeze

Brandeis University

In contrast to the rich literature on the history of social stratification in western Europe,[1] Russian historiography has remained remarkably unreflective and derivative in its assumptions about the structure and processes of social change in Imperial Russia. Curiously enough, Soviet and western historians have generally shared a common assumption that Russian social development conformed to a standard western model of evolution from medieval estates to modern classes. To be sure, they note that the Russian case had its peculiarities: first, its chronology was different, with the transition from estates to classes not coming until well into the nineteenth century; and second, the Russian state, in contrast to the west, played the primary role in directing this whole process.[2]

This traditional estates-to-classes paradigm stands in need of radical revision.[3] The *Begriffsgeschichte* of the social lexicon shows that estates terminology – above all, the key term for estate, *soslovie* (pl. *sosloviia*)

---

[1] See e.g. R. Mousnier, *Social Hierarchies, 1450 to the Present* (New York, 1973); R.J. Morris, *Class and Class Consciousness in the Industrial Revolution, 1780–1850* (London, 1979); *Le Concept de classe dans l'analyse des sociétés méditerranéenes XVIe–XXe siècles* (Nice, 1978); H.-U. Wehler, *Klassen in der europäischen Sozialgeschichte* (Göttingen, 1979).

[2] For a classic pre-revolutionary statement, echoed in modern historiography as well, see P.N. Miliukov, *Ocherki po istorii russkoi kul'tury* (Moscow, 1918), vol. I, p. 219, and N. Lazarevskii, 'Sosloviia', *Entsiklopedicheskii slovar' Brokgauz-Efrona* (St Petersburg, 1900), vol. 60, pp. 911–13.

[3] See G.L. Freeze, 'The *soslovie* (estate) paradigm and Russian social history', *American Historical Review* 91 (1986): 11–36; idem, *From Supplication to Revolution: a Documentary Social History of Imperial Russia* (New York, 1988). See also M. Confino 'Issue and non-issues in Russian social history and historiography (1890–1920s)', *Occasional Papers of the Kennan Institute* 165 (1983), and L. Haimson, 'The problem of social identities in early twentieth-century Russia', *Slavic Review* 47 (1988): 1–20.

– did not even emerge until the first half of the nineteenth century and only then became the decisive category in shaping group identities and state policy. Furthermore, the tendency to equate *soslovie* with stagnation and backwardness is unwarranted. Rather, the estates structure was protean and dynamic: it gave the state an effective instrument for mobilising manpower and resources, and it offered social groups a legal form of collective organisation – even for new groups, such as modern professions.[4] That double utility explains the tenacious vitality of the *soslovie* structure and its perpetuation until the very end of the *ancien régime*. It was only in the wake of the October Revolution in 1917 that the new Soviet government formally abolished estates, although it might well be argued that in many respects the *soslovie* model continued to inform much of its policy-making.[5] The survival of *soslovie* identities (in law, group consciousness and subculture) did not prevent the emergence of alternative hierarchies, some overlapping, some competing – based on power, wealth, occupation, ethnicity and confession. In brief, it is essential to advance beyond the unidimensional and unidirectional estate-to-class paradigm and to recognise the polymorphic structure of the social order in late Imperial Russia. Indeed, far from coalescing into neatly identifiable (and self-identifying) classes, society in late Imperial Russia manifested a contrary tendency toward disaggregation, toward the proliferation of micro-forms of social organization. It was not classes, but smaller social units (especially occupational and professional groups) that coalesced, organised and lobbied their special interests in the waning years of the Russian pre-revolution.

This chapter seeks to explore these processes by examining the archetypical Russian estate – the clergy. The objective here is to consider how that estate reflected and fitted into the larger social matrix of Imperial Russia; how a hereditary (even caste-like) estate aspired to professionalise its structure, status and identity; how this new *Berufsstand*, nevertheless, ultimately remained far more *Stand* than *Beruf*; how, indeed, it even underwent a regressive process of deprofessionalisation in the last decades of the *ancien régime*.[6] In part,

---

[4] For the case of doctors, see N. Frieden, *Russian Physicians in an Era of Reform and Revolution, 1856–1905* (Princeton, 1981), and J.F. Hutchinson, 'Society, corporation or union? Russian physicians and the struggle for professional unity, 1890–1917', *Jahrbücher für Geschichte Osteuropas* 30 (1982): 37–53.

[5] Consider e.g. the powerful role of social origin in determining an individual's status (and fate) in the first decades of Soviet rule as the regime employed old *soslovie* categories to identify class enemies.

[6] For details on the Russian clergy, see E. Bryner, *Der geistliche Stand in Rußland im 18. Jahrhundert* (Göttingen, 1982); N.D. Zol'nikova, *Soslovnye problemy vo vzaimootnosh-*

this analysis of the Russian clergy can be placed within a larger comparative framework, providing a useful counterpoint to the Catholic and Protestant clergies in western Europe, especially with respect to changes in their respective status, composition and professionalism.

Although Russian historians have conventionally applied the Western model of orders to pre-Petrine Russia,[7] they do so at considerable peril. Quite apart from problems of anachronistic terminology (the modern *soslovie*, in the sense of estate, lacked any obvious equivalent in medieval Russian), it is most assuredly a precarious enterprise to stuff Muscovite society into a strait-jacket of three or four estates. If some historians (with good reason) express discomfiture in applying such a simplistic model to western society,[8] one should be still more sceptical about its applicability to medieval Russia.

At the most obvious level, pre-Petrine Russia lacked either the terminology or configurations of the estate. To be sure, if Muscovy did not yet know the term *soslovie*, it did have the term *chin* (customarily translated as rank). *Chin*, however, most certainly cannot be equated with estate or order, for it lacked both the connotation of strict hereditariness and aggregation into corps or constituted bodies.[9] Rather, Muscovite *chiny* referred to the males holding official rank and encompassed a plethora of individual offices (numbering in the hundreds). Although some aggregates appear (for example '*gorodovye sluzhilye liudi*' – the official servicemen in [provincial] towns), broader and cohesive collectivities failed to gain a foothold in Muscovite law. Nor was it simply a matter of Russian

eniiakh Tserkvi i gosudarstva v Sibiri (XVIII v) (Novosibirsk, 1981); G.L. Freeze, *The Russian Levites: Parish Clergy in the Eighteenth Century* (Cambridge, Mass., 1977) and his *The Parish Clergy in Nineteenth-Century Russia: Crisis, Reform, Counter-Reform* (Princeton, 1983); J.H.M. Geekie, 'Church and politics in Russia, 1900–1917: a study of political behavior of the Russian Orthodox Church in the reign of Nicholas II', PhD, East Anglia (1976).

[7] See the discussion and debate in G. Stökl, 'Gab es im Moskauer Staat Stände?', *Jahrbücher für Geschichte Osteuropas* 11 (1963): 321–42, and H.-J. Torke, *Die staatbedingte Gesellschaft im Moskauer Reich: Zar und Zemlja in der altrussischen Herrschaftsverfassung, 1613–1689* (Leiden, 1974), pp. 271–83.

[8] See e.g. H.-U. Wehler, 'Vorüberlegungen zur historischen Analyse sozialer Ungleichheit', in *Klassen in der europäischen Sozialgeschichte* (Göttingen, 1979), pp. 9–32.

[9] Of particular importance was Russia's lack of corporateness (either in social lexicon or formal institutions) to engender the western notions of corps and constituted body. See the analysis of the western terms in W.H. Sewell, 'Etat, corps and ordre: some notes on the vocabulary of the French old regime', in H.-U. Wehler (ed.) *Sozialgeschichte Heute* (Göttingen, 1974), pp. 49–68.

legal backwardness, for official *chin* in fact did not constitute the primary determinant of social identity and affiliation. Rather, it was clan – not *chin* – that provided the definitive social unit; even the Russian nobilities found themselves fragmented into a hierarchy of discrete clannish units ranked by *mestnichestvo* (the Muscovite system of precedence).[10] Moreover, most of the population remained completely outside the *chin* ranks, their status highly differentiated and dependent upon local custom and particularistic state policy. Apart from the formal structure, this traditional order had gaping holes that allowed a high velocity of undetected (and undetectable) social and geographic mobility. In particular, Muscovite autocracy (conventionally credited with awesome feats of social control) lacked the capacity – even desire – to regulate social relations, as its reluctance to codify and enforce enserfment demonstrates.

Within Muscovy's society, the Orthodox clergy probably came closest to approximating western notions of an order or estate, its special status rooted in the Church's claims to juridical separateness and institutional autonomy. The term of *dukhovnyi chin* (clerical rank), with connotations of a large and distinct social aggregate, might appear to resemble a separate estate. Nevertheless, the term's primary referent was really the special juridical status of the Church, not a social group. Indeed, the Russian Orthodox clergy did not yet form a corporate group – in marked contrast to their peers in western Europe. To be sure, the Russian clergy enjoyed a special legal status (the most distinct juridical status of any *chin*), and its married secular clergy showed a clear tendency toward hereditariness. None the less, this clerical *chin* was so rent with internal division – between secular and monastic clergy, between priests and sacristans – that it had neither collective identity nor corporate organisation and assemblies. Nor was it demographically encapsulated into an endogamous estate. The celibate monastic clergy, by definition, remained open and recruited episcopal elites and ordinary monks from such diverse social groups as aristocratic boyars and illiterate peasants. Nor was the secular clergy a closed group; given the abysmal educational standards of Muscovy,[11] virtually anyone could qualify to become a priest –

[10] It was no accident that well into the eighteenth century, amidst the brutal power struggles after Peter the Great, various factions dealt summarily with whole clans, not mere individuals. For the case of estate confiscations, see B. Meehan-Waters, *Autocracy and Aristocracy* (New Brunswick, 1982), pp. 92–6.

[11] The Church had virtually no system of formal education before the eighteenth century; apart from elitist academies in Kiev and Moscow (designed as much to serve secular as ecclesiastical needs), candidates for the priesthood had only to demonstrate bare literacy, often little more than rote memorisation of liturgical texts.

provided that he had a letter of recommendation from parishioners and the requisite funds to pay the ordination and installation fees. Apart from a natural tendency for a son to follow in his father's footsteps and receive the requisite training at home,[12] the parish clergy none the less remained accessible to the rest of society.[13] No less important was the clergy's lack of a corporate spirit and organisation, partly because of the profound gap between the monastic and secular clergy, partly because of the clergy's dispersion among thousands of parishes and monasteries across the vast terrain of Muscovy.

The eighteenth century brought fundamental changes, as the clergy congealed into a hereditary social population. This process was complex and gradual, but by the early nineteenth century the clergy had become isolated from the rest of society, drawing almost entirely on its own progeny to fill vacancies in parish churches.[14] Only the monastic clergy, especially women, showed a significant rate of vocations from other social groups.[15] Yet offspring of the clergy still

[12] It was common for a son to assume his father's post; service in the home parish taught the youth how to perform the liturgy and various rites.

[13] To be sure, Church authorities made a nominal attempt to prevent the ordination of commoners with binding obligations (townsmen, peasants and indentured servants [*kholopy*]) at the interrogation of ordinands, where they were specifically asked whether they belonged to any of those status groups. Examples of such seventeenth-century interrogations (*stavlennicheskie doprosy*) in Moscow are to be found in N.A. Skvortsov, *Dukhovenstvo Moskovskoi eparkhii v XVII v* (Moscow, 1916), pp. 10–12.

[14] Legally, men from *any* social group could enter the clergy; even serfs, had they been formally manumitted, could do so. For confirmation of this policy, see the policy statements in ecclesiastical archives (e.g. TsGIA SSSR, f. 797 [Kantseliariia Ober-Prokurora], op. 1, d. 3759 [1809 reply to the Ministry of Interior] and ibid., f. 796 [Kantseliariia Sv. Sinoa], op. 105, g. 1824, d. 894 [Synod reply to query from the Ministry of Finance in 1824]) and the formal reaffirmation in state law (e.g. 1826 decree in *Polnoe sobranie zakonov Rossiiskoi Imperii*, Vtoraia seriia, 55 vols (St Petersburg, 1830–84), 1: 139).

But such outsiders remained, statistically, virtually unknown. For example, in 1842 only 0.8 per cent of newly appointed parish clergy (35 of the 4,577) came from outside the clerical estate; the proportion rose to 2.7 per cent in 1847 (72 of 2,693) but sank back to a more customary rate of 0.5 per cent in 1855 (19 of 4,065). See the reports in *Izvlecheniia iz otcheta po vedomstvu dukhovnykh del pravosalvnogo ispovedaniia* (St Petersburg, 1837–63) for 1842 (p. 25), 1843 (p. 20) and 1855 (pp. 17, 22). It bears noting that the bulge in 1847 was due chiefly to policy in minority areas of the Empire, such as the Baltics, where the Church had modest resources and deliberately sought to strengthen its influence by recruiting candidates from local ethnic groups. See, especially, the materials on Riga diocese in TsGIA SSSR, f. 796, op. 131, g. 1850, d. 1895 and the typical case in ibid., op. 128, g. 1847, d. 276.

For a discussion of Soviet archival materials (and explanation of the Soviet form for notation), see Freeze, *Parish Clergy*, pp. 477–80.

[15] The Church published data on the social origin of monks and nuns from the mid-1830s to the mid-1850s, showing that clerical progeny represented over half of the monks, but only one-sixth of the nuns (see the materials in each annual of the chief-procurator's *Izvlecheniia iz otcheta*). But at this point the monastic clergy remained

constituted the majority of monks and served as virtually the sole source of the monastic elite – archimandrites and bishops who governed the Church. Hence, from the humblest village sacristan to the illustrious metropolitans in St Petersburg, virtually all clerics were men born to the clerical rank and educated in special ecclesiastical schools.

A number of processes functioned to disqualify candidates from other social groups. One was government fiat, especially legislation from the 1720s that restricted the ordination of lower status groups, chiefly to prevent their escape from the poll-tax system.[16] Although the laws had loopholes and only gradually took effect, it did serve to slow upward mobility of peasants and townsmen – that is the commoners who were most likely to seek the more privileged status of the clergy. A second barrier was education: in the second half of the eighteenth century the Church constructed a new network of seminaries and eventually was able to make study at the seminary a virtual prerequisite for ordination to the priesthood.[17] These seminaries were all the more socially significant because (almost without exception) they admitted only clerical offspring, thereby disqualifying non-clerical children from appointment to the clerical rank.[18] The third obstacle was the clergy itself, which became increasingly determined to reserve church positions for their own children and kinsmen. This exclusivist tendency was partly cultural: bishops suspected that candidates from more secular status groups lacked the proper upbringing and, indeed, were far more likely to be contaminated by secular values and vices. But no less important was the

___

exceedingly small – roughly one-seventh the size of the secular clergy. For statistical data, see the materials in I.V. Preobrazhenskii, *Otechestvennaia tserkov' po statisticheskim dannym, 1840–1 po 1890–1 g.* (2nd edn, St Petersburg, 1901).

[16] The new poll-tax system, introduced in 1718, led to a seminal decree of 1727 regulating the exit of those paying the poll tax (essentially townsmen and peasants). In essence, to prevent the disappearance of taxpaying commoners into the untaxed clergy, the government required that the community assume the tax burden for anyone transferring to the clergy until the next national poll-tax census (about every twenty years). The poll-tax records are fairly complete and record the steady decline of such poll-tax elements in clerical ranks. For the most exhaustive study of the data, see F.E. Den', 'Podatnye elementy sredi dukhovenstva Rossii v XVIII v', *Izvestiia Rossiiskoi Akademii nauk*, 5–7 (1918): 13–14.

[17] The process was, to be sure, complex; it proceeded most quickly in the central provinces, only gradually (and incompletely) affecting the outlying provinces and borderlands. But by the mid-nineteenth century virtually all newly ordained priests had a full seminary education and even the lowly sacristans had to demonstrate some years of formal study at the specialised ecclesiastical schools.

[18] For analysis, data and references see Freeze, *Russian Levites*, ch. 4.

clergy's own vested interest: because the Petrine state strictly limited the numbers of churches and priests, clerics scrambled to reserve places for kinsmen and hence to exclude outsiders from entrance. The result was a tightly knit endogamy, where the transfer of vacant positions was intimately linked to consanguinial and especially affinal ties.[19] As a result, the secular clergy became a closed, hereditary estate and even acquired the invidious epithet of caste. Similar processes affected all other social groups (from military personnel to minorities, from merchants to cossacks), but the effect was exceptionally great in the case of the clergy.

Simultaneously, the clergy acquired a distinctively separate status and code of conduct. Thus their juridical status evolved with that of the Church itself, which found itself increasingly segregated from the secular state and society.[20] That exclusivist status conferred certain privileges, such as exemption from corporal punishment, the poll tax and from various civic obligations.[21] But exclusion also entailed disabilities; it meant, for instance, a strict ban on participation in community affairs or involvement in trade and business.[22] Furthermore, the Church prescribed a normative code of conduct in its new pastoral guides and also issued formal decrees to regulate dress and social behaviour.[23] Authorities also endeavoured to regulate clerical

[19] Church prelates, chiefly from a desire to provide for orphans and widows, but partly out of a preference for girls reared within the cocoon of the clerical estate, forced ordinands to marry women from their own estate. See e.g. the materials on Perm in 1801 (I. Lagovskii, *Istoriia Permskoi dukhovnoi seminarii* (Perm, 1867–77), vol. 1, p. 9); Saratov in 1840 (A. Pravdin, 'Rezoliutsii Saratovskogo preosv. Iakova', *Saratovskie eparkhial'nye vedomosti* 4 (1878): 78), Riazan in 1841 (TsGIA SSSR, f. 797, op. 11, d. 28303, 1. 3–3 ob.), and Orenburg in 1850 (TsGIA SSSR, f. 796, op. 132, g. 1851, d. 2357, 1. 424).

[20] It bears emphasising that, contrary to traditional assumptions about the secularisation of the Church (especially by the Petrine reforms), in fact the Church experienced precisely the contrary process – that is a gradual exclusion from temporal affairs, aptly described in German as the *Entkirchlichung* of society. See also G.L. Freeze, 'Handmaiden of the state? The Church in Imperial Russia reconsidered', *Journal of Ecclesiastical History* 36 (1985): 82–102.

[21] See e.g. the decrees exempting the clergy from civic duties (fire-brigades, guard duties, etc.) in urban communities (*Polnoe sobranie postanovlenii i rasporiazhenii po vedomstvu pravoslavnogo ispovedaniia. Tsarstvovanie Elizavety Petrovny* (St Petersburg, 1899–1911), vol. 1, p. 72; TsGIA SSSR, f. 79, g. 1798, d. 1044).

[22] Most famous were the decrees forbidding the clergy to act as community clerk or draft petitions for serfs (see e.g. the decree of 1767 in *Polnoe sobranie postanovlenii i rasporiazhenii po vedomstvu pravoslavnogo ispovedaniia. Tsarstvovanie Ekateriny Alekseevny* (St Petersburg, 1910–15), vol. 2, p. 1,002). For the exclusion from business and trade, see *Opisanie dokumentov i del, khraniashchikhsia v arkhive Sv. Sinoda* (St Petersburg, 1869–1916), vol. 23, p. 503.

[23] Typical were the manifold attempts to regulate clerical dress *outside* the liturgy. See e.g. the following materials on Moscow diocese in 1744 (N. Rozanov, 'Preosv.

sociability, admonishing priests to eschew intercourse with lower status groups and encouraging them to socialise with people from their own estate.[24]

Despite the changes in recruitment and education, in 1800 the clergy still bore its traditional collective term of *dukhovnyi chin*. In the early nineteenth century, however, state authorities devised a new terminology to categorise (and control) social reality, eventually choosing the term *soslovie* and establishing its legitimacy in the official and demotic lexicon. The term was so puissant because it fused several key concept – status (*chin*), occupation (*zvanie*), clan (*rod*), and culture (*byt*) – to constitute the fundamental category for defining and identifying social groups. In theory, the *soslovie* category denied mobility and divided Russian society into a congeries of discrete social units; in reality, of course, the group boundaries were more porous, admitting varying degrees of upward and downward mobility. In the case of the Russian clergy, however, the estate boundaries were extraordinarily rigid; no other status group proved so hereditary, so inaccessible to outsiders.

Egress from the clerical estate was less difficult, though that too became increasingly restictive. Priests and monks, for example, could sue for voluntary defrocking and freely exercised that right in the eighteenth century.[25] But in the 1830s, largely at the behest of Nicholas I, the Church adopted new rules to discourage facile resignation by establishing severe disabilities on those who resigned

---

Iosif', *Moskovskie eparkhial'nye vedomosti* 21 (1869): 6–7), Poltava diocese in 1758 ('Nastavleniia iereiam Gervasiia, episkopa Pereiaslavskogo i Borisopol'skogo', *Rukovodstvo dlia sel'skikh pastyrei* 20 (1860): 34–5), Vladimir diocese in 1758 and 1884 ('K istorii nebogosluzhebnogo odeianiia Vladimirskogo dukhovenstva', *Vladimirskie eparkhial'nye vedomosti* 18 (1899): 17–21); P. Malitskii, 'Zaboty ep. Ieronima o vozvyshenii nravstvennosti i blagochiniia vladimirskogo dukhovenstva', ibid. 5 (1907): 68, Kazan in 1781 (A.N. Minkh, 'Byt dukhovenstva saratovskogo kraia v XVIII i nachale XIX v', *Trudy Saratovskoi uchenoi arkhivnoi komissii* 24 (1908): 56), and Astrakhan diocese in 1797 (I. Savvinskii, *Istoricheskaia zapiaka ob Astrakhanskoi eparkhii za 300 let ii sushchestvovaniia* (Astrakhan, 1903), p. 213). These local prescriptions became empire-wide in 1825, as central authorities issued a general decree on clerical dress (TsGIA SSSR, f. 796, op. 106, g. 1825, d. 969).

[24] See e.g. the advice in 'Zhizn' pastyria v mire', in *Khristianskoe chtenie*, 1844, ch. 3, pp. 436, 441–2, and a 1773 decree by Moscow authorities admonishing clergy to avoid public gathering-spots (*gul'bishche*) (N.A. Skvortsov, *Materialy po Moskve i Moskovskoi eparkhii za XVIII v* (Moscow, 1911–14), vol. 2, pp. 373–4).

[25] Curiously enough, as late as 1767, when the Synod compiled its instruction (*nakaz*) for the ecclesiastical deputy to the Legislative Commission, it included proposals to facilitate exit for clergymen unable or unwilling to remain in the priesthood. See *Sbornik Imperatorskogo russkogo istoricheskogo obshchestva* (St Petersburg, 1867–), vol. 43, pp. 42–62.

from Church service.[26] Nor could their children easily transfer to a civil status. Although a substantial number in the eighteenth century did enter civil or military service,[27] thereafter authorities generally made it increasingly difficult for them to seek their fortunes in a secular career.[28] That indeed created a grave new problem: a surfeit of qualified candidates. It was quite a paradox for the Russian Church, which had earlier bemoaned the lack of educated candidates, by the 1850s complained of too many qualified graduates (the surplus running into several thousand). In times past the state had summarily conscripted the unneeded (and uneducated) surplus into the army or lower status groups; by the mid-nineteenth century, however, this brutal procedure appeared so demeaning that the state had in effect renounced the process. The result was acute demographic imbalance – the hereditary clerical caste was too fecund, overproducing candidates for the static staffing needs of the Church.

It is highly instructive to compare the Russian Orthodox clergy with their counterparts in the Churches of western and central Europe in the first half of the nineteenth century. The Catholic clergy, despite superficial similarities in ecclesiastical organization and liturgical practice, followed a very different line of development. Much of the difference lies in dissimilar structures: in contrast to the complex organisation and universal celibacy of the Catholic clergy, the Russian clergy had a large clerical estate from which it could recruit monks, priests and bishops. By contrast, the celibate Catholic clergy had to recruit from lay social groups and hence proved highly susceptible to the vicissitudes of politics and piety. As a result, in the first half of the

---

[26] Responding to isolated cases of tainted clergy who defrocked to avoid punishment, but also inspired by the belief that the rites of holy ordination were indelible (and not to be lightly expunged by a wilful monk or priest), authorities imposed serious penalties – most importantly, by excluding priests from state service for a full ten years – to discourage all voluntary defrocking. See the materials in TsGIA SSSR, f. 112, g. 1831, d. 961; *PSZ(2)*, 14:12148. The result was a sharp drop in such defrocking, as attested by statistics compiled over the next two decades (TsGIA SSSR, f. 796, op. 141, g. 1860, d. 1021, 1. 17).

[27] Apart from voluntary transfers (especially, to serve in the bureaucracy and medical profession), clerical youth were also subject to periodic conscription levies (*razbory*) into the army. See the description and references in Freeze, *Russian Levites*, pp. 37–41.

[28] The obstacles, especially legal ones, were exhaustively described and analysed in the 1860s by bishops in their reports to a special reform commission. See the discussion and reference in G.L. Freeze, 'Caste and emancipation: the changing status of clerical families in the Great Reforms', in D.L. Ransel (ed.) *The Family in Imperial Russia: New Lines of Historical Research* (Urbana, 1978), pp. 124–50. At the same time, the government gradually moderated and finally abandoned its earlier practice of involuntary conscription of 'surplus' clerical children into the army, see Freeze, *Parish Clergy*, pp. 167–71.

nineteenth century, at the very time that the Russian Orthodox was groaning under the weight of a surfeit of candidates, the Catholic Church experienced an acute shortage of qualified ordinands.[29]

The Protestant clergy developed in a manner that seemed more analogous to the Russian Orthodox clergy: both suffered from a surplus of candidates[30] and displayed strong endogamous tendencies. Although the Protestant doctrine of calling ran contrary to familial claims and interests,[31] the post-reformation clergy nevertheless exhibited strong endogamous tendencies, as one-third to one-half of candidates in some areas were the sons of pastors.[32] Although that

[29] The diocesan archive for the archbishopric of München-Freising shows the acute dearth of candidates; one whole set of files for the early decades is appropriately labelled 'Priestermangel' (Archiv des Erzbistums München-Freising, Ordinatsakten, Faszikel 'Priestermangel', 1 and 2). For statistics on the high rate of attrition through death and much lower rate of new ordinations, see 'Errichtung eines Knaben-Seminars in Freising', in *Schematismus München-Freising* (München, 1828), pp. 109–22, and the data in M. Ratzka, 'Die Herkunft der Priester des Erzbistums München-Freising im Zeitalter der Restauration (1821–1846)', unpublished manuscript, Archiv des Erzbistums München-Freising. For the similar picture in contemporary France, see B. Guillemain *Le Diocèse de Bordeaux* (Paris, 1979), p. 197. For a more general picture, see H. Jedin, *Handbuch der Kirchengeschichte* (Freiburg, 1971), vol. 6, p. 77.

[30] For the problem in Germany, see R. Binder, *Die unglückliche Lage der protestantischen Pfarramts-kandidaten und die verfehlte Stellung der Vikarien in Württemberg* (Ulm, 1841); O. Fischer, 'Bilder aus der Vergangenheit des evangelischen Pfarrhauses', *Jahrbücher für brandenburgische Kirchengeschichte* 21 (1926): 14; R. Bigler, *Politics of German Protestantism: the Rise of the Protestant Church Elite in Prussia, 1815–1848* (Berkeley, 1972), p. 157.

[31] See R. O'Day, 'The reformation of the ministry (1558–1642)', in R. O'Day and F. Heale (eds) *Continuity and Change: Personnel and Administration of the Church of England 1500–1642* (Leicester, 1976), pp. 55–75; idem, *The English Clergy: the Emergence and Consolidation of a Profession, 1558–1642* (Leicester 1979).

[32] For example, for the period 1705–1714, the English clergy recruited 31 per cent of its members from their own group (J.H. Pruett, *The Parish Clergy under the Late Stewarts* (Urbana, 1978) p. 35). By the early nineteenth century this proportion had fallen sharply; in Worcester, for example, only 23 per cent came from clerical backgrounds (M. Ransome (ed.) *The State of the Bishopric of Worcester, 1782–1808* (Worcester, 1968), p. 8). Far higher rates were recorded among German Protestants. For example, data on clergy in Sachsen-Thüringen for 1540–1740 show that 58.4 per cent (2,511 of 4,299) were sons of clergymen (A. Schieckel, 'Die Pfarrerschaft und das Beamtentum in Sachsen-Thüringen', in G. Franz (ed.) *Beamtentum und Pfarrerstand 1400–1800* (Lemburg/Lahn, 1972), pp. 178–9). Even the more westerly Württemberg reported that 44 per cent of its Protestant pastors were from the clerical estate (G. Bormann, 'Studien zu Berufsbild und Berufswirklichkeit evangelischer Pfarrer in Württemberg. Die Herkunft der Pfarrer', *Social Compass* 10 (1966): 129). For further data, see K.E. Demandt, 'Amt und Familie; eine soziologisch-genealogische Studie zur hessischen Verwaltungsgeschichte des 16. Jahrhunderts', *Hessisches Jahrbuch für Landesgeschichte* 2 (1952): 79–133; S.K. Boles, 'Lutheran pastors in Ernestine Saxony and Thuringia 1521–1546', PhD Indiana University (1971); J. Schneider, *Die evangelischen Pfarrer der Markgraftschaft Baden-Durlach in der zweiten Hälfte des achtzehnten Jahrhunderts* (Lahr in Baden, 1936).

endogamy gradually steadily atrophied after 1800, with the quotient from clerical families gradually shrinking to one-quarter of candidates in most churches,[33] the selectivity index still shows a disproportionate recruitment from the clergy itself. Even so, that proportion in western churches constituted a dramatic contrast to the nearly 100 per cent found in contemporary Russia. More to the point, even though both had a surplus of candidates, the causes were radically different. Thus in Protestant churches it was the pastor's high status that proved attractive to men of all ranks, not just pastors' sons, and the office was open to all who attended the university and not some specialised ecclesiastical shool. That was very different from the Russian case, where a caste-like population simply over-produced sons for the available positions.

The late 1850s heralded the epoch of 'Great Reforms' in Russia – when, in the wake of the Crimean *débâcle*, state and society concurred on the necessity of radical reform in fundamental institutions of state and society. These reforms eventually enveloped virtually every segment of society – serfs and soldiers, Jews and judges. As a result, it ineluctably had to address the very structure of the *soslovie* order itself, which was universally castigated as a primary cause of the stagnation that led to the *débâcle* of the Crimean War. Even Tsarist bureaucrats wary of massive social change concurred on the need to loosen the *soslovie* bonds that seemed peculiar to Russia and to retard her social and economic development. Only by removing artificial walls between *sosloviia* and reducing state tutelage, it was argued, could authorities unleash the natural creative potential of the populace and thereby accelerate development. But authorities defined these objectives in narrow, gradualist terms; their aim was not to abolish

[33] For the English clergy, see A. Russell, *The Clerical Profession* (London, 1980); B. Heeney, *A Different Kind of Gentleman* (Hamden, Conn., 1976); and A. Haig, *The Victorian Clergy* (London, 1984). Hereditary lines remained firmer, but subject to steady erosion, among the continental Protestant clergy as well. For the whole period of 1800–1910 some 28 per cent of the pastors in Norway were clerical sons (D. Mannsaker, *Det norske presteskapt i det 19. Hundret* (Oslo, 1954), p. 143). A study of the Swedish clergy shows a sharp decline from 27 per cent in 1821–45 to 15 per cent by 1881–1915, see R. Norrman, *Fran prästöverflöd till prästbrist. Prästrykryteringen i Uppsala Ärkestift 1786–1965* (Uppsala, 1970), p. 210. A similar, if more sluggish, pattern emerges for nineteenth-century Germany. Thus the Württemberg clergy dropped from 44 per cent to 34 per cent for the period 1834–96 (Bormann, 'Studien', pp. 98, 129; see also A. Neher, *Die katholische und evangelische Geistlichkeit Württembergs 1817–1901* (Ravensburg, 1904), pp. 36–9). This process continued so that, by the late nineteenth century, only some 20 per cent of the Protestant pastors were born into that estate (K.-W. Dahm, *Beruf: Pfarrer. Empirische Aspekte* (Munich, 1971), pp. 86–8).

sosloviia by fiat, but to draw them closer together and thereby to overcome the mutual prejudices that inhibited cooperation and mobility. Thus the state sought to disregard, not disestablish, *soslovie* differences; the codeword was *vnesoslovnost'*, not *besslovnost'* – that is supra-*soslovie* rather than anti-*soslovie*. Their hope was that in time *soslovie* lines would gradually fade away – a pious gradualism so characteristic of the cautious reformers of the 1860s.

These ideas also shaped reform policy toward the clergy. Few, inside or outside the Church, challenged the view (ubiquitously expounded in private memoranda, official commissions and the press) that the Russian clergy fell woefully short of their high calling and hence were in urgent need of radical reform. And while many reasons were adduced to account for their poor performance (such as the ill-conceived curriculum in the seminary or the priest's poverty and economic dependence upon his parishioners), most contemporaries laid particular stress on the clergy's *soslovie* structure – the exclusiveness and endogamy that subverted merit and segregated the priest from his flock. In the late 1860s a joint Church–state commission attempted to transform the clergy from a hereditary estate (*Geburtsstand*) into a professional corporate body (*Berufsstand*) by abrogating the special claims of kinsmen to Church positions, by authorising the matriculation of outsiders in seminaries, and by facilitating the transfer of clerical offspring to secular schools and lay careers.[34]

It is important to note that this *soslovie* reform aimed at once to democratise and to professionalise the clergy. If the clergy were freely recruited from all social groups, if clergy intermarried with other segments of society, the reformers believed that the bonds between Church and lay society could be significantly strengthened. In theory, such democratisation would not only diminish the social distance between clerics and laymen, but also help to overcome the clergy's apparent indifference to worldly problems and to bolster their weak influence over their flock. That beneficent influence seemed all the more urgent in the wake of the emancipation of serfs in 1861, impelling many to conclude that only a more effective priesthood could guide ex-serfs to responsible citizenship.

The second goal – professionalisation – aspired to transform the clergy from a hereditary caste into a corps of professional servitors. By selecting ordinands with a sense of vocation (not mere familial claims), the Church should be able to staff its parish churches with a more dynamic corps of committed priests. Professionalisation also

[34] See Freeze, *Parish Clergy*, chs. 5–7.

entailed reform in the seminary, especially its curriculum, which was redesigned to provide more practical vocational training for the priest who would not merely perform liturgies and rites, but also preach and teach, catechise and counsel. The reforms also granted the clergy a modest degree of corporate self-government, including the right to elect peers to local clerical office (such as deanship) and to convene regular diocesan and district assemblies (primarily to address the financial needs of local seminaries, but potentially as well to deliberate common pastoral problems). And of special promise were plans to improve economic support for the clergy, above all by replacing the traditional forms of support (essentially, a combination of gratuities and cultivation of the glebe) with a state salary or parish tithe. Such a reform, it was widely agreed, would liberate the priests from their economic dependence on local parishioners and give them the time and opportunity to concentrate upon their non-liturgical duties.

For all their promise and ambition, these Great Reforms in Russian Orthodoxy (as indeed parallel efforts in other sectors) proved largely abortive. Above all, the scheme to redesign the *soslovie* into an open social group went awry: it did enable clerical sons to leave, but it failed miserably in attracting candidates from other social groups. This one-sided mobility derived from the fact that a clerical career continued to hold little appeal for educated laymen: its status was too low, its rewards too meagre, especially when compared with the other new professions. The impact on recruitment was catastrophic: within a decade of the reforms, the Orthodox Church experienced acute shortages of qualified candidates. It was not simply a matter of quantity: by the late 1870s bishops complained that it was precisely the most talented seminarians who abandoned the Church to pursue secular careers. In the event, the Church had the worst of both worlds: it still had to recruit from the same *soslovie*, but this pool had been stripped of its most talented personnel. The result was in fact a veritable de-professionalisation – an inexorable decline in educational standards.[35] Worse still, this de-intellectualisation transpired at the very time of an educational explosion among the laity, and the sharp plunge in educational standards (both absolutely and relatively) in the

---

[35] Among priests, for example, the proportion bearing a full seminary education shrank from 88.1 per cent to 63.8 per cent between 1890 and 1904; since many older priests remained in service, the proportion of *new* ordinands with inferior education was singularly high (TsGIA SSSR, f. 796, op. 172, g. 1891, d. 2883; *Vsepoddanneishii otchet oberprokurora Sv. Sinoda po vedomstvu pravoslavnogo ispovedaniia za 1903–1904 god* [St Petersburg, 1906], p. 112).

clergy could not but reflect badly on their status, especially with respect to middling and upper strata of society.

Although the reform diverted the flow of qualified candidates away from the Church, it nevertheless failed to dissolve *sosloviia* bonds for those who stayed behind. On the contrary, the very experience of the Great Reforms served to reinforce, not weaken, the clergy's estate mentality. By abrogating traditional privileges (above all, the hereditary right to a free ecclesiastical education and to transfer family positions), coupled with the failure to improve the clergy's material support, the reform only stiffened the clergy's sense of vested interest. This defence of estate interest found broader resonance in the late 1870s, for the surge of revolutionary terrorism drove the government to shift policy in search of more stable foundations for autocracy. Church authorities, for their part, were also sympathetic to estate interests, partly because of their anxiety over the shortage of candidates, and partly because most bishops themselves came from this very estate. At any rate, whether by formally rescinding or quietly failing to implement reform directives, the Church renewed its commitment to the clerical *soslovie* and its special interests. That was apparent, for example, when it elected to set quotas on the matriculation of outsiders in church schools. The quotas were partly a response to demands from the clerical *soslovie*, but they also resulted from a disillusionment with the open-enrolment policies, since many of the seminarians from other groups simply exploited an opportunity for a free education and then refused to enter Church service.[36]

To be sure, the renewed devotion to the *soslovie* principle (*soslovnost'*) had its limits, as enlightened clergymen – especially in the face of popular dechristianisation – attributed part of the Church's failings to their very own casteness. Yet that liberal fibre proved exceedingly tenacious; even priests deeply committed to social justice and political reform found it difficult to ignore the special interests of their own estate. To the very outbreak of the First World War, powerful vested

---

[36] By 1900 outsiders comprised nearly one-quarter of the seminaries and elementary ecclesiastical schools – which, until 1867, had been populated exclusively by children from the clerical estate. Dismayed that so few of the outsiders actually chose a clerical career, and determined to stem the disturbing influence of secular culture and political agitation inside ecclesiastical schools, the Church imposed a 10 per cent quota on boys from other estates. See the materials and legislation in TsGIA SSSR, f. 796, op. 179, g. 1898, d. 415. Despite such edicts, outsiders still exceeded the quota, comprising, for example, over 16 per cent of seminarians in 1911–12 (*Vsepoddanneishii otchet ober-prokurora Sv. Sinoda po vedomstvu pravoslavnogo ispovedaniia za 1911–1912 gg.* (St Petersburg, 1913), appendix).

interests in the clergy disposed many in that group to defend their special privileges and rights.[37]

Concomitantly, professionalisation proved as elusive as democratisation. In part, authorities annulled concessions toward professional corporateness, chiefly by rescinding the clergy's right to elect local officials and by narrowly defining the competence of the diocesan assemblies. This retrenchment, which accelerated amidst the counter-reforms of the 1880s, vitiated both the clergy's professional identity and autonomy. The regression was all the more disheartening for the clergy when they saw that other (and newer) professions were making gains toward corporate rights of assembly, self-regulation and representation before the state. Furthermore, the seminaries – which was supposed to produce the new breed of professional priests – were regarded more as hothouses for radicalism than religion. Indeed, so many alumni became revolutionaries that in 1879 the government limited the transfer of seminarians to Russian universities.[38] Of cardinal importance was the failure to professionalise the clergy's material support, to free them from demeaning gratuities and glebes, to ensure income that was both honourable and adequate. Nor did the effort to augment the priest's extra-liturgical functions fare well. Apart from the competition of newer professions (most notably, lay schoolteachers), authorities found that most priests had neither the time nor often even the qualifications (given the educational decline) to perform these newer functions. Many priests, especially the younger ones, did make an honest effort to raise the 'dark masses' from a superstitious ritualism and to inculcate to a more conscious Orthodoxy. But even the most zealous found it difficult to sunder the bonds of parish dependence or find time for their new professional duties.[39]

The malfunctions of the reform aside, it is arguable that the new professional model – as represented by elites like doctors and lawyers, even lesser groups like statisticians and teachers – ultimately was not applicable to the clergy. Much ink has been spilled in efforts to define

---

[37] See e.g. the collective statements in Freeze, *From Supplication to Revolution*, pp. 228–38, and *Zapiska dumskogo dukhovenstva, podannaia v avguste 1915 g. ober-prokuroru Sv. Sinoda A.D. Samarinu* (Petrograd, 1916).

[38] That measure did not, of course, stop the 'flight' (*begstvo*) of seminarians from Church service, and indeed became a principal cause of seminary disorders.

[39] To cite only the most well-known problem, parishes traditionally preferred a cleric, especially for the deacon's position, who had a strong bass voice – regardless of education and even moral reputation. That ran directly contrary to Church efforts to promote more educated candidates who could assist the priest and, simultaneously, serve as the religious teacher in elementary schools.

professions and the process of professionalism, and to determine which social or occupational categories qualify for inclusion in this new rank.[40] At the very least, the concept of profession presupposes several key characteristics – monopolistic possession of esoteric knowledge, autonomous organisation (to regulate recruitment, to define and enforce norms, and to defend the vested interests of the group), a shared sense of community, and an ethos of altruistic, self-less service. While that model fits the newer technical professions and often inspired imitation by other occupational groups (including the clergy),[41] even in the west the clergy found it difficult to fit into this new mould. To be sure, the Protestant and Catholic clerics – free from the bonds of hereditariness and *soslovnost'* – found it feasible to emulate some elements of professionalisation. Thus they already subscribed to an ethos of altruistic service; they often exercised control over licensing and standards; they found it useful and feasible to establish more specialised occupational training[42] and to convoke assemblies.[43] What proved most elusive was the occupational pro-

[40] See e.g. M.S. Larson, *The Rise of Professionalism: a Sociological Analysis* (Berkeley, 1977); B. Barber, 'Some problems in the sociology of professions', *Daedalus*, Autumn, (1963): 669–86; A. Etzioni, *The Semi-Professions* (New York, 1963); R.H. Hall, *Occupations and the Social Structure* (New York, 1969); P. Elliott, *The Sociology of the Professions* (London, 1972); E. Freidson (ed.) *The Professions and their Prospects* (Beverly Hills, 1971); R. Dingwall and P. Lewis (eds) *The Sociology of the Professions* (London, 1983). Some literature is devoted specifically to the clergy as a profession: T. Ferrence, F. Goldner and R. Ritti, 'Priests and the Church: the professionalization of an organization', in Freidson, *Professions*, pp. 173–90; idem, 'Priests and laity: a profession in transition', *Sociological Review Monographs* 20 (1973): 119–37; M. Marty, 'The clergy', in N. Hatch (ed.) *The Professions in American History* (Notre Dame, 1988); P. Jarvis, 'The parish ministry as a semi-profession', *Sociological Review* 23 (1975): 911–22.

[41] For an early expression of such sentiments, see the materials in J.M. Stroup, 'The struggle for identity in the clerical estate: northwest German Protestant opposition to absolutist policy in the eighteenth century', PhD Yale University (1980). For detailed analyses of the professionalisation processes in America, see J.W.T. Youngs, *God's Messengers: Religious Leadership in Colonial New England* (Baltimore, 1976); D. Scott, *From Office to Profession: the New England Ministry, 1750–1850* (Philadelphia, 1978); D. Merwick, *Boston Priests, 1848–1910* (Cambridge, 1973). For the English case, see Heeney, *Different Kind*, pp. 4–8; Russell, *Clerical Profession*, pp. 247–8; Haig, *Victorian Clergy*, pp. 1–26; and R. Blakely, *The Man in the Manse* (Edinburgh, 1978).

[42] On the need for more professional training, see G. Schulz, *Die praktische Ausbildung der Predigtamts-Kandidaten für das evangelische Kirchenamt* (Königsburg, 1844), and W. Bornemann, *Die Unzulänglichkeit des theologischen Studiums der Gegenwart* (Leipzig 1886).

[43] For the establishment of the *Konferenzen* and *Pastorunion* in Germany, see H. Werdermann, *Der evangelische Pfarrer in Geschichte und Gegenwart* (Leipzig, 1925), pp. 124–5, and H. Bruchner, *Die synodalen und presbyterialen Verfassungsformen in der Protestantischen Kirche des rechtsrheinischen Bayern im 19. Jahrhundert* (Berlin, 1977); for England see P.J. Welch, 'The revival of an active convocation of Canterbury', *Journal of Ecclesiastical History* 10 (1959): 188–97.

fessionalism, for their education and usual role (as preacher, counsellor, fund-raiser, and so on) made them a jack-of-all trades, not a technical expert indispensable to his clients. More important still, they suffered an inexorable role atrophy and redefinition, not through their actions, but as the inexorable result of macrosocial processes of professionalisation: other professions, such as teachers and psychiatrists, emerged to challenge and largely usurp roles once ascribed to the clergy.

That professional model proved even more elusive for the Russian Orthodox clergy.[44] One reason was its organisational structure, the discrete hierarchy that left yawning fissures between substrata (between the black and white clergy) and vitiated a sense of collective identity. Although most professions have internal hierarchies, few have the enmity that polarised the white and black clergy in late Imperial Russia. Nor did the clergy even succeed in sustaining their spiritual monopoly, as independent spiritual movements (such as Old Believers and sectarians) contested the Church's claim to the folk and their beliefs. Moreover, the clergy also failed to achieve total control over the process of recruitment, licensing and regulation; although the bishop had far-ranging authority, the clergy as an estate did not. Indeed, appointment was de facto subject to the irresistible influence of the parish itself.[45] Perhaps most significant of all, the professionalist ethic – especially its elitist superiority – ran contrary to an explicit desire to reorient the Church to 'this-wordly' concerns, with a deeper involvement in society and closer fusion with the laity. Although most clergy looked askance at radical proposals for immediate recognition of lay rights (for example to choose their parish priest), many tended to concede that the laity should have a greater participatory role in directing Church affairs.[46]

Viewed in a broader European perspective, the development of the Russian clergy – at first glance – appears to conform to a universal

---

[44] For the special development of Russian professions, see Dietrich Geyer, 'Zwischen Bildungsbürgertum und Intelligenzija: Staatsdienst und akademische Professionalisierung im vorrevolutionären Rußland', in W. Conze and J. Kocka (eds), *Bildungsbürgertum im 19. Jahrhundert* (Stuttgart, 1985), pp. 207–30.

[45] To be sure, proposals emerged sporadically for the clergy, either at the district or provincial level, to administer ecclesiastical justice, elect church officials and provide nominations for clerical positions. But these proposals, along with the larger agenda for ecclesiastical reform, failed to achieve enactment under the old regime.

[46] For an overview of this process, from the mid-nineteenth but especially early twentieth centuries, see F. Jockwig, *Der Weg der Laien auf das Landeskonzil der Russischen Orthodoxen Kirche Moskau, 1917–1918* (Würzburg, 1971); also J.A. Loya, 'Theological clarification of lay status in the Russian Church pertaining to the Moscow Reform Council of 1917–1918', PhD Fordham University (1985).

pattern of inexorable decline in the status and quality of new recruits. Indeed, by the early twentieth century, virtually every Church – Catholic, Orthodox, Protestant – faced a veritable crisis in the recruitment of qualified new ordinands.[47] But the operative dynamics were fundamentally different: whereas cultural processes (dechristianisation) and political anticlericalism played a key role in the west, the crisis of the clergy in Russia derived chiefly from the abortive effort to professionalise and democratise a *soslovie*.

This study of the Russian parish clergy suggests a number of broader conclusions about the social hierarchy in Imperial Russia and contemporary Europe. First, it demonstrates the need to recognise the complex interplay of multiple social identities – both ascriptive and self-conscious – in the process of social change. This pattern, evident in central and eastern Europe, was especially pronounced in Tsarist Russia, where both old and new status groups tended to assume the physiognomy (and legal form) of *soslovie*. That facilitated their integration into the existing order, conferred specific privileges and specifically promoted the advancement of collective organisation and autonomy. It is, conversely, important to note how traditional *sosloviia* – like the clergy – aspired to emulate the newer corporate professions, especially the forms of association that strengthened group identity and advanced its common interests. And the contrary was also true: professions reached backward to lay claim to *soslovie* titles and status. In a word, social mimicry, whether of past forms (estates) or newly emergent ones (professions), operated interactively between categories of social groups.

[47] For the Catholic clergy in France, see R. Gibson, *A Social History of French Catholicism, 1789–1914* (London, 1989); P. Huot-Pleuroux, *Le Recrutement sacerdotal dans le diocèse de Besançon de 1801 à 1960* (Paris, 1966); R.A. Hanneman and E.T. Gargan, 'Recruitment to the clergy in nineteenth-century France', *Journal of Interdisciplinary History* 9 (1978): 275–96; Abbé Bougard, *Le Grand péril de l'Église de France au XIXe siècle* (Paris, 1978); F. Boulard, *Essou ou declin du clergé français* (Paris, 1950); G. Cholvy, *Le Diocèse de Montpellier* (Paris, 1976) p. 242; B. Bligny, *Le Diocèse de Grenoble* (Paris, 1979) p. 259; A. Poitrineau, *Le Diocèse de Clérmont* (Paris, 1979), p. 265. For the German case, see the account in 'Zum Bildungsdefizit der Katholiken in Deutschland', *Historisch-politische Blätter* 118 (1896): 102–11. But the Catholic case was highly uneven, with surges as well as declines, in the recruitment pool. See G. Merkel, 'Studien zum Priesternachwuchs der Diözese Freiburg 1870–1914', *Freiburger Diözesan-Archiv* 94 (1974): 15–265.

The Protestant clergy, whose social position had once been so high, suffered a sharp decline in status and, accordingly, the number and standards of new ordinands. For the English case, see the discussion in Russell, *Clerical Profession*, pp. 241–2. For the problems with the German clergy, see the discussion in J. Schneider, *Kirchliches Jahrbuch* 31 (1904): 345; and Dahm, pp. 48–58, 80.

That process, in turn, suggests the need to consider the interaction, not the simple transition or exclusivity, of different kinds of social identities. Different kinds of social hierarchy interacted to define and diffuse social identities; the process of social restructuring was less one of replacement than the lamination of different elements. It is clear, for example, how confused (and, to contemporaries in *fin-de-siècle* Russia, how confusing) social identities had become by the final decades of the *ancien régime*.[48] The result was a swirling, fluid set of competing social hierarchies – not the simple displacement of one type by another. In Imperial Russia, that lamination and proliferation meant the interaction and competition of different identities, different principles of discrimination and affiliation – not mere class or estate, but also locus, culture, ethnicity and confession as well. The structural complexity proved inimical to group cohesion and, in some degree, accounts for the problems of group identity and social disorganisation in the Russian pre-revolution.

Acknowledgement

For financial support making the research for this chapter possible, the author is particularly grateful to the Alexander von Humboldt-Stiftung, the International Research and Exchanges Board, and the Fulbright-Hayes Faculty Research Programme.

[48] See the discussion and references in Freeze, 'The *soslovie* (estate) paradigm'; for an interesting discussion of the implications, see J. Neuberger, 'Stories of the street: hooliganism in the St Petersburg popular press', *Slavic Review* 48 (1989): 177–94.

CHAPTER FIVE

Between estate and profession: the Catholic parish clergy of early modern western Europe

Joseph Bergin
University of Manchester

In the long-running, now somewhat becalmed, debate over the nature of *ancien régime* society, scant attention has been paid to the clergy. This may seem a curious omission, as they were still recognised, in post-Reformation Catholic western Europe at least, as the first of the three orders. Membership of the first estate was personal and limited to an individual's lifetime, not collective and hereditary; entry was by taking of tonsure or religious vows; and as an estate, the clergy possessed privileges common to other social groups, but also legal and social features peculiar to themselves. French historians of the society of orders were all the more likely to accept the verdict of the *ancien régime* social and political thinkers on whom they drew, since the French clergy had crystallised far more sharply and visibly than either of the other two estates: alone of the three orders they possessed the right to assemble at regular intervals, to elect deputies, to maintain a permanently manned standing agency, and so on. These activities, and the need to defend them from erosion over several centuries, not only heightened the *ancien régime* clergy's self-consciousness, but also seemed to leave little for either theorists or historians to argue about.

While it would be interesting to investigate the defining characteristics of the clergy as an order, it is arguably more profitable to examine, from an empirical and social rather than from an explicitly theoretical angle, the structure and evolution of the most numerous section of that clergy, the parish clergy. Although historians involved in the society of orders debate may have neglected the clergy, it would be mistaken to regard them as a static, unchanging estate, protected against change by their constitutive privileges. For a considerable body of research now exists on the clergy, both higher and lower, and the aim of this chapter is to suggest how the experiences of the parish clergy may help us to understand what kind of order the clergy was. Its main title, 'between estate and profession', is intended to convey an initial hint of what was happening to them during the early modern period. Because of the sheer size of the subject, it has also seemed sensible to concentrate on a limited number of questions, and to focus on the French clergy, the subject of the most impressive research, while using comparative material from the Spanish and Italian churches where that is both possible and instructive.[1]

Some preliminary observations are indispensable before embarking on such a study. First, it is obvious that the term 'parish clergy' lacks precision and, on a purely theoretical level, is probably indefensible. But a definition that would satisfy the social theorist or jurist is rendered virtually impossible by the sheer variety of the lower echelons of early modern Europe's clergy. Even within parishes themselves, there were considerable differences in status and functions between clergy, so that the term 'parish clergy' must be viewed in the broadest sense, that is those holding parishes with formal title, their curates, and the other categories of clergy resident within parishes. Observed from a negative angle, it embraces those not sufficiently fortunate, clever or well-connected to belong to either the upper or the corporate clergy, secular or regular – in a sense, the first estate's own third estate.

It is also important to have some general idea of the institutional geography of the *ancien régime* churches in France, Spain and Italy. The French church was the largest within a single political framework, with around 110 dioceses in the mid-sixteenth century, and 130 by 1789; the Spanish kingdoms contained fifty-five dioceses around 1600, and sixty a century or so later, while Italy eclipsed both France and Spain together with about 315 dioceses. Many Italian dioceses were little more than glorified collections of urban parishes with a limited rural hinterland, but in Spain and in especially southern France the map was not much different. Clearly problems of governing, disciplining and reforming clergy here should have been simpler than in the vast, largely rural, dioceses of central and northern France and Spain. Similar variations can be found at parish level, with important consequences for the status and occupations of clergy resident in them. Disproportionately large parishes required annexes and chapels in outlying districts, but their vicars or curates were often

---

[1] Both the number and the range of references have been kept to a minimum; priority has been given to documenting statements involving quantitative evidence.

distinctly unwilling to reside in them, preferring the comforts of the local parish towns, and reluctantly commuting on horseback to perform services. This seems to have been the case in parts of Brittany and western France generally, but was not unknown in Italy and Spain. The consequences of such geographical and institutional inertia can be readily imagined, especially since few new dioceses or parishes were created from the seventeenth century onward. Parish structures were thus often seriously out of line with changing patterns of population settlement and density, especially after the population boom of the sixteenth century. Lastly the parish clergy also found themselves constrained by an age-old benefice system that was as rigid and unequal as it was complex.

These difficulties notwithstanding, it appears that almost everywhere in later medieval and sixteenth-century Europe, access to the ranks of the clergy was relatively easy, for both practical and theoretical reasons.[2] The church hierarchy as a whole was incapable of limiting numbers by imposing a strict set of entrance criteria. Where ordination statistics exist, they show that the numbers of those taking major orders were at their highest in French dioceses up to the wars of religion, while those taking the tonsure, and thereby obtaining the privileges of clergy, outnumbered those taking priestly orders by anything from ten or twenty to one in an average year.[3] Many of these clerics would never become priests or members of religious orders, and would exercise the option of returning to the lay state at a later time. Thus, while theorists and historians agree that conditions of entry are crucial to defining the clergy as an order, it is important to note – compared, for example, with the nobility – that conditions of exit were just as undemanding for clerics at any point before taking priestly orders or final religious vows. Moreover, before the Counter-Reformation the Church exercised little pressure on these clerics to make a choice one way or the other: clerical orders themselves had to be taken in correct sequence, but there was no timetable beyond that of reaching a stipulated minimum age. Children of as little as 8–11 years of age were still taking the tonsure in huge numbers in mid-sixteenth century France, Spain and Italy. The clerical estate thus extended far beyond those in priestly orders, and contained a vast underbelly of men who were technically clerics, but who in effect lived as laymen. The effect of this was severely to blur

---

[2] See the example of England before the Reformation, R.N. Swanson, *Church and Society in Later Medieval England* (Oxford, 1989), pp. 30ff.

[3] See nn. 10–11 below.

the line which in theory separated the clerical estate from the rest of society.

But this ease of access to the clergy was not simply a result of administrative neglect or failure. Until well into the Counter-Reformation, it was universally held that the clerical estate, as instituted by Christ and defined by the Church, was good and desirable in itself, and did not require of candidates anything more than a 'right intention' and the minimum capacity needed to fulfil the appropriate duties. Moreover, such attitudes found institutional support in the extraordinary complexity of the benefice system, particularly in its distinction between offices with and without cure of souls. Ranging from the wealthiest bishopric to the humblest chaplaincy, it created huge disparities between clergy, and gave rise to a corresponding complexity of motives on the part of those taking orders. It renders the litmus test most favoured by nineteenth- and twentieth-century Catholic historians and commentators – namely that vocations to the clergy are a prime index of religious fervour – largely inapplicable to the *ancien régime* Church. Viewed alongside the disjunction of the holding of office from the performance of a function so characteristic of the Church, these facts meant that the clergy would long remain far too heterogeneous to be regarded as a profession. They were an estate characterised by their way of life and privileges. Matters would slowly begin to change under the combined impact of social pressures and new ideas in the post-tridentine Church.

For all Charles Loyseau's flattering description of the clergy as the most perfect of orders, the later-medieval and sixteenth-century clergy were less than universally respected as an estate, or regarded as adequate as a profession. This has partly to do with the sheer size and variety of the clerical estate, but also with its geographical distribution. Historians have had considerable difficulty in establishing the size of early modern Europe's nobilities, and differ greatly in their estimates and conclusions. No less formidable a problem arises in respect of the clergy, and where figures exist, there are familiar difficulties in interpreting and deciphering early modern categories. Figures for Spain, Italy and France do not always cover the same realities, thus making direct comparisons on a number of questions impossible.

Historians of Spain are best served when it comes to assessing the global presence and distribution of clergy. Sixteenth-century Castile experienced a series of surveys culminating in the great household census of 1591, which gives a unique idea for the time of clerical density and geography. Such curiosity did not return until the eighteenth century, when it culminated in the census of 1797. In 1591, about 74,000 of Castile's population of some 6.5 million people were clergy, male and female; 33,000 of these were secular clergy of all ranks, of whom all but a few thousand can be classed as lower clergy. For the Spanish kingdoms as a whole, the clerical estate probably amounted to around 100,000 people, just over 1.1. per cent of the total population.[4] While this was probably not exceptional for Europe at the time, eighteenth-century surveys show that the total had continued to rise in both numerical and relative terms – for all of Spain, the clergy as a whole accounted for over 1.5 per cent in 1758, and nearly 1.4 per cent in 1797. Put differently, this means that Castile had one member of the secular clergy per 200 inhabitants in 1591, while the Spanish kingdoms as a whole had 1 to 141 in 1758 and 1 to 150 in 1797.[5] Most of this increase seems to have occurred in the seventeenth and early-eighteenth centuries, and was part of a wider increase centred primarily on the female religious orders. Equally interesting is the geography of this clerical population. The majority of the secular clergy were to be found in northern Spain, where an age-old system of dense, patrimonial parishes and benefices was the bedrock of the ecclesiastical estate, while the religious orders were heavily concentrated in the south, where parishes were large and poorly endowed. Moreover, both types of clergy were overwhelmingly concentrated in towns. This may come as more of a surprise in the case of the secular lower clergy than in that of the religious orders. If towns positively teemed with clergy, entire rural areas were short of them, with poor provinces like Extremadura, La Mancha and parts of Galicia being partly deserted. Nor does the pattern appear to have changed much over two centuries.[6] It is hardly surprising that this urban-based lower clergy, plethoric and mediocre in quality, were successively attacked by *arbitristas*, Church reformers and eighteenth-century enlightened ministers.

Italy had a reputation similar to Spain when it came to clergy, but there it is more difficult to get beyond the impressions of travellers

---

[4] See A. Dominguez Ortiz, 'Aspectos sociales de la vida ecclesiastica', in R.G. Villoslada (ed.) *Historia de la iglesia en España* (Madrid, 1979), vol. iv, pp. 17–19. A. Molinié-Bertrand, *Au siècle d'or: l'Espagne et ses hommes* (Paris, 1985), contains much information on the regional distribution of sixteenth-century clergy.

[5] Dominguez Ortiz, pp. 54ff; C. Hermann, *L'Eglise d'Espagne sous le patronage royal 1469–1834* (Madrid, 1988), p. 25.

[6] W.J. Callahan, *Church, Society and Politics in Spain 1750–1874* (Cambridge, Mass., 1984), pp. 8–9.

and commentators. Figures compiled for the kingdom of Naples between the 1620s and 1650s show an even higher density of both clerics and clergy. Clerics amounted to 3 per cent and more of the civil population, and about half of them were in full sacerdotal orders. Around 1650, the religious orders claimed 0.6 per cent of the peninsula's entire population. Towns were especially favoured: 12 per cent of the population of Lecce, in the Puglia, was clerical in the broad sense around 1630.[7] But such densities were probably untypical outside the southern kingdoms.

By comparison, historians of the French clergy lack global statistics of any real worth. The Crown never attempted major surveys or censuses, either in the sixteenth or eighteenth century. This did not prevent some from attempting to guess the clerical population. Colbert, convinced that France, too, had an excess of clergy, reached an impressionistic and exaggerated total of 260,000 clergy of all kinds, including tonsured clerics and members of religious orders, that is 1.2 per cent of the population.[8] Eighteenth-century estimates, albeit confined to particular provinces or localities and to the clergy in full orders or in vows, put the percentages a good deal lower, less than 1 per cent. Obviously, such guesswork is not very helpful; fortunately there are more limited, but well-founded, sources which enable us to form a better idea of the presence of the lower clergy in France. Surviving ordination statistics leave little doubt but that the numbers of clergy rose to a peak during the sixteenth century. In the middling-sized Norman diocese of Seez, 270 ordinations were recorded in 1445, but 1,196 in 1514.[9] In St Malo diocese, an average of fifty-seven priests were ordained a year in the 1550s, sixty-two a year in the 1570s, but with the religious wars worsening, forty in the 1580s and twenty in the 1590s. By way of comparison, we may note that the St Malo average for the eighteenth century varied between twenty and thirty-five.[10] In Grenoble diocese, there were fifty-five ordinations a year in the 1570s, seventy-nine in 1580s, eighty-one in 1590s, forty-nine in 1600s, but a growing percentage of these numbers was from the religious orders, leaving fewer secular clergy to serve in the

---

[7] R. Martucci, 'La formazione del clero meridionale tra sei e settecento', *Archivio Storico Italiano* 144(1986): 454–6; Y.-M. Bercé, G. Delille, J.M. Sallmann and J.C. Waquet, *L'Italie au xviie siècle* (Paris, 1989), pp. 239–42, 255.

[8] J. Quéniart, *Les Hommes, l'église et dieu dans la France du xviiie siècle* (Paris, 1978), p. 15.

[9] F. Rapp, *L'Eglise et la vie religieuse en occident à la fin du moyen âge* (Paris, 1971), p. 213.

[10] J. Delumeau (ed.) *Le Diocèse de Rennes* (Paris, 1979), p. 108.

parishes of a diocese with 312 parishes.[11] Although comparable figures are lacking for other dioceses, it is clear that clerical hopefuls from the uplands of the Auvergne, Massif Central, the Dauphiné and Provence, poured into the papal enclave of Avignon during much of the sixteenth century where ordinations were easily obtained with few questions asked until at least the 1560s.

In the absence of ordination lists, visitation records occasionally convey some impression of the scale of the clerical presence: the ratio for Nantes diocese in 1554 was one priest to 270 inhabitants, in 1563 it was 1:143, in 1572, 1:197, in 1640, 1:250, while the ratio for the whole of Brittany around 1700 was about 1:212. These were high densities by comparison with the dioceses of Chartres and La Rochelle, where it was 1:400 around 1650, though it had apparently been around 1:100 in La Rochelle in the early sixteenth century.[12]

In virtually every area of France for which figures exist, the Wars of Religion, especially from the 1580s onwards, seem to have triggered a sharp drop in entry into the clergy. The totals would rise again thereafter, but never to their mid-sixteenth-century peaks. Thereafter, France's experience would be the reverse of that of Spain and Italy: the clergy would decrease both absolutely and relatively. Whether their numbers would have risen again to previous levels after the Wars of Religion, had all other things been equal, is debatable, but there was a new factor present in the early decades of the seventeenth century: the French Counter-Reformation Church was now making entry into the clerical estate more difficult than hitherto.

But general diocesan averages of ordinations or ratios of clergy to laity tell only part of the story. A major feature of French history since the Revolution has been a well-defined geography of clerical recruitment, as indeed of religious observance generally, with certain localities and regions regarded as over-producers or under-producers of clergy. Early indications of both processes have been documented for the eighteenth century. Despite problems with sources, there is some evidence to suggest that such patterns of clerical recruitment were already present in the seventeenth century, and may even represent much longer-term patterns. This can be observed at both an intra- and an inter-diocesan level. Louis Pérouas discovered in the La Rochelle diocese for the period 1650–1720 what he called a 'religious dimorphism', with the hinterland of La Rochelle and

---

[11] B. Bligny (ed.) *Le Diocèse de Grenoble* (Paris, 1979), pp. 118–19.
[12] A. Croix, *La Bretagne aux xvie et xviie siècles* (Paris, 1981), vol. ii, pp. 1,157–61.

southern parts of the diocese depending heavily on the northern deaneries to supply them with clergy; in some districts, up to 70 per cent of clergy serving in parishes came from the north.[13] In Reims in the same period, the north-eastern and south-eastern deaneries provided a disproportionate number of the parish clergy, while certain localities, notably around the town of Reims itself, provided scarcely any.[14]

There were inter-diocesan, even regional, disparities, too. Throughout the seventeenth century, over one-third and occasionally even half of the rural parishes of Paris diocese were filled by migrant clergy, especially from Normandy; in one archdeaconry, the figure was around 80 per cent. In 1708, 30 per cent of the Beauvais parish clergy were outsiders, most of them also Norman.[15] Other areas like the Orléanais and parts of the Loire valley also had high numbers of outsider clergy. There were Norman clergy in significant numbers in some Breton dioceses from the late sixteenth century onwards; from Liège and Luxembourg in Reims; from the Auvergne, Provence and Dauphiné in Avignon and the Rhône valley, from Auch and Béarn in Tarbes, and so on.[16]

It is not easy to evaluate the significance of these patterns. Not only are the statistics needed to plot a map of clerical abundance and scarcity for France as a whole before the nineteenth century lacking, but also clerical migration was a perfectly normal and enduring feature of the medieval and early modern Church. Clerical autonomy was still a reality, and boundaries between dioceses were highly porous, as the cases of Beauvais, Paris, Reims and Tarbes show; it was normal practice for areas producing an excess of clergy not only to export some of their own, but even to attract others from outside. Brittany, never short of clergy under the *ancien régime*, witnessed considerable clerical migration from diocese to diocese, while also attracting clergy from neighbouring Norman dioceses. Much of this movement was due to the gross inequalities of the benefice system, which could take clergy on surprisingly long-distance journeys in search of better livings. Consequently, the threshold between the

---

[13] L. Pérouas, *Le Diocèse de La Rochelle de 1648 à 1724* (Paris, 1965), pp. 199–200.

[14] D. Julia and D. McKee, 'Le clergé paroissial dans le diocèse de Reims sous l'épiscopat de Charles-Maurice Le Tellier: origines et carrières', *Revue d'Histoire Moderne et Contemporaine* 29(1982): 534–7.

[15] Julia and McKee, p. 533.

[16] T. Tackett, 'Social history of the diocesan clergy in eighteenth-century France', in R.M. Golden (ed.) *Church, State and Society under the Bourbon Kings of France* (Lawrence, Kansas, 1982), pp. 329–31.

over-producing and the under-producing dioceses and regions cannot be firmly established for the *ancien régime*. At best, one can detect areas which consistently failed to produce enough clergy to meet their needs at parish level. To date, these include Paris *extra-muros* and perhaps the Ile-de-France generally, the Orléanais, parts of the Loire and southern Rhône valleys, the Toulouse plain and the Garonne valley, all of which were consistently dependent on large numbers of immigrant clergy from at least the seventeenth century onwards.

But what about the presence of the clergy at parish level, in both town and country? In certain parts of France, it was not uncommon to have anything from ten to twenty secular priests living within a parish, as the bishop of St Pol de Léon in Brittany claimed in 1630, but with considerable variations in their status and functions.[17] While only one of them would hold the title of parish priest, all would have aspired to a parish or benefice of their own – a prime incentive to geographical mobility. Despite this, it seems that in the sixteenth century in Brittany, the south-west and perhaps elsewhere, a high proportion of parish priests and perhaps their curates were natives of the parish they served in. In both France and Spain, this was probably closely connected to extensive presentation rights to parishes and other benefices belonging to local families or religious institutions. In Spain, however, there was far greater pressure to exclude outsiders altogether and although the Crown and the Church refused to legislate to that effect, custom probably ensured that parishes, curacies and other benefices were reserved for native-born clergy.[18] This phenomenon was much more muted in the French Church. Indeed, its consequences – a parish clergy that too closely resembled their parishioners – would be quite unpalatable to the Counter-Reformation Church, which did much to undermine such arrangements.

But with far too many clergy chasing too few parishes, even a curacy could prove attractive to some. Outside large parishes which traditionally possessed curates, it is unclear before the mid-seventeenth century how common or numerous curates were. Many parish priests were either unwilling or unable to pay for their upkeep, and it took sustained pressure from both Counter-Reformation bishops and parishioners to overcome their resistance.

But this still leaves many other members of the lower clergy to be accounted for in the average parish. The endowment of numerous

---

[17] Croix, vol. ii, p. 1,159.
[18] Hermann, pp. 22ff.

chapellenies throughout later medieval Europe catered for some of them, but these were not necessarily open to all comers, and were often intended by families, especially nobles, for their own younger sons. Consequently, many of the unbeneficed clergy were reduced to membership of societies of priests (*communautés de prêtres, prêtres filleuls*, chantry priests) which, in France at least, emerged clearly only in the early sixteenth century. They flourished in Brittany, the uplands of the Auvergne, Dauphiné, and the Pyrénées, La Rochelle diocese and perhaps elsewhere. There were at least 165 such communities in the Rouergue in 1522, 141 in 1675, and 53 in 1771. In Limoges diocese there were still 114 of them in the late eighteenth century, but by then membership had generally dwindled to twos and threes, where two centuries earlier some communities had between 50 and 100 members.[19] Similar patterns may have obtained elsewhere before the Counter-Reformation began to take effect.

The presence and survival of these communities is usually a good indicator of areas producing a surplus of clergy, for nearly everywhere only clergy born in the parish were admitted to membership; outsiders, even where acceptable, often had to pay a stiff entry fee; and everywhere, membership was incompatible with the holding of a benefice of any kind, even without cure of souls. Despite this, the presence of communities reduced rather than removed altogther the urge to migrate to other dioceses. The French communities were often precarious financially, living off the proceeds of pious benefactions and foundations which might or might not be paid, saying masses for the dead, attending ceremonies and, in a vague way, assisting the parish priest. Because of these factors, it was frequently they, rather than the parish priests or curates, who were the subject of reformist criticism and anticlerical satire; although their destitution was relative rather than absolute, it was they who came closest to being a kind of clerical proletariat. Church authorities and reformers were perennially suspicious of them, and made strenuous efforts to discipline them, without however eliminating them altogether. In southern Italy and northern Spain similar societies existed, but in many instances enjoyed greater autonomy and corporate status. Often, they collectively controlled the parish living, with the functions of parish priest rotating among members. Here bishops disliked

[19] N. Lemaître, 'Les communautés des prêtres-filleuls dans la Rouergue d'ancien régime', *Ricerche di Storia Sociale e Religiosa* 17 (1988): 33–58; N. Lemaître, 'Les communautés des prêtres filleuls d'Ussel à la fin de l'ancien régime', *Actes du 102e Congrès National des Sociétés Savantes* (Paris, 1977), vol. i, pp. 295–309.

them as much for their independence as for their behaviour, but found them harder to deal with than their French counterparts, who lacked comparable status.[20]

But the different careers and fortunes of the lower clergy cannot be understood in purely institutional terms; a study of their social origins provides some useful insights into the evolution of the early modern clergy. Once again, the best research has been done for the eighteenth century, where documentation is relatively good if not uniform throughout France, while for Spain and Italy, the lack of detailed studies makes even guesswork hazardous. For earlier centuries, historians often have to make do with fragmentary and often laconic ordination lists or bishops' registers, so any conclusions are necessarily speculative.

The high rates of entry into the clergy in the sixteenth century suggest there were few impediments to candidates of modest social background. The low standards of education and competence demanded of ordinands by the Church, the fact that most of them received their rudimentary clerical apprenticeship from the priests of their parish (often their blood relatives), and their tendency to stay on in their native parishes, in whatever capacity, after ordination – all made the taking of orders relatively easy to envisage. If the proportion of nobles who became priests was generally higher than their proportion of the total population, relatively few of them were content with being parish priests. However, these did exist. In Breton and south-western dioceses, as well as in northern Spain, noble parish priests were often to be found in parishes where their own families enjoyed patronage rights; but they were just as happy to hold minor benefices, without cure of souls but guaranteeing a reasonable income, benefices mostly situated in their native parishes and regarded virtually as family heirlooms. Whether the phenomenon of noble parish- or parish-based priests was more widespread than this remains to be established. There are indications that they had become increasingly rare, even where they had once been numerous, by the eighteenth century. In the northern Breton diocese of Tréguier, they fell by half between 1710 and 1789, and by even more than that in the southern Breton diocese of Vannes.[21]

One of the most significant features of the French Counter-

---

[20] Bercé *et al.*, pp. 255–6.

[21] G. Minois, *La Bretagne des prêtres en Trégor sous l'ancien régime* (n.p., 1977), pp. 202–9, 236–7; T.J.A. Le Goff, *Vannes in the Eighteenth Century* (Oxford, 1981), pp. 248–51.

Reformation parish clergy is how large a proportion of it was drawn from the *bourgeoisie* of town and country. They appear to have made their greatest gains in the century and a half after the Wars of Religion. By the late seventeenth or early eighteenth century, they accounted for over 80 per cent of the Reims parish clergy; 85 per cent in the diocese of Autun; 78 per cent in Lyon, and probably the same in Tarbes in the south-west.[22] Such high ratios left little enough room for social groups below the *bourgeoisie*: only sons of prosperous and, less frequently, of middling peasants and artisans stood much of a chance of taking orders at all, let alone acquiring a parish, from the mid-seventeenth century onwards. Unless they found benefactors or obtained free places in colleges or seminaries, sons of urban or rural labourers were virtually excluded. Between 1650 and 1750 in the Forez district of Lyon diocese, sons of the peasantry averaged about 22 per cent of the parish clergy, a disproportionately low figure for an overwhelmingly rural area, while there was not one ordination of priests from a lower social class; between 1650 and 1789, less than 1 per cent of those becoming tonsured clerics were from humble social backgrounds.[23]

Against this pattern of bourgeois near-monopoly should be set the evidence from certain northern and western dioceses of France where sons of well-to-do peasants continued to enter the clergy in considerable numbers. But as much of the evidence comes from the eighteenth century, when there are signs that the Church was obliged to make it easier for the sons of peasants and artisans to take orders, we cannot be sure if this represents a longer-term pattern.

Despite these uncertainties, it is clear the parish clergy of Counter-Reformation France were not drawn from 'la lie du peuple'. Indeed, it seems that from the seventeenth century onwards even the parish clergy of rural France were increasingly of urban *bourgeois* origin, which may explain their detachment from their parishioners and their disdain for the rituals of popular religion. But how are we to explain this social profile of the French lower clergy? In particular, why were sons of the 'bourgeoisie' so dominant among the lower clergy?

Several complementary explanations, not all of the same order, are possible. Careers in the Church, like those in royal or seigneurial service, were an intrinsic part of the *bourgeoisie*'s search for social status and recognition. An undoubted, often significant, rise in clerical

[22] Quéniart, pp. 78–80.
[23] N. El Hajje-Kervevan, 'Sociologie du clergé forézien 1650–1789', *Histoire, Économie Société* 4 (1985): 504.

incomes following the Wars of Religion, also rendered the Church attractive, all the more so as the French clergy were relatively protected from the fiscal burdens endured by seventeenth-century taxpayers; parish priests, and even curates, could enjoy very comfortable incomes by mid-century. Moreover, a rapprochement between the Church and the urban lay elites, which can be traced to the later Wars of Religion, spawned the intense religious activism so central to the French Counter-Reformation, and enabled these elites to provide the Church with most of its highest-quality clergy.[24]

But a social history of the parish clergy cannot, any more than institutional history, fully explain the changes that were taking effect among them. It is essential to realise that the Church itself was trying to change them in significant ways. Its efforts have usually been seen in terms of new institutions like seminaries for the education and systematic training of the clergy. But that is too facile and limited an explanation; indeed, the much vaunted tridentine seminaries must be seen as a complement to, not a substitute for, other measures of a more prosaic, conventional kind. Bishops and Church authorities were both obliged to, and proved perfectly capable of, working within traditional institutions and the benefice-system to produce change; it was because they were having some success, rather than the opposite, that they gradually began reaching out for novelties like seminaries. We can only briefly review the most important of them here.

First, there is no doubt that after 1600 episcopal authority over French dioceses and clergy was greatly revived and reinforced after the high rates of pluralism and absenteeism of previous generations. It was a slow process, punctuated by rows between bishops and clergy, few of whom welcomed what they regarded as episcopal absolutism. If change was slow, it was because it depended heavily on Crown support, and until the age of Louis XIV, the Crown's control of the provinces was too limited for bishops to have it all their own way. But from the 1670s–80s onwards, there is no doubting the solidity of the episcopal-royal alliance for the strengthening of episcopal authority. Despite the security of tenure conferred by the benefice system, the autonomy of the parish clergy was severely weakened, enabling bishops to supervise and discipline them in a way that would have been unthinkable a century earlier. In Spain and Italy different political conditions prevented the emergence of comparable

---

[24] For one case of this, see P.T. Hoffman, *Church and Community in the Diocese of Lyon 1500–1789* (New Haven, 1984), p. 44.

episcopal power, and a greater measure of presbyteral autonomy obtained. The changes in France did much to reshape the lower clergy.

The post-tridentine Church attempted to curtail the vast numbers of persons taking the tonsure, by insisting on a minimum age of 14 years for those acquiring benefices, and on an examination to test educational achievement. It was only gradually enforced, but the result was that by around 1700, the numbers of those taking minor orders began to tally fairly closely with those proceeding later to the priesthood. The proliferating mass of mere clerics in minor orders of earlier centuries was slowly wiped out, thus rendering the clergy a more visibly separate estate within society. Minor clerical orders were increasingly seen as a stepping stone to the priesthood, and the clerical estate was slowly becoming a sacerdotal one.

No less significant was the gradual enforcement of an obligation on all those wishing to take orders to prove that they already possessed a secure source of income called a clerical title. The idea was not new, but the manner of its enforcement certainly was. The income from a clerical title might be provided by a benefice, generally without cure of souls, or by an annuity of some kind – called a patrimonial title – which would enable aspiring priests to live decently until such time as they could acquire a benefice. Since gaining benefices either before or after ordination was not a simple matter, especially for those from modest or poor backgrounds, this condition effectively obliged families or, more rarely, patrons, to provide a fixed source of income for those intent on taking orders. The Council of Trent saw this measure as a way of cleaning up the lower ranks of the clergy, and of ensuring a minimum of decency and good behaviour among the inflated ranks of non-beneficed clergy. The ruling was enforced in Naples from the late sixteenth century, and also in Spain, but either the annuity required was very low or the ruling was feebly enforced, for the clerical population continued to rise during subsequent centuries. Although Trent's decrees were never officially promulgated in France, royal legislation on this point closely followed Trent, and initially fixed the annuity at 60 *livres* a year. However, royal legislation was not uniformly implemented in individual dioceses, and the ensuing variations may help to explain the differing social backgrounds of the French lower clergy: in Lyon, the requirement still stood at sixty *livres* in the 1730s; in the 1630s it was already eighty *livres* in La Rochelle diocese, but was raised to 100 *livres* by the 1680s, a figure to be found in numerous other dioceses.[25] But whatever their

[25] El Hajje-Kervevan, pp. 500–1; Pérouas, p. 197.

monetary value, there is no doubting the importance attached to these titles by bishops and by those seeking orders. They had to be properly registered and produced before orders could be taken. What this policy meant was that families or personal patrons wishing to provide a stable income of, say, 100 *livres* for prospective clerics had to set aside capital of around 2,000 *livres*. This was a very substantial sum, several times the annual income of any labourer or all but the most prosperous artisan. In some dioceses, there were a few endowed places in seminaries for poorer students, for whom these places would provide the equivalent of a clerical title. But given the financial precariousness of most seminaries for a long time, these places were statistically insignificant. Consequently, unless families were comfortable enough to sacrifice a large amount of capital, over and above the often considerable costs of schooling, they stood little chance of seeing their sons ordained.

The impact of this piece of Church policy cannot be underestimated, and was at least twofold: it helped to thin the ranks of the clergy, though how severely and at what speed varied considerably from diocese to diocese; it also eliminated all but a handful of priests from among the lowest classes. Sons of the labouring poor, of poorer peasants or even modest artisans could no longer really aspire to the priesthood. As we saw, no one from these groups was ordained in the Forez area between 1650 and 1750, while sons of the peasantry fell as a proportion of ordinands from 23 per cent in the 1650s and 1660s to under 10 per cent in the later seventeenth and early eighteenth centuries, before recovering to above 20 per cent in the later eighteenth century.[26] Indeed, there are signs that this restrictive policy may even have been too successful, for some eighteenth-century bishops began easing entry to the clergy for certain social categories, like artisans and peasants, at a time when the nobility and sections of the bourgeoisie were becoming less keen on clerical careers for their sons, by providing more free places in seminaries or allowing the real value of the clerical title to slide. A combination of these factors may explain why sons of the peasantry figured more prominently in places like Vannes, Coutances and elsewhere in the eighteenth century, especially when ordinations began to drop sharply after 1740–60.[27]

During the early Counter-Reformation, French bishops were hampered by their limited rights to appoint to parishes: in some dioceses,

[26] El Hajje-Kervevan, pp. 502–6.
[27] Le Goff, pp. 254, 260.

they could appoint to only one in ten, in others to over three-quarters, with numerous variations within that range; but even these percentages were often theoretical, since long-standing practices of resigning or exchanging benefices were both widespread and subject to minimal interference, and greatly facilitated the perpetuation of dynasties of parish priests. Nepotism was not a papal monopoly, and families were determined to retain those benefices they laid their hands on. Nevertheless, Counter-Reformation bishops were gradually able to alter clerical standards by increasing their control of the benefice system. It was Church policy after Trent to institute competitive examinations called *concours* for those seeking parishes. French bishops began, again with great variations in time-scale, by doing this for benefices at their own disposal; in places like Brittany, Provence and other areas not subject to the 1516 concordat of Bologna, *concours* were instituted for parishes and other benefices in the gift of the papacy. Where it proved impractical to have a full-blown *concours*, candidates for benefices had to pass a qualifying exam after which they were declared fit for parish service. By the later seventeenth century, it seems that in some dioceses lay and other patrons were coming round to accepting that the *concours* should apply to benefices in their gift, too.[28] But even before that point was reached, bishops had been insisting on setting minimum standards for priests 'presented' to them by patrons; acceptance of a full-blooded *concours* by patrons was, in a sense, a logical extension of such efforts. Apart from extending episcopal control of the benefice system, the major consequence of recruitment by *concours* was to raise the educational standards of the clergy seeking parishes. Curates or *vicaires* provide a good illustration of this. Traditionally, they were a category of parish clergy that escaped episcopal control almost entirely, being hired and fired directly by parish priests often reluctant to have them at all. Visitation records show this to be a constant preoccupation of bishops and their officials, while there was similar pressure from parishioners, especially in the larger rural parishes of the west and centre. This combined pressure gradually told, no doubt helped by the rise in clerical revenues. But here, too, bishops reserved the right to examine and approve curates being proposed by parish priests, whose independence was curtailed accordingly. Indeed by the later seventeenth century, some bishops were insisting that they would not allow anyone to take up a parish – whoever the

[28] O. Chadwick, *The Popes and the European Revolution* (Oxford, 1981), pp. 121–33; Callahan, pp. 17ff; Minois, pp. 237ff.

patron might be – unless the candidate had previously served time as a curate.[29]

These somewhat unspectacular measures were extensions of traditional episcopal prerogative, but produced results because they were applied at the traditional intersection of Church and society – the benefice system. But the same benefice system sharply limited the possibilities of total episcopal control over the lower clergy. Benefices conferred tenure, and there is plenty of evidence from the eighteenth centrury, after over a century of efforts at reform, that French parish priests were still able to get away with behaviour deemed unclerical by their superiors.

For that reason, continuing pressure, both disciplinary and educational, had to be exerted on the parish clergy. The practice of pastoral visitations was resumed on a large scale during the French Counter-Reformation, and served both a disciplinary and an educational purpose. Large-scale and organised missions were another major feature of the Counter-Reformation, often carried out by whole teams of clergy drawn mostly from the newer religious orders; in France, at least, they spent a great deal of time, especially up to the 1640s and 1650s, knocking clerical heads together and virtually acting as itinerant seminaries in backward areas. Likewise the practice of dividing dioceses into territorial units for the purpose of holding regular, often monthly, ecclesiastical conferences among the parish clergy, where the better educated were expected to instruct the more benighted on pastoral and ethical questions, was first tried in Italy after Trent and later taken up by the French; it seems to have worked reasonably well as an educational tool until issues like Jansenism made many bishops either curtail or close them down altogether for fear of doctrinal contamination.

The development of seminaries should be seen within this context of disciplinary and educational policies towards the lower clergy. French historians of the Counter-Reformation have often confused those of the *ancien régime* with the full-blown *grands seminaires* and *petits seminaires* of the nineteenth century, when in fact they differed to a significant degree. The Council of Trent recommended seminaries for future clergy, but provided no specific guidelines. Many were founded in Italy and especially Spain in the last decades of the sixteenth century, and again in the eighteenth century. But they were frequently no more than glorified grammar schools for boys, and for that reason opposed by existing schools, religious orders with col-

[29] Julia and McKee, p. 582.

leges, and even universities. Many were severely short of competent directors and teachers. Nor were they obligatory for those seeking to take priestly orders, while even those attending them continued to take philosophy and theology courses in external colleges or institutions. Most of them appear to have stagnated during the seventeenth and early eighteenth century. The few French seminaries founded after Trent did not survive the religious wars, and a new wave of foundations only began in the 1630s. But by then, the French Church could at least rely on the Jesuits, the Oratorians, the Lazarists and the Doctrinaires, all capable of running seminaries with reasonable efficiency. Even so, progress was slow: many seminaries were severely underfunded, relying more on private benefactors than on either bishops or clergy; frequently small in scale, few could house more than a dozen or so intending clergy; furthermore, they served a variety of objectives, and were used, for example, to discipline existing, especially disreputable, clergy. As far as aspiring clergy were concerned, most seminaries initially received them for only a few weeks before ordination, offering them a crash course on the basics of the liturgy, but they were probably incapable of training them how to preach; even when the typical course was increased later to one year, the 'year' seems to have consisted of several sandwich courses staggered over several years. The nineteenth-century seminary, with its comprehensive academic, pastoral and liturgical formation, and its aim of producing a distinctively clerical personality, was still a long way off. It is not hard to see why bishops who valued seminaries could not rely on them alone to transform their clergy.[30]

Yet, taken as a whole, the development and intensive use of pastoral visitations, synods, missions, ecclesiastical conferences and seminaries, suggests that the Counter-Reformation Church was, however unconsciously at times, attempting to impose the marks of a profession on the lower clergy. In practice, something like a career structure for the lower clergy began to appear, one which was roughly as follows: the tonsure would be taken at about the age of 14, and would overlap with study at a college or *régence latine*; stays of variable length might follow later in a seminary, usually in between taking sub-diaconate and diaconate, with final orders coming finally at the age of 25. Then, for a growing percentage of priests already partly uprooted by attendance at college or seminary, there would follow many years as a curate in one or more

[30] See Chadwick, pp. 112–21; A. Dégert, *Histoire des séminaires français jusqu'à la Révolution* (Paris, 1912) 2 vols; Villoslada, *Historia de la iglesia en España*, vol. iv, pp. 525ff.

parishes before the ultimate objective of securing a parish for oneself was realised. Previous rates of mobility between benefices were thus sharply reduced, and by the eighteenth century, bishops and their officials had secured far greater control over the movements of the lower clergy.

But if a career structure and a certain professionalisation gradually appeared among the lower clergy, it was not merely the result of administrative pressure from above. There is a final, indispensable element, which can be only briefly sketched here by way of conclusion. At the level of ideas, a slow but important shift was taking place, particularly in the French Church, which was to export its ideas to eighteenth-century Spain and Italy. While remaining within a traditional framework which they were not free to discard, even had they wished to, the leading thinkers and reformers of the seventeenth century – many of whom took a direct hand in forming new generations of clergy – attempted to revalue the priesthood, at the expense of both the laity and the religious orders. They were primarily concerned to elevate the priesthood itself to a separate plane; while this involved far more than defining it as just another profession requiring trained and competent members, it could not but have consequences for the clergy's performance of its duties. Linguistic conservatism might ensure that the terms estate and profession were still interchangeable, but the *école française* increasingly insisted that the priesthood was a condition which required a positive sense of calling on the part of candidates. No longer would it do to embrace such a condition merely because it was good in itself; candidates must experience a 'particular attraction', as it was called, to it within themselves.[31] Even then, that vocation had to be scrutinised and tested to ensure it was genuine, and not a smokescreen for less worthy motives. Needless to say, in practice, such high ideals were unattainable in a Church where the benefice-system and family pressures remained powerful forces. But even those eighteenth-century clerics who acknowledged that family decisions determined their destinies, clearly betray their awareness of the Church's official line. Without it, the French seminary movement, which would be copied in eighteenth-century Spain and Italy, would have been unthinkable. If the duration of seminary courses tended to lengthen by the eighteenth

---

[31] For the early stages of this change, see M. Dupuy, *Bérulle et le sacerdoce* (Paris 1969). For subsequent developments, see Quéniart, chs 2–4. Comparison with Protestant churches could yet yield fruitful results: see A.J. La Vopa, *Grace, Talent and Merit* (Cambridge, 1989).

century, it was not because of any desire to turn seminaries into learned academies, but rather to test individuals' sense of vocation and, above all, to create habits and attitudes which would ensure that, on leaving the seminary, the clergy would live *selon leur profession* – a bland, time-honoured expression which had imperceptibly moved towards what later generations would understand by the term 'clerical profession'.

CHAPTER SIX
The middle classes in late Tsarist Russia

Charles E. Timberlake
University of Missouri – Columbia

By the end of the nineteenth century, industrialisation and its con-comitant division of labour had produced in Russia middle-class groups that performed the same functions as their counterparts in western Europe. But the longevity of the Tsarist autocracy delayed the dissolution of the society of orders (*soslovie*, plural *sosloviia*) and, in combination with other factors, gave a peculiar physiognomy to Russia's middle groups.

Attempting to maintain social stability while promoting rapid industrial development, the Tsarist government attempted to coopt emerging middle-class elites by assimilating them into its existing web of privileges. Thus, privilege, higher educational degrees and a rank (*chin*) in the Table of Ranks became closely interlinked in late Tsarist Russia. Privileged social status, on the basis of estate origin, helped gain access to universities and special institutes. In turn, recipients of higher educational degrees automatically acquired a *chin* in the Table of Ranks. Since the government also granted *chin* to persons of outstanding achievements in the world of commerce and industry, it merged into one rank on the Table of Ranks people with disparate routes to privilege: sons of nobles who obtained higher educational degrees, sons of merchants with little formal education, and persons of noble or non-noble status promoted to a rank for lifelong service in the Tsarist bureaucracy. Government dispensation of privilege contributed to, and then rewarded, upward social mobil-ity through the system of higher educational institutions, through Tsarist bureaucratic service (military and civil), and through the world of commerce and industry. No matter what the route, the government's aim was to coopt the new elites into traditional positions of privilege rooted in the society of orders.

Government social legislation consciously fostered vertical social mobility and obstructed horizontal integration. It did not wish horizontal integration geographically nor among disparate groups on the same stratum within the same estate. For example, legislation arranged people in commerce and industry into hierarchical layers based on their wealth; within those vertical columns, it established self-governing boards at each social layer.[1] Encouraging such tiny legislatively created, heterogeneous groups on each social stratum, the government categorically forbade formation of national associations of professions and of commercial-industrial groups.

Government legislation, coupled with the cultural, ethnic and religious proclivities of Russian middle groups that made them social non-participants by choice, prevented the formation of autonomous professional and commercial-industrial associations. The absence of such groups, in turn, deprived society of the means to participate in national politics before 1905 when the government, weakened by the war with Japan and unable to maintain social control, was forced by general social upheaval to grant social groups at least a modicum of participation in national politics.

Rather than build new social and political institutions prior to 1905, segments of the Russian middle class participated with Tsarist bureaucrats to modify the autocracy's stratified system of estates to create within it niches for themselves. This collaboration produced a middle class whose members were frequently attired in garb historically reserved for the nobility, ornamented by medallions, and endowed with ranks historically tied to noble service in the Tsarist bureaucracy. That collaboration also perpetuated the myth among some middle groups that the Russian estates system (*soslovnost'*) was a more rational means of integrating modern society than the principle of *obshchestvennost'*, an estate-less society of citizens equal before the law. Thus, they deduced, Russian society needed no middle-class revolution to overthrow autocracy.

Without a sense of shared values to unify them, Russian middle groups remained even more fragmented than those of western Europe and England, and liberalism, therefore, had no middle-class bastion in Russia. While some small segments of Russian society – the reforming noblemen involved in capitalist agriculture, merchants, bankers and the professional men coalescing around institutions

---

[1] The *kupechestvo* and *meshchanstvo* elected officials to boards for each status, but their powers were quite limited, see K.Vr., 'Gil'dii', *Entsiklopedicheskii slovar'* (St Petersburg, 1893), vol. 16, p. 600.

created in the mid-nineteenth century by the Great Reforms (city dumas, university academic associations, provincial and county self-governing assemblies) – developed a perception of a modern integrated Russian society (*obshchestvennost'*)[2] that eschewed the principle of estates, most layers of the middle class did not acquire such a consciousness. Like other segments of Russian society, they were deeply ingrained with the tradition of bureaucratic centralism, with the *soslovie* system at its core, and a consciousness of Russian uniqueness. For this reason evolving an alternative world-view was a formidable intellectual and cultural task for them, one requiring considerable contact with the outside world. Consequently, the concept of an integrated society free of estates was propagated primarily by Russian lawyers, doctors, university professors and journalists, almost all of whom descended from one of the privileged estates and had completed a course of study at a Russian university or special institute. Historians of Russian liberalism attribute the failure of liberalism in Russian to its diminutive middle class. Of at least equal significance is the fact that its segmented nature and proclivities prevented many of its component groups from embracing the tenets of west European liberalism.

This chapter's objective is to describe the estates system that lingered in Russia long after the abolition of serfdom, to identify the groups that emerged during rapid state-sponsored industrialisation in the last half of the nineteenth century, and to explain how Tsarist legislation sought, while producing specialists necessary for industrialisation, to integrate those specialists into the estate-based system of privilege that survived the institutional reform that occurred from 1861 to 1874 during the period of the Great Reforms.[3]

At the beginning of the nineteenth century, the formal social structure of European Russia, the core area of the Russian Empire, was a system that listed all persons in one of four estates: nobility, clergy, urban estate, rural estate. Although not pristine groupings, these categories shaped the way people perceived Russian society and located their place within it during the last century of Imperial Russia.

At the top of the formal system were the two 'serving *sosloviia*': the nobility (*dvorianstvo*) who provided the state with secular service, and

---

[2] Such clusters characterised the 'left' faction in Chernigov provincial *zemstvo* in the 1870s and Tver *zemstvo* for most of its history.

[3] In a book that appeared while my work was in final editorial stages, Pamela Pilbeam argues this point for the middle class of three other European countries as well: *The Middle Classes in Europe, 1789–1914: France, Germany, Italy and Russia* (Chicago, 1990).

the clergy (*dukhovenstvo*) who provided spiritual service. The clergy was subdivided into *monastery* ('black') and *parish* ('white') clergymen, and the *dvorianstvo* was subdivided into *hereditary* and *personal* nobility.[4] The characteristics of the clerical estate at the beginning of the nineteenth century were still primarily those set in legislation by Peter the Great in 1721. But in 1762 the nobility had shed the service obligation that Peter had imposed upon it, and in 1785 its rights, privileges and liberties had been guaranteed in the Nobles' Charter. While Peter had intended that membership in these upper two estates should carry various privileges, he had been even more interested in attaching to them special service obligations. To ensure that the upper estates would provide a reservoir of able, well-trained state servitors, he had sent some of their members abroad to be educated, founded schools for them at home, and provided means whereby he and his successors could add new talent to this pool by ennobling talented commoners. Into the Table of Ranks that Peter created in 1722 he wrote the provision that a commoner awarded rank received personal nobility and, upon being promoted to rank eight, became eligible to request hereditary ennoblement.[5] Although this practice was restricted in the nineteenth century, the principle remained until the fall of the Russian autocracy.

The division of the nobility into hereditary and personal statuses is a consequence of this fluidity of movement into the nobles' estate. A hereditary noble was one born into the noble estate, or a person awarded nobility in reward for outstanding state service. A personal noble achieved that status for himself, again through state service, but could not bequeath it to his children.[6] Used rather generously in the last four decades of Tsarist Russia to reward middle-class specialists for their achievements and service to the government,[7] the power of ennoblement both transformed and prolonged the *soslovie* system,

[4] For historical sketches of the *soslovie* system see N. Lazarevskii, 'Sosloviia', *Entsiklopedicheskii slovar' Brokgauz-Efrona* (St Petersburg, 1900), vol. 60, pp. 911–13, and for an effort at a new interpretation of the significance of the system for nineteenth-century Russia, see G.L. Freeze, 'The Russian *soslovie* (estate) paradigm', *American Historical Review* 91 (1986): 11–36.

[5] A translation of the original Table of Ranks is in B. Dmytryshyn, *Imperial Russia: A Source Book, 1700–1917* (2nd edn, Hinsdale, 1974), pp. 17–19. The best catalogue, with commentary and historical sketches, of individual ranks in the table is by L.E. Shepelev, *Otmenennye istoriei: chiny, zvaniia i tituly v Rossiiskoi imperii* (Leningrad, 1977).

[6] In Dmytryshyn, p. 19.

[7] S. Becker, *Nobility and Privilege in Late Imperial Russia* (Dekalb, Ill., 1985), pp. 101–3. Also see J.A. Ruckman, *The Moscow Business Elite: A Social and Cultural Portrait of Two Generations, 1840–1905* (Dekalb, 1984), *passim*.

confusing social roles as well as retarding the development of middle-class associations and a middle-class identity.

Movement across estate boundaries was frequent for other estates as well. As Gregory Freeze's chapter on the clergy shows, sons of clergymen increasingly chose careers outside Church service in the late nineteenth century, and some clergymen legally renounced their estate in order to find careers elsewhere (see Chapter 4 in this volume). Given the conditions that motivated these actions, it is not surprising that few persons born into other estates chose to enter the clergy estate. No such formal renunciations were necessary for sons of nobles who wished to pursue a career different from those traditionally practised by the nobility: state service and agriculture. Upon receiving a professional degree, they could begin a practice in an urban area. Functionally they had become urban professionals, but legally they remained nobles.

The lowest position in the formal social structure at the beginning of the nineteenth century was the rural estate, composed primarily of the peasantry (*krest'ianstvo*) which was subdivided into three major groups: state peasants (peasants living on land belonging to the state), landlords' serfs, and serfs living on land belonging to the Imperial family. Even after Emancipation in 1861, the Tsarist government retained these labels, merely inserting the adjective 'former' before each as a way of directing legislation at specific groups.

The urban population constituted a fourth *soslovie* subdivided into three legal statuses (*sostoianiia*): first, the merchantry (*kupechestvo*, later called, in the popular use of the term, a *soslovie* of their own) which was, in turn, divided into guilds according to individual wealth; second, the small businessmen (collectively, *meshchanstvo*); and third, the artisans (*remeslenniki*, later called *tsekhovye*). Outside this system of four estates was a category for those who did not fit. This was termed the *inorodtsy* (literally 'members of other tribes') and included gypsies, Jews and Siberian peoples.[8]

Within the formal society of estates that existed in Russia in the mid-nineteenth century, where could socio-historical 'middle' groups appear, and from which estates? The concept of middle groups was

---

[8] Literally, *inorodtsy* means 'other tribes' than the Slavic tribes, but it had a legal definition establishing a status for specific tribes. Functionally, it was a miscellaneous category for stashing all the Tsar's subjects who had not been specifically enumerated within another status. Included in this status were such groups as Siberian nomads, Jews, gypsies. See A. Ia., 'Inorodtsy', *Entsiklopedicheskii slovar'* (St Petersburg, 1894), vol. 25, pp. 224–5. In English, R. Pipes, *The Formation of the Soviet Union: Communism and Nationalism, 1917–1923* (revised edn, New York, 1968), ch. 1.

born in western Europe when the society of estates was experiencing the beginning of industrialisation. As early as the eighteenth century, observers referred to 'middle classes of people' (that is neither members of the aristocracy and clergy above, nor the peasantry below) who performed new functions associated with emerging industrialisation and with rendering services to the masses that had formerly been reserved for the privileged, especially medical care and education.[9] Further, the new groups and the services they performed were urban-centred.

While the urban estate in Russia was not meant to be above or below the peasantry, but merely different from it, stratification within the urban population had long been recognised in law. Clearly, the wealthy urban merchants had privileges and prestige greater than other strata within the urban estate and greater than the peasantry. Thus, they occupied a middling position between nobility and the urban and rural masses. The upper echelon of the middle class as it emerged during the last sixty years of Tsarist Russia was composed of big businessmen, some of whom were honoured citizens,[10] and established practitioners of the old professions (doctors, professors, lawyers) and later the new professions (such as journalists, engineers) in Russia's major urban centres. However, because most of these professional men were of noble status, they were not numbered among the urban estate in Tsarist nomenclature before the census of 1897. The middle rungs of the middle class were the small businessmen (*meshchane*) and lesser professional specialists. In the provincial capitals these specialists were often *zemstvo* employees (statisticians, teachers in special and elementary schools, paramedical workers, bookkeepers). The lower echelon, 'the lower middle class' in western usage, was composed of urban artisans and small shopkeepers, and in the provincial capitals people with lesser specialisations employed in business and *zemstvo* service (e.g. clerks).

Rapid industrialisation and expansion of higher education in the four decades after Emancipation produced significant demographic changes that rendered the terminology of the *soslovie* system anachronistic. Despite government legislation prohibiting the emancipated peasantry (approximately 88 per cent of the population in 1861) from leaving its land and becoming industrial labourers, the urban population (persons living in towns of 15,000 or more) of European Russia

---

[9] A. Meusel, 'Middle class', *Encyclopedia of the Social Sciences* (New York, 1933), vol. 10, pp. 410–15.
[10] See below.

Table 1   Urbanisation, 1858–97

Groups of sosloviia	Urban population (in thousands)			
	1858	%	1897	%
Urban estate (honoured citizen, merchant, small businessman, etc.)	3,052	55	7,859	47
Rural estate (peasants)	1,131	20	7,145	43
Nobility and clergy	383	7	1,215	7
Others (military, mixed origin)	1,018	18	610	3

Source: Vodarskii, Naselenie Rossii, p. 114

virtually doubled in the thirty-year period of 1867 to 1897, increasing from an estimated 6.67 million to around 12.49 million. In the next twenty years, it doubled again to 25.84 million by 1917. During this approximately fifty-year period, the urban population growth rate of some 400 per cent far exceeded a national growth rate of 90 per cent.[11] Where in 1867 the urban population constituted only approximately 10 per cent of the total, it constituted some 21 per cent by 1916, in a country that experienced a population boom during that period. While Moscow (which grew from 350,000 to 2.2. million inhabitants during the period) and St Petersburg (growth from 0.5 million to 1.25 million)[12] were by far the largest cities, had a lion's share of the large industries, and were home to the major journals, newspapers and cultural and educational institutions, all Russia's major European cities underwent dramatic population growth and relatively signifi-cant cultural development during this period.[13]

Analysing the list of urban dwellers by soslovie (see Table 1) illustrates the anachronism of retaining the soslovie categories to describe the urban populace in the 1890s. While the number of people in social layers the government officially designated the urban estate actually doubled during the forty-year period of 1858 to 1897, their total percentage of all urban dwellers dropped from 55 per cent to 47 per cent.

Reflecting nobles' and priests' preference for occupations in the professions, commerce, industry and other urban-based activities,

[11] P. Gatrell, The Tsarist Economy, 1850–1917 (London, 1986); Ia. E. Vodarskii, Naselenie Rossii za 400 let (XVI-nachalo XX vv) (Moscow, 1973), p. 133.
[12] Gatrell, p. 67.
[13] Ibid., pp. 67–8. See M. Hamm (ed.) The City in Late Tsarist Russia (Bloomington, 1986) for sketches of development of eight cities of the empire. Also see P. Hurlihy, Odessa: A History, 1794–1914 (Cambridge, Mass., 1986).

figures for the combined estates of nobility and clergy show a fourfold increase of this group among urban dwellers to retain its 7 per cent share of the total. The *soslovie* with the largest increase among urban dwellers was the peasantry. These figures show that despite government legislation to restrict peasant migration to the cities, the peasants found ways to absent themselves from the village commune.[14] Although many peasants migrated permanently to nearby cities and became an industrial proletariat, the government listed them as belonging to the *soslovie* into which they were born. The Tsarist government never created a separate legal status for the industrial proletariat.

The Russian middle class was composed of three major categories, each with its own strata, each geographically dispersed, each without institutional linkage of its members or with groups in another category. Further, to varying degrees, these groups were composed of persons with different *soslovie* origins who, in a period of rapid social transformation, added functional identities that clashed with their *soslovie* identities. It was this period of Russian history that produced Anton Chekhov's play *The Cherry Orchard* which masterfully portrays the social and psychological anxieties this confusion of roles created.[15] The three major categories, each of which is examined in turn below, are: professionals and para-professionals, who will henceforth be indicated by the term 'the intelligentsia'. Although these specialists practised in urban areas, they were listed in government statistics by their *soslovie* status (see the 'nobility and clergy' entry in Table 1) and not as members of the urban estate. The second category is groups within the urban estate ranging from an elite of merchant-industrialists through middle layers of small businessmen (the *meshchanstvo*). The third category is the army of *zemstvo* employees dispersed throughout the thirty-four provinces of European Russia that received *zemstvo* institutions in the reform of 1864 (forty-three provinces had them after 1912). Within this category, some jobs were unique, but many employees were professionals, para-professionals, or had some type of specialised training that would also place them in the category 'intelligentsia'. But the combination of intelligentsia specialists with people performing business functions (insurance agents, banking personnel) and with people performing

---

[14] Violation of the passport rules was the most common crime among the Russian peasantry in the late nineteenth century.

[15] Several essays in E. Clowes, S. Kassow and J. West (eds) *Between Tsar and People* (Princeton, 1990) analyse the portrayal in Russian literature of confusion and anxiety produced by changing social roles at the beginning of the twentieth century.

government administrative functions (tax assessors, public school teachers, public health specialists, postal workers, librarians) made *zemstvo* servants a unique subset within Russian society and within the individual specialist's field.[16] To some degree all three segments overlapped, but each possessed features that differentiated it from the others.

The government's need for specialists, especially in technology, became acute after it began a policy of rapid industrialisation in the mid-1880s, and even more acute after 1890 when it began building a double-tracked railway across the vast reaches of Siberia and Northern China to the Sea of Japan. Other agencies, such as *zemstvos* and private enterprises, also had increased needs for specialists. Assimilating this new social stratum was a challenge to the defenders of the *soslovie* system.

To increase the numbers and types of specialists, the government created new higher special institutes in the 1890s and early 1900s, opened two new universities, and after the Revolution of 1905, admitted significantly larger numbers of students to the universities.[17] Upon graduation from a university, students received an academic degree (*uchenaia stepen'*) of active student (*deistvitel'nyi student*) or candidate (*kandidat*) from 1863 to 1884. After 1884, the two degrees were merely called 'first' and 'second', determined by students' performance in the final examinations.[18] The higher special institutes bestowed upon their graduates a diploma (*diplom*) with a specialist designation (*zvanie*, plural: *zvaniia*). For instance, the Alexander III Electro-Technical Institute awarded its graduates one of two possible diplomas: diploma with the *zvanie* Electrical Engineer of the First Order (*razriadka*) or diploma with the *zvanie* Electrical Engineer of the Second Order. To graduates whose performance in the examinations was marginal, they granted a certificate (*svidetel'stvo*).[19]

To assimilate these specialists into the modified estate system, the Tsarist government resorted to the same device Peter I had employed in 1722 when he faced the same practical task: how to integrate into

[16] These categories are slightly different from those explained by Laura Engelstein in her study *Moscow, 1905: Working-Class Organization and Political Conflict* (Stanford, 1982), p. 16, because I attempt to include provincial cities as well.

[17] J. McClelland, 'Diversification in Russian-Soviet education', pp. 180–95, and P. Alston, 'The dynamics of educational expansion in Russia', pp. 89–107, both in K. Jarausch (ed.) *The Transformation of Higher Learning, 1860–1930* (Chicago, 1983).

[18] A.I. Bogomolov, 'Uchenye stepeni i zvaniia', *Pedagogicheskaia entsiklopediia* (Moscow, 1968), vol. 4, pp. 434–8.

[19] D. Margolin, *Spravochnik po vysshemy obrazovaniia* (3rd edn, Petrograd-Kiev, 1915), p. 191.

Tsarist service, and how to rank for purposes of reward, large numbers of specialists hired from western Europe and Russian specialists drawn from the new schools in the Russian Empire? To solve the problem, Peter engaged in wholesale borrowing of terms for government positions (*chiny*) and degree designations from western Europe, especially Germany. He arranged all the *chiny* into three columns – civil, military and court – and ranked them in each column in descending order from 1 through 14. The final product was his Table of Ranks.

Since Peter's Table was still in use in amended form in the late nineteenth century, the government utilised it to establish a hierarchy among the plethora of specialist degrees it had borrowed wholesale from west European languages and begun to grant to graduates of its universities and, especially, higher special institutes. The hierarchy determined levels of reward and prestige, and served as an incentive for young students to enter a course of studies at a university or one of the higher special institutes.

Table 2 (appendix at end of this chapter) shows the hierarchy of specialist degrees and the rank assigned them in the Table of Ranks as of 1915. In order to compare two periods of heavy borrowing of terms from the west, I have transliterated and retained in the two columns on the left side of the table the terms Peter used for his civil and court *chiny* in the original Table of Ranks of 1722. Juxtaposed to those are the terms, translated (virtually the same as to transliterate), in the two columns on the right side of the table that were in use in 1915. Comparing the ancient German terms with the modern Latin-derived terms provides one type of evidence of two significant periods of westernisation separated by 150 years. As Peter's economic reforms and western borrowing introduced confusion into the social structure of his time, so did the reforms and foreign terms of the last fifty years of Tsarist Russia.

Tables 3-1, 3-2 and 3-3 (see appendix) are an index of specialist degrees, arranged by rank as assigned to them in the Table of Ranks.[20] After each degree, the name of the institution authorised to grant that degree is given. This hierarchy of specialist degrees, supported by rights to wear special items of clothing and medals, to invest in special mutual funds, and receive a state pension, was intended to distinguish specialists from the lower strata of the population. The use of *zvanie* and other paraphernalia publicly declared the institution, from which

[20] Tables compiled from information supplied by Margolin for each higher educational institution.

95

the person bearing the *zvanie* and decorations had received his degree. Since some specialist degrees were granted by only one institution, the graduates of which had exclusive right to wear various paraphernalia, the bearer of the qualification was instantly identifiable as a graduate of a particular school. For instance, any person who listed his designation as 'mining engineer' was a graduate of the Mining Institute. A person walking along the street wearing a particular clothing, even without reinforcing the appearance by wearing the official medal, was immediately recognisable, to anyone who cared enough to learn the system of designations, as a graduate of the Alexander III Electro-Technical Institute.

This hierarchy of specialist degrees was separate from the estate system, but supplemented it by allowing people who earned a specialist degree to change their social status. For instance, the son of an artisan who became a doctor could erase the estate designation 'artisan' after his name and replace it with the term 'doctor' that carried with it a rank in the Table of Ranks, and that rank, in turn, entitled him to certain perquisites. And in reward for state service a commoner could be promoted through the Table of Ranks to a position entitling him to ennoblement.

As socio-economic complexity developed within the urban estate during the nineteenth century, the Tsarist government added new legal statuses within that *soslovie* in proportion to the accumulation of wealth the commercial-industrial elite had achieved. As it had adapted the Table of Ranks to reward professionals and specialists, the government also created new *chiny* in the Table of Ranks for the benefit of merchants and industrialists. In this way they were assimilated into government service and awarded appropriate ranks and salaries for their work.[21]

By the beginning of the nineteenth century, the traditional division of the urban *soslovie* into the categories of merchantry (*kupechestvo*), small businessmen (*meshchanstvo*), and artisans (*remeslenniki*) did not adequately depict the major differentiation in wealth and power that had developed within the merchantry and between it and the other urban groups. In the first place, the original term of *knpechestvo* had expanded to include a much broader group of businessmen than merchants. Within this designation the government also included industrialists and entrepreneurs and virtually everyone else involved in a major way in business activity. Despite economic diversification in the late nineteenth and early twentieth centuries, the government

[21] Shepelev, p. 100; Ruckman, pp. 33–40.

continued to apply only this label to industrialists, entrepreneurs, bankers and others with the personal wealth required for this status.

From Peter I's rule to 1917, the *kupechestvo* was subdivided into guilds (two from 1721–42, three from 1742–1863, two from 1863–1917), and all businessmen in that category were assigned to a guild based purely upon wealth. Capital assets required for the guilds increased over time.

Year	1st guild	2nd guild	3rd guild
1742	10,000	1,000	500
1785	10,000	5,000	1,000
1807	50,000	20,000	8,000

Businessmen with capital assets less than the minimum for the lowest guild were assigned to the *meshchanstvo* status.[22]

Beginning with legislation in 1832 the government sought to establish greater distinctions among businessmen and to reward the business elite. One tactic was to extend privileges to the elite in the form of exemption from fees and from performance of the uncompensated obligations (such as financial agent, collector of direct and indirect taxes and other revenues, agent for the government in various domestic and foreign trade arrangements) that Peter's legislation had introduced and that had been retained for members of the merchant guilds.[23]

The government's second act in 1832 to reward the business elite was creation of the status of honoured citizen (*pochetnyi grazhdanin*) as the ultimate status, above that of first-guild merchant, to honour particularly successful businessmen. The bearer of this title had not only the distinction of using it, but also the major personal rights enjoyed by all who attained official membership in the *kupechestvo*, namely freedom from corporal punishment, exemption from paying the soul tax, the right to engage in business on a national scale. In addition, the bearer of this honour was exempted from paying the guild fee. For those who attained this status, membership in a guild was not necessary.

The title of Personal Honoured Citizen was available upon application to any businessman who had been a member of the first guild for ten years. After ten years of continued business activities as a Personal Honoured Citizen, or after twenty years of maintaining

[22] 'Gil'dii', pp. 679–80.
[23] Ibid.

membership in the first merchant guild, a businessman was eligible to apply for the title of Hereditary Honored Citizen.[24]

A law of 1863 reduced the number of guilds from three to two. While requiring all persons conducting commercial-industrial activities to purchase special licenses, this law opened membership in the merchant guilds to any person, male or female, of any *soslovie* so long as they could pay the licence fee. Guild licences were denied only to a very few such as certain Church officials and Protestant clergymen. People not born into a merchant family and who bought guild licences could retain their existing estate titles or accept the title 'merchant of the first [or second] guilds'. Members of the nobility who bought a guild licence could enjoy all the rights and privileges accruing to a holder of that licence, while retaining the rights, privileges and title of a noble.[25]

Despite the considerable complexity that entered the Russian social system, the *Collection of Russian Laws* that the central bureaucracy reissued in 1892 retained the simplistic schematisation of four *sosloviia*: nobility, clergy, urban and rural. The laws also recognised four status categories (*sostoianiia*) within the urban estate, organised in the following descending order of status: honoured citizen (subdivided into hereditary honoured citizen and personal honoured citizen); merchant (*kupets*, subdivided into first guild and second guild merchants); small businessman (*meshchane*), and artisan (*tsekhovyi*).[26] The law code of 1892 retained the arrangements of the law of 1863 regarding membership in the merchant guilds: to wit, virtually anyone with the means could buy a licence and enter it.[27]

Legislation during the Great Reforms and afterwards that removed many of the estate distinctions by abolishing the poll tax, introducing universal military service, and limiting corporal punishment rendered membership in merchant guilds less beneficial for members of the business elite. But for the later middle class the ladder of statuses within the urban estate remained useful as a means to achieve upward social mobility. Thus *meshchanstvo* status could be replaced by *kupechestvo* status simply through accumulating the requisite amount of

[24] Korkunov, 'Nashe zakonodatel'stvo o pochetnom Grazhdanstve', *Vestnik prava* 4 (1899). This title was available to people other than merchants, such as sons of personal nobles.

[25] 'Gil'dii', pp. 679–80; A. Ianovskii, 'Grazhdanstvo pochetnoe', *Entsiklopedicheskii slovar'* (St Petersburg, 1893), vol. 18, pp. 523–4.

[26] E. Dement'ev, 'Tsekhy v Rossii', *Entsiklopedicheskii slovar'* (St Petersburg, 1903), vol. 75, pp. 131–4.

[27] 'Gil'dii', p. 680.

Figure 1

Stratification of the Russian Urban Population, *c.*1900

> **ELITE**
>
> > **ACQUIRED PERSONAL OR HEREDITARY NOBLE STATUS**
> > (Rank 3 in the Table of Ranks)
> >
> > **ACTIVE STATE COUNCILLOR**
> > (Rank 4 in the Table of Ranks)
> >
> > **COMMERCIAL COUNCILLOR**
> > **MANUFACTURING COUNCILLOR**
> > (Rank 8 in the Table of Ranks)

> **HEREDITARY HONOURED CITIZEN**
> **PERSONAL HONOURED CITIZEN**

> *KUPECHESTVO:*
> **MERCHANT OF THE FIRST GUILD**
> **MERCHANT OF THE SECOND GUILD**

> **THE *MESCHANSTVO***
> (businessmen with capital assets below *kupechestvo* minimum)

> **ARTISANS**

> **THE INDUSTRIAL PROLETARIAT**

> **THE LOWER CLASSES**
> prostitutes, pimps, beggars, thieves
> occasional day labourers, hawkers, rag–pickers

wealth for admission to the second merchant guild. Potentially, such a person could advance to the first guild, then to the titles of personal and hereditary honoured citizen, and eventually become ennobled. Figure 1 shows stratification by statuses within the urban estate and the *chiny* on the Table of Ranks that granted ennoblement to people in the business world.

By 1900 all of the leading businessmen in Moscow had acquired the title of personal or hereditary honoured citizen. Government service *chiny* of Manufacturing Councillor and Commercial Councillor were also available to the extraordinarily successful businessman. One who was designated Manufacturing Councillor or Commercial Councillor achieved rights and privileges (including 'personal noble' status) attached to Rank 8 of the Table of Ranks. Still higher ranks could be achieved through acts of public service outside government or through occasional consulting work within a government ministry. The ultimate social achievement for many commoner businessmen was to be named personal and then hereditary member of the nobility.[28]

While the elite of the Moscow business community controlled the Moscow city government (the duma) by 1905, they had not established linkages with businessmen outside Moscow. Neither had the business leaders in St Petersburg, the Urals or the southern region. No one of these four major groups had made efforts to establish broader associations with the other three. Exclusiveness of one region, as well as of segments within a local community, was the result of ethnic and religious factors. In Moscow, some 50 per cent of all members of the *kupechestvo* were Old Believers who, being an illegal cult, had long grouped together in small sections of the city and whose lives were directed inward toward the family. Even their churches were constructed inside their homes.

Rather than play a role in politics, the railway barons and captains of the textile and steel industries pursued their personal idiosyncrasies by becoming patrons of the arts, such as Savva Mamontov (supporter of Moscow painters and the art community at Abramtsevo), P.M. Tretiakov (collector of contemporary paintings), K.S. Stanislavskii (founder of the Moscow Art Theatre).

While these business–intelligentsia connections in Moscow were an early form of horizontal social integration within a stratum, neither these efforts nor some efforts at collaboration among businessmen during the First World War provided the disparate middle groups in Russia with any cohesion of values or purpose. The survival of the altered *soslovie* system, coupled with ethnic, religious and other factors, promoted exclusiveness within the urban estate, and thereby helped to shape group perceptions and to determine political behaviour.[29]

[28] Ruckman, pp. 32–4.
[29] See W.B. Lincoln, *In War's Dark Shadow: the Russians Before the Great War* (New York, 1983), pp. 69–102, for a succinct presentation of the rapid rise of the new merchant-industrialists.

By 1917, the provincial and county *zemstvo* institutions employed some 90,000 to 100,000 full-time specialists, a veritable second civil service, parallel to the Tsarist civil service. Stratified from professionals at the top to laundresses at the bottom, certainly not all such employees fell into the middle-class category. Table 4 (see appendix) shows, for illustrative purposes, that by 1891 Tver *zemstvo* employed nearly a thousand full-time servants with forty-two job classifications. Retirement benefits, arranged in five pension groups, allow us to see the hierarchy of job classifications and relative rewards for the *zemstvo* civil service staff. In addition to the official statuses into which the government divided the urban *soslovie* (honoured citizen, merchantry, and so on), we can attribute the growing diversity evident within the middle-class to the job designations of *zemstvo* personnel. This was especially so in the provincial capitals where the *zemstvo* was often the major employer of specialists.[30]

While doctors, in the first stratum for pension purposes, could be numbered among the professional/para-professional segment of the middle class, and in fact, doctors from Tver province were among those who joined with doctors in Moscow to form the Pirogov Society in 1885, their work in the *zemstvos* gave them a service elan that set them apart from other doctors. Initially, some Russian doctors sought to organise the medical profession around those practising 'zemstvo medicine'. Dispersed among thirty-four provincial towns and more in contact with other *zemstvo* specialists than with other doctors, *zemstvo* doctors, as other *zemstvo* specialists, developed dual identities. *Zemstvo* professionals/specialists might organise with others along professional lines, or they might organise with other types of *zemstvo* specialists using the *zemstvo* itself as an organising centre. An identity of *zemstvo* servants, already forged before 1901, acquired its own name, 'the third element', after Vice-Governor Kondoidi used that term to describe the *zemstvo* servitors. In 1905, some 'third element' groups formed to make various economic and political demands.[31]

Specialists such as those in groups II and III on the Tver table (see Table 4 in appendix) had no occupational associations. Their group identity was shaped by *zemstvo* service. Given the chance to apply for

---

[30] Details on numbers of specialists in provincial and county towns of Tver province are to be found in C. Timberlake, 'The zemstvo as promoter of a Russian middle class', in Clowes, Kassow and West (eds) *Between Tsar and People*.

[31] N.M. Pirumova, *Zemskaia intelligentsiia* (Moscow, 1986), pp. 233–5; S. Seregny, *Russian Teachers and Peasant Revolution: the Politics of Education in 1905* (Bloomington, Ind., 1989).

rank in the Table of Ranks in 1894, the *zemstvo* board declined, citing its desire to retain the clear distinction between Tsarist civil service and *zemstvo* service.[32]

The distribution of some 90,000 specialists among thirty-four provinces with *zemstvos*[33] added an average of more than 2,000 people per province to the groups that were emerging from such activities as industry, trade and Tsarist civil service to form a provincial middle class.[34]

Despite government efforts to tuck new groups into niches in the *soslovie* system and Table of Ranks, some groups sought to organise independent associations. Among the professionals, the lawyers, doctors and engineers were the first to attempt to form occupational associations. Such associations required government approval. Unable to hold their own meetings, Russian engineers, doctors and lawyers used academic societies inside Russia's universities and special institutes as organising centres.[35]

The first to attempt forming a national association, Russian lawyers, through the Moscow Legal Society in Moscow University, petitioned the Tsarist government to convene 'the first congress of Russian lawyers' in 1874 with the purpose of initiating a series of periodic congresses. The Minister of Education approved the proposal merely as an experiment, and when the first meeting, of 228 lawyers, in 1875 gave the government unsolicited advice on the organisation of the revised and supplemented *Code of Russian Laws* that was scheduled for publication the following year, the government denied all future requests for a second meeting.[36] Only under the Provisional Government in 1917 did Russian lawyers establish a national association.

The medical profession used the same strategy in trying to organise a national association. Utilising the prestigious medical society within Moscow University as the focal point for medical specialists throughout Russia, a coalition composed of doctors on the medical faculty of

[32] Timberlake, op. cit., *passim*.

[33] B.B. Veselovskii, *Istoriia zemstv za sorok let* (St Petersburg, 1909–11), vol. 3, p. 465, estimates the number of *zemstvo* employees at 65,000–70,000. The census of 1897 listed some 104,000 such employees. See H. Seton-Watson, *The Russian Empire, 1801–1917* (Oxford, 1967), p. 536.

[34] Timberlake, op. cit., *passim*.

[35] By 1895 Russia's nine universities had founded thirty-eight scholarly societies. See C. Timberlake, 'Higher learning, the state and the professions in Russia', in K. Jarausch (ed.) *The Transformation of Higher Learning, 1860–1930* (Chicago, 1983), p. 338.

[36] For a fuller version of the lawyers' efforts, see ibid., pp. 338–40.

Moscow University and of *zemstvo* doctors got permission to found a national association of doctors in 1882: The Russian Surgical Society in Memory of N.I. Pirogov, the late professor of medicine at Moscow University. This association survived into the Bolshevik period.

In 1884 Russian engineers organised the Society of Technologists by combining government-chartered societies and groups utilising higher educational institutions. The society's role was limited to seeking jobs for technicians, providing support for needy members and their families, increasing cooperation between factory owners and engineers, and fostering cooperation to solve technical problems. Only in May 1917, after the fall of the autocracy, did the Russian engineers finally establish the All-Russian Union of Engineers.[37]

The business segment of the middle class, existing in regional clusters and isolated in cocoons even within those regions by religious, social and ethnic distinctions, exhibited no desire to form a national association before the First World War. In his study of Russian businessmen, Alfred Rieber groups them in four centres: St Petersburg (metallurgy), Moscow (textiles), the southern region (mining, metallurgy), and the Urals (mining, metallurgy).[38] He concluded that the Revolution of 1905 awakened the country's business elite to the realisation that the *soslovie* system could not shield Russia from the social unrest brought by industrialisation.[39] During the First World War, despite continued rivalry between the business elites of St Petersburg and Moscow, some cooperation and consolidation was beginning to occur among the business leadership in the four major industrial areas.[40] But, the fall of the autocracy and nationalisation under the Bolsheviks ended any role an organised group of factory-owners might play.

The studies by Thomas Owen and Jo Ann Ruckman focus on the business elite in Moscow to 1905.[41] While both scholars discovered some consolidation among Moscow businessmen, they found still greater evidence that segments within that community remained isolated from others for religious, ethnic and cultural reasons. A still greater chasm existed between business organisations in Moscow and

[37] Ibid., pp. 340–3.
[38] A. Rieber, *Merchants and Entrepreneurs in Imperial Russia* (Chapel Hill, 1982), pp. 219–55.
[39] Ibid., pp. 261–332.
[40] Ibid., pp. 418–27.
[41] T. Owen, *Capitalism and Politics in Russia: A Social History of the Moscow Merchants, 1855–1905* (Cambridge, 1981); J.A. Ruckman, *The Moscow Business Elite: A Social and Cultural Portrait of Two Generations, 1840–1905* (Dekalb, 1984).

those in the provinces.[42] During the First World War, contacts between regional organisations began, but competition for government orders, along with traditional rivalries and exlusiveness, prevented formation of a national organisation or even of national coordination to supply needed war materials before the Bolshevik seizure of power in 1917 and subsequent nationalisation of the factories.

What efforts were made by our third group, *zemstvo* servants, to form national associations? In the pre-1905 period when organised political activity was illegal, *zemstvo* employees utilised their own agencies to disseminate ideas. Because *zemstvo* employees worked directly among the peasantry as teachers, nurses, statisticians, veterinarians and so on, many young people of populist/socialist persuasion became *zemstvo* employees for political reasons. In the chaos of 1905 *zemstvo* employees formed occupational associations among *zemstvo* schoolteachers, and some employees called for the organisation of all *zemstvo* employees into a coalition.[43]

In the elections to the First Duma in 1906, the constitutional-democratic (Kadet) party found its strongest provincial support among *zemstvo* employees.[44] The activities of this group during the period of 1906 to 1914 when political activity became legal have not been studied, but the role of *zemstvo* specialists was crucial during the First World War in the quasi-legal bodies that managed medical aid for wounded soldiers, distribution of foodstuffs, and providing assistance in other areas where the Tsarist bureaucracy proved incapable of managing affairs. When the agencies of central government collapsed in 1917, these *zemstvo* specialists quite naturally assumed officially the positions in which they had functioned already for some time. The first premier in the Provisional Government was G.N. Lvov, who had served during the war as head of the Union of *Zemstvos* and Towns. At the local level, people with *zemstvo* experience served as key officials during the period of the Provisional Government and in the early soviets created after the Bolshevik Revolution of 1917.

In the last sixty years of Tsarist Russia, increasing numbers of Russians took up occupations and played some of the roles historians

---

[42] Owen, p. 222; see also Rieber, pp. 424–7.

[43] Seregny discusses the *zemstvos* as a factor in teachers' organisations. Pirumova discusses their efforts to organise as 'Third Element' units, *Zemskoe liberal 'noe dvizhenie: Sotsial'nye korni i evoliutsiia do nachala XX veka* (Moscow, 1977), pp. 74–126.

[44] C. Timberlake, 'Constitutional Democratic Party', *Modern Encyclopedia of Russian and Soviet History*, 8 (1978): 30–44.

and sociologists associate with the west European middle class. On the other hand, the Tsarist bureaucracy achieved some success in its efforts to disguise the emergence of a society of classes by bedecking the new groups with costumes, medallions and titles similar to those worn by others in pre-Emancipation Russia as *soslovie* privileges, Russia's version of a society of orders. While some university-educated professionals sought consciously to replace the society of estates with a modern form of integrated society, Russian business-men prided themselves on the difference evident between themselves and the greedy European bourgeoisie. The transformation of percep-tions that the Revolution of 1905–6 and the First World War produced in the business elite of the two national capitals came too late, and no such change seems to have affected provincial businessmen who were more likely to join nationalistic, anti-Semitic parties[45] than constitu-tional parties pursuing programmes of west European liberal democ-racy. Middling groups were only just emerging from the cocoons of the *soslovie* system when the Bolshevik Revolution swept away the associations and institutions in which their middle-class identity had been incubating.

[45] Owen, p. 222.

APPENDIX

Table 2 Table of Ranks 1722 and 1915

	Civilian chiny	Court chiny	Higher education Zvaniia	
			University	Special institutes
1	Kantsler			
2	Deistvitel'nyi tainyi sovetnik	Ober-kamerger Ober-gofmarshal Ober-shtalmeister Ober-egermeister Ober-gofmeister Ober-shenk Ober-tseremonii-meister Ober-forshneider		
3	Tainyi sovetnik	Gofmarshal Shtalmeister Egermeister Gofmeister Obertseremonii-meister Ober-forshneider		
4	Deistvitel'nyi statskii sovetnik Ober-prokuror Gerol'dmeister		Rektor	Rektor
5	Statskii sovetnik	Tseremonii-meister	Ordinarnyi Professor	Ord. Professor
6	Kollezhskii sovetnik Voennyi sovetnik		Ekstarodin-arnyi Professor	Eks. Professor
7	Nadvornyi sovetnik		Dotsent	
8	Kollezhskii assessor		Lektor	Doktor (Religious academy degree)
9	Tituliarnyi sovetnik			Magistr (Religious academy) Graduate with #1 degree: Imperial Alexander Lyceum; Imperial Institution for Study of Jurisprudence

Table 2   (Continued)

Civilian chiny	Court chiny	Higher education Zvaniia	
		University	Special institutes
10 Kollezhskii sekretar		First degree Kandidat (Warsaw & Iuriev)	Engineers (11)★ Agronomists (3) Foresters (2) Veterinarians (1) Lawyers (2) Teachers (2) Economists (1) Paramedics (2) Clergymen (1) Linguists (1)
11 Korabel'nyi sekretar			
12 Gubernskii sekretar		Second degree	Engineers and Technicians (12) Agronomists (2) Foresters (2) Lawyers (1) Economists (1) Clergymen (1) All graduates of certain schools
13 Provintsial'nyi sekretar Senatskii registrator Sionodskii registrator Kabinetskii registrator			
14 Kollezhskii registrator			Engineers and Technicians (3) Economists (1)

★ Numbers in parentheses in this column designate numbers of *zvaniia* for the category. That is there are eleven separate *zvaniia* for engineers, such as electrical, mining, transportation; two *zvaniia* for foresters: forester, and research forester, etc. See Tables 3-1, 3-2 and 3-3.

Table 3-1 Degrees Granted by Higher Special Educational Institutions
Earning Rank 10 on the Table of Ranks in 1915

Specialist Degree	Granting Institutions
Engineers:	
Transportation engineer 'with excellence'	Institute of Engineers of Ministry of Transportation
Mining engineer	Mining Institute; Kiev and Warsaw Polytechnic Institutes
Mechanical engineer	Imperial Moscow Technical Institution; Riga Polytechnic Institute
Construction engineer	Kiev, Riga and Warsaw Polytechnic Institutes
Civil engineer ('most successful')	Institute of Civil Engineers
Metallurgical engineer 'with excellence'	Petrograd Polytechnic Institute
Electrical engineer 'with excellence'	Petrograd Polytechnic Institute
Electrical engineer 'of the first order'	Electro-Technical Institute
Naval engineer 'with excellence'	Petrograd Polytechnic Institute
Surveying engineer	Konstantinov Surveying Institute
Chemical engineer	Riga Polytechnic Institute
Engineer of technology	Petrograd and Khar'kov Technological Institutes; Imperial Moscow Technical Institution; Kiev & Warsaw Polytechnic Institutes
Agronomists:	
Agronomist	Riga Polytechnic Institute; New Alexandria Institute of Agriculture and Forestry; Moscow Agricultural Institute
Research agronomist	Kiev and Warsaw Polytechnic Institutes
Agronomist-technician	Moscow Agricultural Institute
Foresters:	
Forester 'of the first order'	New Alexandria Institute of Agriculture and Forestry;
Research forester 'of the first order'	Imperial Petrograd Forestry Institute
Veterinarians:	
Veterinarian	Veterinary Institues in Khar'kov, Kazan, Iuriev and Warsaw

Table 3-1 (Continued)

Specialist Degree	Granting Institutions
Lawyers:	
(graduates) 'of the second order'	Imperial Institution for the Study of Jurisprudence
Candidate	Demidov Lyceum of Jurisprudence
Teachers:	
Gymnasium teacher	Imperial Petrograd Institute of History and Philology; Historico–Philological Institute of Prince Bezborodko in Nezhin Special Courses in Lazarevskii
(graduates)	Institute of Oriental Languages
Economists/commercial specialists:	
Candidate of economic sciences	Petrograd Polytechnic Institute
Medical specialists:	
Doctor (*lekar*)	State Medical Examining Board
Doctor (*lekar*) 'with excellence'	State Medical Examining Board
Clergymen:	
Candidate	Religious Academies in Moscow, Kazan, Kiev, Petrograd

Table 3-2 Degrees Granted by Higher Special Educational Institutions
Earning Rank 10 on the Table of Ranks in 1915

Specialist Degree	Granting Institutions
Engineers and Technicians:	
Transportation engineer of the second order	Institute of Engineers of Ministry of Transportation
Mining engineer of the second order	Mining Institute; Ekaterinoslav Higher Mining Institution
Civil Engineer 'with good success'	Institute of Civil Engineers
Metallurgical engineer of the second order	Petrograd Polytechnic Institute; Ekaterinoslav Higher Mining Institute
Electrical engineer	Petrograd Polytechnic Institute
Electrical engineer of the second order	Electro-Technical Institute
Naval engineer	Petrograd Polytechnic Institute
Senior surveying assistant	Konstantinov Survey Institute
Construction engineer	Imperial Moscow Engineering Institution
Student with certificate of programme completion	Petrograd Polytechnic Institute
Technician (*teknelog*)	Petrograd and Khar'kov Technological Institutes; Imperial Moscow Technical Institution
Mechanic	Imperial Moscow Technical Institution
Agronomists:	
Agronomist	New Alexanderia Ag. and Forestry Institute; Moscow Agricultural Institute (when teaching in state special schools)
Agronomist-technician	Moscow Agricultural Institute (when teaching in state special schools)
Foresters:	
Forester of the second order	New Alexandria Ag. and Forestry Institute
Research forester of the second order	Imperial Petrograd Forestry Institute
Lawyers:	
Student with certificate (*deistvitel'nyi student*)	Demidov Juridical Lyceum; Imperial Alexander Lyceum; Imperial Institution for the Study of Jurisprudence

Table 3-2 (Continued)

Specialist Degree	Granting Institutions
Economists/commercial specialists: (graduates) 'with excellence'	Commercial Department of Riga Polytechnic Institute
Clergymen: Student with certificate	Religious Academies: Moscow, Kazan, Kiev, Petrograd
Miscellaneous unspecified: 'All graduates of'	Riga Polytechnic Institute not in Rank 10, except its Commercial Department
'All graduates of'	Kiev and Warsaw Polytechnic Institutes not in Rank 10

Table 3-3 Degrees Granted by Higher Special Educational Institutions Earning Rank 10 on the Table of Ranks in 1915

Specialist Degree	Granting Institutions
Engineers and Technicians: Students with certificate	Institute of Civil Engineers
Electrician (third order of this degree)	Electro-Technical Institute
Junior surveying assistant	Konstantinov Surveying Institute
Economists/commercial specialists: All graduates who failed to receive 'with excellence'	Commercial Department, Riga Polytechnic Institute

Table 4   Tver *Zmestvo* Employees, 1891

	Job title	province	uezdy	total
I	1. Board chairmen	1	12	13
	2. Prov. Board members	3	—	3
	3. Senior doctors (Prov. hospitals and Burashevo colony)	2	—	2
	(1,000 roubles pension)			18
II	1. Uezd board members	—	24	24
	2. Secretaries	1	12	13
	3. Bookkeepers	1	12	13
	4. Manager of statistical dept	1	—	1
	5. Manager of insurance office	1	—	1
	6. Senior technician	1	—	1
	7. *Zemstvo* insurance agents	13	—	13
	8. *Zemstvo* doctors and veterinarians	6	44	50
	9. Principal of Maksimovich teachers' school for girls	1	—	1
	10. Head teacher, Maksimovich school	1	—	1
	11. Teachers, Maksimovich school	3	—	3
	12. Provincial board cashier	1	—	1
	13. Assistant to manager of the statistical department	1	—	1
	14. Manager of the economic department, Burashevo colony	1	—	1
	(600 roubles pension)			124
III	1. Desk heads, assistant secretaries, assistant bookkeepers	8	26	34
	2. Assistants to senior technician	2	—	2
	3. Supervisor of printing plant	1	—	1
	4. Female warden of the orphanage	1	—	1
	5. Provincial pharmacist and pharmacists in uezd hospitals	1	12	13
	6. Supervisor, provincial hospital	1	—	1
	7. Teachers (four women, three men) in Maksimovich girls' school	7	—	7
	8. Clerks in provincial hospital and Burashevo colony	2		2
	9. Assistant insurance agents	4	—	4
	10. Librarian	1	—	1
	(400 roubles pension)			66

Table 4 (Continued)

	Job title	province	uezdy	total
IV	1. Clerks and receiving clerks	15	32	47
	2. Type-setters and printers	5	—	5
	3. Medical and veterinary fel'dshers, fel'dshers and midwives	15	144	159
	4. Supervisors of uezd hospitals	—	—	11
	5. Teachers and their assistants	1	494	495
	6. Counters, statistical department	3	—	3
	7. Manager of the school fund	1	—	1
	8. Burashevo pharmacist's assistant	1	—	1
	9. Burashevo laundress	1	—	1
	10. Burashevo housekeeper	1	—	1
	11. Supervisor, Novotorzhok orphanage (200 roubles pension)	1	—	1
				725
V	1. Clerk in Burashevo colony	1	—	1
	2. Supervisors in the provincial hospital and Burashevo colony	5	—	5
	3. Provincial hospital laundress	1	—	1
	4. Housekeeper, Maksimovich school (120 roubles pension)	1	—	1
				8
	Totals	117	824	941

CHAPTER SEVEN

From 'middling sort' to middle class in late eighteenth- and early nineteenth-century England

John Seed

Roehampton Institute of Higher Education

What do we mean when we talk about 'the middle class'; and, as a corollary, how useful a category is it in analysing processes of change in England during the eighteenth and nineteenth centuries? From the beginning we have a problem with available terms such as 'middle class' or bourgeoisie. 'Bourgeois is a very difficult word to use in English', Raymond Williams comments.[1] It is difficult, first, because it is still quite clearly a French word, largely unassimilated to the British vocabulary. Even in France the word 'bourgeois' has shifting historical meanings. In medieval France it denoted an urban dweller – whether merchant, artisan or even wage labourer. In the eighteenth century it had come to mean an urban dweller of a very particular kind: one who was a rentier, a commoner without an active occupation living off his investments. This meaning was transformed in the aftermath of the revolution and in the nineteenth century 'bourgeoisie' came to denote an economically active group of industrialists, merchants and financiers.[2] It is a difficult term also because of its association with particular kinds of radical or bohemian diction in which it has often served less as a social catogory than as a term of abuse. 'Bourgeois' or 'bourgeoisie' thus evokes a complacent materialism or narrow-minded philistinism: the 'muddle crass' in James Joyce's formulation.

---

[1] Williams *Keywords: a Vocabulary of Culture and Society* (London, 1976), p. 37.

[2] On shifting usages of 'bourgeois' in France, see M. Vovelle and D. Roche, 'Bourgeois, rentiers, and property owners: elements for defining a social category at the end of the eighteenth century', in J. Kaplow (ed.) *New Perspectives on the French Revolution: Readings in Historical Sociology* (New York, 1965), pp. 25–7.

The term 'middle class' presents other problems. It originates as an anomaly, a discord, within the supposed harmony of the traditional order. It is the MIDDLE class, between rich and poor, upper and lower; in the words of the eighteenth-century poet Cowper, 'Tenants of life's middle state, / Securely plac'd between the small and great'. During the eighteenth century the term appears again and again: 'the Middling People of England', 'the middling sort', 'men of a middling condition', 'the middle Station of Life', and so on. Only towards the end of the eighteenth century does this become 'the middle classes' or 'middle class'. The term 'middle class' originates, then, as an inter-position between rich and poor, between persons of rank and the common people. This leaves at least two problems. First, how appropriate is the term 'middle class' for modern social structures? It implies a continuing tripartite division in which the 'upper class' – the landed aristocracy or some other kind of narrow propertied elite – remains dominant, or at least significantly separate.[3] Second, the term 'working class' at least connotes some kind of economic role or activity. But 'middle class' remains merely positional – a space, a 'between'; not something that exists in its own right but a grouping that fails, or refuses, to fit the dominant social division between upper and lower, rich and poor, land and labour.

These problems of vocabulary are not merely a matter of untidy definitions. They are rooted in the very history we are trying to understand.[4] In this chapter I want to begin with a minimal definition of the middle class in England between the mid-eighteenth and mid-nineteenth centuries. Its constituent elements were distinguished from the landed aristocracy and gentry by their need to generate an income from some kind of active occupation(s). And they were distinguished from the labouring majority by their possession of property – whether mobile capital, stock in trade or professional credentials – and by their exemption from manual labour. Their economic activity thus involved the possession and management of material resources and the labour of others.

Whatever the difficulties of the social vocabulary we have inherited,

---

[3] For discussion of the 'middle class' within the class structure of contemporary societies, see N. Abercrombie and J. Urry, *Capital, Labour and the Middle Classes* (London, 1983), and R. Carter, *Capitalism, Class Conflict and the New Middle Class* (London, 1985).

[4] For accounts of the language of class in this period, see A. Briggs, 'The Language of class in early nineteenth-century England', in A. Briggs and J. Saville (eds.) *Essays in Labour History* (London, 1960); S. Wallech, 'Class versus rank: the transformation of eighteenth-century English social terms and theories of production', *Journal of the History of Ideas* 47 (1986).

certain long-term social processes in the eighteenth and nineteenth centuries are obvious and relevant. Britain was increasingly an urban society. The total population living in towns rose from around 19 per cent in 1700, to 23 per cent by mid-century, reaching 30 per cent by 1800. There were some sixty-seven towns with a population of 2,500 or more in 1700. By 1800 this had increased to 187. By that date London's population was almost 1 million, around 10 per cent of the population of the nation. The 1841 census showed that by that year some 48 per cent of the population of England and Wales lived in towns with a population of over 2,500; by 1871 this had reached 65 per cent. This was also a society in which landowners, farmers and farm labourers were a shrinking proportion of the population. By the 1760s, according to Massie's contemporary calculations, workers involved in trade and manufacture outnumbered those involved in agriculture. The 1801 census indicated that 40 per cent of families were involved in trade, commerce and manufacturing, compared to 36 per cent in agriculture. This was, then, an increasingly urban society in which economic life was more and more structured around all kinds of trading and manufacturing activities. This is a significant direction of social change – though it is important to remember the continuing economic significance of all kinds of agricultural raw materials and the complex articulations of agriculture, manufacturing and trade and of the urban and rural.

Data on the social structure of eighteenth-century England are notoriously hard to come by. The estimates of Gregory King in 1688, Joseph Massie in 1760 and Patrick Colquhoun in 1803 provide some useful information.[5] It is true their calculations were not constructed in order to provide a description of social structure and have all kinds of limitations as a source for the historian. But they can be used to sketch in a shadowy picture of the social hierarchy. At its apex there was a tiny elite of landowners numbering around 1 or 1.5 per cent of the population, though receiving some 15 per cent of national income. At its base were the 'Labouring Poor': all kinds of casual and unskilled labourers, seamen and soldiers, paupers and vagrants. Between these strata were the ranks of 'the middling sort'. They stretched from judges, state officials and great merchants at the top, on the margins

[5] See G. Holmes, 'Gregory King and the social structure of pre-industrial England', *Transactions of the Royal Historical Society* 5th series, 27. (1977); P. Mathias, 'The social structure in the eighteenth century: a calculation by Joseph Massie', in Mathias, *The Transformation of England: Essays in the Economic and Social History of England in the Eighteenth Century* (London, 1979); H. Perkin, *The Origins of Modern English Society, 1780–1800* (London, 1969), ch. 2.

of the landed elite, to small farmers and semi-independent craftsmen at the bottom, blurring into the ranks of the labouring poor. For the eighteenth century it is within these intermediate strata, 'the middle ranks', that an emergent middle class is to be traced. Perkin uses figures from King and Colquhoun for the 'Middle Ranks' as a whole to estimate an overall increase from 435,000 in 1688 to around 634,640 by 1803. Within this total the middle ranks in agriculture – freeholders and farmers – increase only from 150,000 to 160,000. The professions similarly show a modest increase: from 55,000 to 62,000. It is overwhelmingly from within the ranks of those involved in trade and manufacturing that increase among 'the middling sort' therefore occurred during the eighteenth century.[6] But this is where the problems begin.

Town directories provide more specific occupational breakdowns. First published for London in the later seventeenth century, these directories began to be published for more substantial provincial towns from the 1760s. How accurate and how complete were such directories? They certainly claimed to represent the commercial and financial elite of their town. And considerable trouble was taken to ensure both completeness and accuracy.[7] Stana Nenadic's careful linkage of the Glasgow Directory of 1832 and 1861 with other sources suggests that its listing was to a degree representative of a broadly conceived middle class in the town.[8] What use, then, can town directories be in specifying the elements of the middle class in the late eighteenth and early nineteenth centuries? The changing numbers of specific occupational groupings can be traced. This is a relatively easy matter for groups such as the legal or medical professions. The problem is to get at the manufacturing and commercial groups. For example, Manchester's directories in the late eighteenth century indicate the preponderant place of the cotton industry in the town's economy. However, closer elucidation of the listings runs into difficulties because of the vagueness of the categories. 'Cotton merchant', 'smallware manufacturer', 'cotton dealer', 'fustian manufacturer', 'yarn merchant', 'merchant', 'merchant and warehouseman', 'merchant and manufacturer', and so on – the terms proliferate with no means of grasping whether we are looking at substantial firms or

---

[6] Perkin, op. cit.

[7] See the discussion in P.J. Corfield and S. Kelly, 'Giving directions to the town: the early town directories', *Urban History Yearbook*, 1984: 22–35.

[8] S. Nenadic, 'Record linkage and the exploration of nineteenth-century social groups: a methodological perspective on the Glasgow middle class in 1861', *Urban History Yearbook* 1987: 34.

small-scale enterprises, employers of many or few labourers, direct employers of labour or simply what Adam Smith called 'speculative merchants' transacting business through intermediaries and agents. To give one example of the potential for error: James Hall, a Quaker fustian dyer in Manchester since 1763, is listed simply as a dyer in the 1788 directory. But we know that as well as employing some forty people in his dyeing firm, in 1784 he was using over 4,000 men, women and children as outworkers in cloth production.[9] Town directories are useful sources for studying the social and economic structure of particular towns but, if the aim is to pinpoint with some precision the different elements of the middle class, they have serious limitations.

Census material on occupations has been extensively used by social historians of the Victorian period. Here too there are difficulties. As Robbie Gray notes: 'The difficulties attaching to Victorian censuses make it impossible to arrive at precise measures of the occupational or class structure at any particular census, still less of changes between censuses.[10] Occupational categories in the decennial census are unstable. In the case of the apparently straightforward 'professional class', for instance, the 1851 census included not only 'the learned professions' and those involved in 'literature, art and science' but also those in defence and government, including the royal family. At the same time it excluded accountants, architects and surveyors – though the two latter were incorporated into the professional category by 1881. Anglican clergy were included but Nonconformist ministers were not. Also 'the professional class' included 'their subordinate services', so that not only were lawyers included but also their clerks.[11] There is a major problem too in distinguishing types of employers in industry – between the owner of a large enterprise with hundreds of workers and a small businessman with many fewer workers or even the artisan with one or two apprentices in addition to family labour. From 1841 enumerators were instructed to distinguish between masters, journeymen and apprentices, from 1851 to specify the number of employees for each master, and from 1861 to distinguish 'employers'. However the census returns were plainly inadequate since many employers failed to indicate the numbers of their employees. There was also some ambiguity about the designation of share-

---

[9] *The Merchant and Manufacturers Magazine of Trade and Commerce* (1785): 135.
[10] R.Q. Gray, *The Labour Aristocracy in Victorian Edinburgh* (Oxford, 1976), p. 191.
[11] See T. R. Gourvish, 'The rise of the professions' in R.G. Gourvish and A. O'Day (eds.) *Later Victorian Britain 1867–1900* (London, 1988), pp. 18–19.

holders or partners in a firm. Census categories therefore need to be used with caution.[12] They are frequently unsafe, reflecting contemporary perceptions of the social order as much as social realities.

Underlying the difficulties of using any of these sources to analyse social structure is the limited value of occupation as an index of social position. This is especially the case for the middle class. Precisely what assumptions can we make about the social and economic position of a merchant, a manufacturer, even a lawyer or physician? A Manchester 'cotton manufacturer' might be a captain of industry managing a huge enterprise employing over a thousand hands and with a princely income. Or he might be renting a few looms, employing a handful of people and surviving on very low profit margins. Similarly among merchants and professional men the congruence of their designated occupation can disguise wide divergences of income and social position. Medical men were sometimes gentlemen of substantial wealth and generally made a comfortable living, but cases of physicians and surgeons struggling on the verge of poverty were not exceptional.[13] Among clerks a significant proportion in mid-nineteenth-century commercial centres were not merely white-collar wage-earners but, coming from propertied families, were in the process of acquiring the necessary expertise and contacts to set up businesses of their own. 'It is under this title', it was observed in 1871, 'that the various scions of the aristocracy who are learning business in Liverpool must be ranged'.[14] Moreover, a single occupation might be convenient for the compiler of directories or census tables but obscures the complexity and variety of middle-class economic activities throughout this period.

Two detailed examples will illustrate this point. First, Joseph Robinson Pease (1752–1807): a Hull 'banker' he held the major share in 'Pease's Old Bank', the first in the town. He was also involved in two seed-crushing businesses and in the whaling industry. He invested heavily in canal development and in the 1790s was the second-largest shareholder in the Calder-Hebble Navigation with an investment of £6,000. He also had £3,800 in the Driffield Navigation as well as lesser sums in the Rochdale Canal. He was heavily involved

---

[12] See E. Higgs, *Making Sense of the Census: The Manuscript Returns for England and Wales, 1801–1901 (Public Record Office Handbook* 23, 1989).

[13] On impoverished medical men see e.g. H. Marland, *Medicine and Society in Wakefield and Huddersfield, 1780–1870* (Cambridge, 1987), esp. ch. 7.

[14] Quoted in D. Lockwood, *The Blackcoated Worker: A Study in Class Consciousness* (2nd ed. Oxford, 1989), p. 26.

in property development in Hull, owning several plots of land and several substantial housing projects. In addition he had a 190-acre estate a few miles west of the town which brought in around 16 per cent of his income in the mid-1790s.[15] James Losh (1763–1833), a Newcastle upon Tyne barrister, provides a second illustration. As well as following his legal business on the northern circuit – from which he drew a considerable annual income – he was a partner in an alkali works on Tyneside, held substantial shares in a Hexham brewery and was a partner in several coal-mines in the area. In 1812 his income was £2,600: £1,400 from his profession, £1,000 profits from his coal interests, and £200 'interest on moneys'. In 1818 he inherited via his brother-in-law considerable land in Lancashire with an annual rental of nearly £2,000. And in 1820 he inherited land in Cumberland from an uncle. In both cases he took an active part in developing the economic value of this land. His brother William was involved in running an iron works, an alkali works and a coal-fitting business, all on Tyneside, in each of which James Losh had some financial involvement and occasionally played an active role in their management. So Losh was not only a barrister but also an improving landlord and an industrialist.[16] The complex range of economic activities of Joseph Robinson Pease in Hull and James Losh in Newcastle cannot then be encapsulated in the simple categories of the town directory or the census – 'banker' or 'barrister'.

The case of Losh suggests a further point: that the distinction between 'profession' and 'business', as if they were two quite autonomous spheres, can easily be overdrawn. Members of the legal profession were frequently involved in a range of economic activities based upon the management of capital and labour. This was equally true of the medical profession. In early-nineteenth-century Manchester William Henry combined medical practice for a number of years with management of the family's chemical manufacturing firm. He was also engaged in scientific research, lectured and published on science and acted as a scientific consultant to local industrialists. Henry may have been untypical in the range of his activities but many other medical men had business involvements, especially in property development.[17] More generally those who possessed a modicum of

---

[15] This material comes from the Pease Papers in the Wilberforce House Museum, Hull.

[16] The most detailed account of the Losh family is in H. Lonsdale, *The Worthies of Cumberland* (London, 1873), vol. IV, esp. pp. 186–96.

[17] For Henry, see W.V. Farrah, K. Farrah and E.L. Scott, 'The Henrys of Manchester', in *Ambix: Journal of Alchemy and Early Chemistry*, 12 (1974), nos. 2 and 3.

capital were rarely confined to a single occupation or single source of income in this period.

If occupation can take us only so far in identifying the different social elements of the middle class and its internal structure, then wealth can provide another dimension. The possession of property, of mobile capital, was an essential constituent of the middle class. Income, especially when realised in consumption, was a recognised marker of social position. For Defoe in the early eighteenth century 'the middling sort' were essentially defined by their visible and public distinction from either the 'mere labouring people' or 'the upper part of mankind'. They were not 'exposed to the miseries and hardships, the labour and suffering of the mechanic part of mankind, and not embarrassed with the pride, luxury, ambition and envy of the upper part of mankind'.[18] By the 1830s there was a broad consensus that £300 per annum was the minimum for sustaining a middle-class standard of living.[19] Dudley Baxter's careful estimate of the distribution of national income of England and Wales in 1867 indicated those with incomes between £300 and £1,000 as numbering some 90,000 families or just under 1.5 per cent of the national total. Below them in the hierarchy were 510,000 families (just over 8 per cent of the total) – clerks and shopkeepers, schoolteachers, commercial travellers, various kinds of small businessmen – with an income of between £100 and £300 per annum.[20] Two main sources provide a more detailed picture of the structure of the middle class: probate records and income tax data. W.D. Rubinstein has made extensive use of both sets of records to develop an analysis of the Victorian middle class.[21] In brief, he suggests that these sources reveal the much greater wealth of the metropolitan and commercial middle class compared to the northern industrial middle class. From this he asserts that there were two segregated middle classes in Victorian England characterised by distinct forms of property, different 'occupational ideologies', separate status priorities, and contrasting relations with the landed aristocracy. Only after 1918 did these distinct middle classes merge

[18] Quoted in P. Earle, *The World of Defoe* (London, 1976), p. 166.

[19] The best account of middle-class living standards remains J.A. Banks, *Prosperity and Parenthood: A Study of Family Planning among the Victorian Middle Classes* (London, 1954).

[20] See H. Perkin, *The Rise of Professional Society: England since 1880* (London, 1989), pp. 28–30.

[21] W.D. Rubinstein, 'Wealth, elites and the class structure of modern Britain', *Past and Present* 76 (1977): 99–126, and his *Men of Property. The Very Wealthy in Britain since the Industrial Revolution* (London, 1981).

into a single 'elite', within which the northern industrial middle class was a subordinate partner.

Some of the wider implications of this argument will be taken up later. What is at issue here is the value of the records which Rubinstein has opened to historical debate. In fact probate material has serious limitations. First, it records an estimate of wealth at time of death but provides no information on precisely what made up that sum and how it had been generated. Second, it excludes realty, that is land and freehold property. This is a significant omission in the case of industrialists and merchants who had substantial amounts of capital tied up in factories, warehouses, and so on. Third, there is a geographical bias built into probate since wealth was recorded at the place of death not at the place where it was generated. If an industrialist died outside the North the valuation was more than likely to be assessed in London, especially after 1858. Moreover, there were material reasons why wealthy industrialists and merchants were less likely to die in industrial Lancashire for instance. The poor climate and poor soil made it unattractive for retirement. It was noted in 1849:

> those who have grown rich in those great marts of industry and commerce, Liverpool and Manchester, and other manufacturing towns of the county, when they seek a permanent investment for their property in land, frequently leave the country in which they have made all their money, and, unwilling in the autumn of their years to engage in new and untried undertakings, are led to seek in more southern counties a more genial climate, a more fertile soil, a higher class of farmers and farming, and a more tempting investment than Lancashire can offer.[22]

Finally, and perhaps most important of all, probate estimates wealth (personalty) at time of death not when the individual is economically most active. Frequently manufacturers and merchants of all kinds retired from business, passing much of the capital on to the next generation well before their deaths. In this way, Samuel Greg saw to it that each of his four sons was trained to join the family's cotton manufacturing firm. On coming of age, between 1817 and 1830, each son was presented with £5,000 and a share of the business. Finally in 1832, two years before his death, Greg retired and his sons took control of the family's mills. Thus what Samuel Greg left on his death in 1834 was only a small part of the value of the business developed

---

[22] W.J. Garnett, 'The farming of Lancashire', *Journal of the Royal Agricultural Society* 10 (1849), p. 6.

by this important representative of the first generation of industrialists.[23] This points to a wider issue. To quote Simon Gunn:

the characteristic form of nineteenth-century business organization was familial and dynastic . . . As a result, capital was rarely concentrated in the hands of a single individual, but dispersed unequally through several branches of an industrial dynasty, or still more complex, through several families interlinked by marriage.[24]

Recall the case of the Newcastle barrister James Losh. From a landed family, his elder brother managed their Cumberland estate and he himself inherited several parcels of land, some of it through marriage. At the same time a younger brother was involved in chemical manufacturing and coal-mining. Losh himself was involved in land, the professions, commerce and manufacturing. To know only what this Newcastle 'barrister' left at death is to know little or nothing about his location within the economic and social life of early-nineteenth-century England. In this sense at least Losh is representative of the middle class.

Probate records, then, have severe limitations, significantly underestimating industrial wealth and producing a distorted picture of the middle class as a whole. They fail to trace out the social patterns of wealth-holding, the intricate social structures through which capital was deployed and profit distributed. The income tax records which Rubinstein exploits to reinforce his model of two distinct middle classes present similar problems – a geographical bias towards London, failure to indicate precisely what the records are assessing, representation of individual incomes rather than family incomes, and so on. In addition income tax was only levied for a few years during the Napoleonic Wars and from 1842 and thus covers a very limited span before the mid-nineteenth century. Finally, then as now, it was subject to evasion. As McCulloch complained in 1863, little confidence can be placed in the accuracy of the Inland Revenue's assessments.[25] Any attempt to draw up a picture of the size distribution of incomes during the eighteenth and nineteenth centuries confronts insuperable problems because of the basic inadequacy of the empirical data. And this is especially the case for the middle class whose sources

[23] See M.B. Rose, *The Gregs of Quarry Bank Mill: the Rise and Decline of a Family Firm, 1750–1914* (Cambridge, 1986).

[24] S. Gunn, 'The "failure" of the Victorian middle class: a critique', in J. Wolff and J. Seed (eds.) *The Culture of Capital: Art, Power and the Nineteenth-century Middle Class* (Manchester, 1988), p. 21.

[25] J. R. McCulloch, *A Treatise on the Principles and Practical Influence of Taxation and the Funding System* (Edinburgh, 1863), pp. 120ff.

of income were so diverse – profits from running a business, rent from urban property, profits on invested capital or government bonds, and so on – and so liable to fluctuation over even short periods of time.

Despite their limitations, it remains the case that the kinds of materials briefly examined so far can take us some way towards identifying the elements of the middle class, assessing their numbers and pinpointing their geographical locations. But it is important to understand social class as something more than a passive and static description based upon certain kinds of quantifiable information. Doubtless probate records, directories, poll books, insurance records, rate books, tax records, apprenticeship registers, census enumerators' books, marriage registers, and so on, will be investigated in the future using computers and sophisticated sampling techniques. Ultimately the difficulties in exploiting these sources are not just a matter of quantification but more importantly of conceptualisation. Though it may uncover patterns and correlations not accessible via other empirical methods, no narrowly quantitative method will illuminate relations within the middle class or with the wider society. Nor will it tell us much about the ways these relations were changing.

Class was, and is, a dynamic process – a matter of shifting social relations. Thus the middle class did not 'rise' out of the level plains of the traditional social order. Its emergence in this period involved a radical reordering of social relations within the eighteenth-century 'middling sort'. For some their small capital and modest enterprise grew and prospered. Indeed in a few instances remarkable wealth accumulated within a relatively short time, especially in the early phases of industrialisation in the textile industries. The meteoric rise of men like Arkwright, Peel, McConnel and Kennedy, George and Adam Murray, Ashtons, Fieldens, Gregs, Birleys, in Lancashire, or John Marshall, Benjamin Gott, Titus Salt, Isaac Holden, Samuel Cunliffe Lister in West Yorkshire was, however, untypical, even among northern industrial employers. Of some 700 cotton firms in Lancashire in 1841 only 51 (around 7 per cent) employed over 500 people. Over 600 (around 85 per cent) employed less than 200 people. Similarly in the Yorkshire woollen and worsted industries large employers were few and far between. Few woollen mills employed more than 75 workers and most had a work force of fewer than 50.[26] The marked concentration of economic power in a number of major

---

[26] D.S. Gadian, 'Class consciousness in Oldham and other north-west industrial towns, 1830–50', *Historical Journal* 21 (1978): 169.

northern textile firms is a fact of importance. But in terms of understanding even the industrial middle class in Lancashire and Yorkshire too narrow a focus on a few well-documented case studies produces an extremely distorted picture.

More typically the middling sort prospered modestly, becoming part of the distinctive Victorian middle class only after several generations of steady accumulation of capital – and good health, shrewd marriages, and good fortune. For many others economic change was more difficult. They were bankrupted or proletarianised by the vicious fluctuations of an unstable economy or by cut-throat competition. One factory inspector estimated that only 127 of the 318 firms in the Yorkshire trade survived the major economic crisis of the late 1830s and 1840s. Similarly in the Nottingham area fewer than half the hosiery firms in existence in 1815 survived into the 1840s and some 500 small-scale lace manufacturers disappeared in the years 1833–6.[27] How extensive was downward social mobility in the transition from 'middling sort' to middle class? 'It is a melancholy truth', Dickens reminds us in *Bleak House*, 'that even great men have their poor relations'. What happened to bankrupt or economically declining families? Beatrice Webb recalled among the mid-Victorian middle class of London 'the making and breaking of personal friend-ships according to temporary and accidental circumstances in no way connected with personal merit: gracious appreciation and insistent intimacy being succeeded, when failure according to worldly stan-dards occurred, by harsh criticism and cold avoidance'.[28]

The weak notion of 'the rise of the middle class' has obscured the complex processes of change in this period and neglected analysis of the way in which as a social category 'the middling sort' were splintering into a number of quite different strata and quite divergent individual fates.[29] It is here that the model of two distinct middle classes – a northern industrial middle class and a southern commercial middle class – needs to be examined. London certainly had a substantial middle class throughout the eighteenth and nineteenth centuries. The 1861 census listed over 70,000 males (over 7 per cent of occupied males) belonging to Class I – large employers, merchants

---

[27] R.M. Hartwell, 'Business management in England during the period of early industrialisation', in R.M. Hartwell (ed.) *The Industrial Revolution* (Oxford, 1970), p. 31 n.; M.I. Thomis, *Politics and Society in Nottingham, 1785–1835* (Oxford, 1969), p. 39.

[28] B. Webb, *My Apprenticeship* (Penguin ed. 1938), vol. I, p. 70.

[29] For an interesting sketch of divergent fates within a particular family see J. Wedgewood, *The Economics of Inheritance* (2nd ed., London, 1939), pp. 180–3.

and bankers, the liberal professions.[30] There were nearly 160,000 males (16.3 per cent of occupied males) belonging to Class II: small employers, wholesalers, all kinds of dealers, shopkeepers, minor officials, lesser professionals, clerks. The most visible part of this propertied class in the nineteenth century was undoubtedly its financial and commercial elite. The 1861 census reveals that there were nearly 12,000 men in the five categories of banker, merchant, accountant, stock and commercial broker, shipowner and broker. Yet what Gareth Stedman Jones terms 'the social domination of London by non-industrial forms of capital' should not obscure the fact that there was a substantial manufacturing sector in the metropolis. While London may not have been a centre of heavy industries associated with industrialisation – textile mills, iron and steel production, coal-mining – it pioneered the development of mechanical engineering in the 1820s and remained second only to Lancashire as an engineering centre until the 1870s. As well as engineering, metal-working and tool-making there was chemical manufacturing, shipbuilding, paper-making, brewing, printing, furniture manufacturing, boot and shoe making, tanning, and various kinds of textile manufacturing. In 1861 around one-quarter of the male population over ten years of age were employed in these kinds of manufacturing activities in London – compared to around 15 per cent in commerce, clerical work, retail and distribution and 13 per cent in transport.

The vast bulk of employers in London's industries were small in scale. In some forty-one of the city's most important trades less than 2 per cent of the workforce were employed in firms with more than fifty workers. Large-scale industrial employers were few and far between and largely restricted to engineering, tanning, building and silk-manufacturing. And yet within the social world of London in the late eighteenth and early nineteenth centuries what is important is not so much the relative scarcity of large-scale industrial employers as the increasingly dominant pattern of the social relations of production and the accompanying ascendancy of the drive to increase productivity via intensified control of the labour process and the erosion of artisan independence. This was as marked within the 'financial services sector' as within the manufacturing sector. Granted, of course, the City was of immense economic importance and a con-

---

[30] These and subsequent figures on London are taken from the appendices to G. Stedman Jones, *Outcast London: A Study in the Relationship between Classes in Victorian Society* (Oxford, 1971). See also F. Sheppard, *London 1808–1870: The Infernal Wen* (London, 1971).

siderable proportion of its profitability stemmed from wealth appropriated overseas. Nevertheless it depended also upon the labour of vast armies of wage labourers – dockers, white-collar workers, porters and transport workers of all kinds. It would be difficult to sustain an argument that in London in this period the powerful presence of the City mitigated to a significant extent the dominance of capitalist property relations and the subordination of labour to the dictates of capital. Mayhew's writings of the early 1850s testify eloquently to the contrary as trade after trade was subjected to that regime.

London was not, from this perspective, markedly different from other urban centres. Throughout England during the late eighteenth and first half of the nineteenth century the diverse ranks of 'the middling sort' were being radically recorded by economic development. Small masters were being squeezed out by market forces and increasing specialisation, pushed down into the ranks of wage labour as traditional protections (such as the Elizabethan Statute of Artificers) were repealed by an increasingly *laissez-faire* state. Or they adapted, more or less successfully, to the new dictates of capital and became, at however humble a level – as garret masters in the sweated trades, owners of workshops or building yards, small-scale employers, wholesalers and retailers of all kinds – employers subsisting on profits derived from the wage labour of others. Or, in some instances they persisted in the old ways, especially some shopkeepers and traditional small-town tradesmen. Often the precise demarcations between small employer and artisan small master were extremely fluid and subject to rapidly shifting determinants – crucially the disposition of their work force.[31] Even in the textile industries the line between employer and employee was sometimes indistinct. At the same time there were emerging quite new and distinctive middle-class groups: new professions, white-collar groupings, specialised functionaries within commerce and so on. It is wrong to draw a simple distinction between a northern industrial middle class and a southern commercial or financial middle class. Even in the classical northern factory town such as Oldham or Bradford the middle class consisted of a much wider grouping than simply the factory owner, including, as well as professionals, a range of commercial and financial groups – brokers, accountants, agents, bankers, merchants and so on. This is even more

---

[31] See C. Behagg, 'Masters and manufacturers: social values and the smaller unit of production in Birmingham, 1800–50', in G. Crossick and H. Haupt (eds.) *Shopkeepers and Master Artisans in Nineteenth-Century Europe* (London, 1984).

important in larger urban centres in the North like Manchester or Leeds where the commercial and financial sectors were of increasing importance. Conversely the absence of the classical industries of the 'industrial revolution' in London and other southern towns should not obscure the significant presence there of employers of labour, including industrial employers.

This is not to propose that there was a more or less uniform middle class evenly distributed across the towns and cities of England. There were significant and identifiable differences in the composition of the middle class between distinct economic regions. The major urban centres of nineteenth-century England each had a variable mix of industrial employers, merchants, professionals and others but the precise character of the middle class varied from district to district, from town to town. Newer factory towns developed a smaller middle class with fewer professionals and commercial men, who tended to be concentrated in regional capitals. Manchester diversified its economic base and by the middle years of the nineteenth century had a much smaller proportion of its labour force employed in textiles than its lesser neighbours such as Stockport, Oldham, Ashton or Bolton. It became a centre for all kinds of professional and commercial services for the region as a whole and hence had a proportionately larger middle class of bankers, lawyers, accountants, agents, merchants and so on. County towns, as traditional market centres with administrative functions, generally possessed a relatively large professional middle class. In mid-nineteenth-century York there were more persons of independent means and proportionately more professionals and domestic servants than in either Leeds or Sheffield; while on these counts Bradford trailed far behind all three.[32] At the same time York included the major manufacturing works owned by the Rowntrees and extensive railway works so that Seebohm Rowntree in 1901 saw the place not as a cathedral town, vestige of another epoch, but as a typical Victorian provincial town. There were also the several hundred provincial market towns with not only their lawyers, bankers and auctioneers, builders and innkeepers but also diverse manufacturing elements – perhaps a brewery, paper mill or textile factory, and some merchants or small employers linked to important regional industries. There were the seaside resorts with their retired businessmen, rentiers (often widows), professionals and local entre-

---

[32] A. Armstrong, *Stability and Change in an English County Town: a Study of York 1801–51* (Cambridge, 1974), p. 30.

preneurs involved in property development, building or services.[33] The character of the middle class in coal-mining districts such as the north east was particularly complex.

To identify the make-up of the middle class in nineteenth-century England an examination is required not only of northern industrialists and City merchants but also of urban centres that have been neglected. Hull, Torquay, Stockport, Reading, Newcastle upon Tyne, Guildford, Halifax or Lincoln are merely emblematic of the variety and complexity of urban society in eighteenth- and nineteenth-century England. John Foster's comparison of Oldham's social structure in 1851 with those of South Shields and Northampton illuminates significant differences in the character of the middle class from this perspective. Fairly similar in size and occupational make-up, nevertheless Oldham was distinguished by a sharp break between 'big' and 'petit' bourgeois groupings. The former were larger, wealthier and much more exclusive than their counterparts in South Shields and Northampton. Indeed a local account from 1852 distinguished three major groups in the town: 11,000 'operative families'; 2,000 ' "middle-class" families' (non-manual groups such as small shopkeepers, small masters, farmers, clerks and so on); and 200 families described as 'upper class'. These latter were not just exclusive but in important respects culturally and politically isolated. This sharp division within the town's 'middling sort' was in marked contrast to South Shields and Northampton. There industry was by and large small in scale and the very wealthy much thinner on the ground. In these towns there was much more continuity between the social elements of the middle class and lower middle class and significantly greater cultural and political cooperation.[34]

This points to the importance of analysing the middle class in terms of the active construction of all kinds of social relations – internal and external. What kinds of organisation cemented relations between urban property-owners and at the same time excluded others? How were the boundaries of middle-class identity produced and maintained?

---

[33] See D. Cannadine, *Lords and Landlords: The Aristocracy and the Towns 1774–1967* (Leicester, 1980), esp. ch. 3. See also J. Field, 'Wealth, styles of life and social tone amongst Portsmouth's middle class, 1800–75', in R.J. Morris (ed.) *Class, Power and Social Structure in British Nineteenth-century Towns* (Leicester, 1986).

[34] J. Foster, *Class Struggle and the Industrial Revolution: Early Industrial Capitalism in Three English Towns* (London, 1974), especially pp. 162–6.

Of primary importance was family.[35] Even after the Joint Stock Acts of 1856 and 1862, limiting the personal liability of individual investors, most textile firms, most engineering firms, nearly all cutlery and pottery firms, with few exceptions shipbuilding, brewing, the Birmingham trades, housebuilding and the clothing trades were private and family affairs, at least until the last decades of the nineteenth century. Mercantile and professional businesses similarly remained, by and large, family based. The fundamental business unit was the individual owner/manager or the small partnership, very often consisting of family members. Management functions were generally carried out by the firm's owner and his immediate family – though supported by a small group of clerks, overseers, foremen. Again and again in the textile industries, for instance, nephews, brothers-in-law, sons-in-law were recruited into the family firm as partners, assistant managers or bookkeepers – especially in cases where there was no son available to follow his father. At the same time as providing managerial personnel the family was important as a source of capital. A central nexus for the reproduction of the family firm was therefore marriage. In other words, the marriage market was articulated with the wider markets for capital and management skills. Marriage partners were chosen not, finally, by individuals but by social, primarily family, pressures. 'It would not signify about her being in love', Mrs Davilow says of her daughter in *Daniel Deronda*, 'if she would only accept the right person'. Kinship, then – the brotherhood and cousinhood of property – constituted one of the inner structures which joined individuals and different forms of capital together in communities of interest. Sociologists have examined how a propertied elite emerged gradually in this way as groups of loosely connected families engaged in similar economic activities became increasingly integrated via partnerships and intermarriage.[36]

A central institution of middle-class life, reinforcing aspects of the role of family, was organised religion. 'Visit the churches and chapels of this great town', wrote a contributor to a Manchester magazine in 1842, 'look around the various congregations, richly and gaily dressed, comfortably seated in easy-cushioned pews, and say how many of the real horny-handed workmen will be found among the

---

[35] The role of the family in middle-class formation is exhaustively discussed in L. Davidoff and C. Hall, *Family Fortunes: Men and Women of the English Middle Class* (London, 1987).

[36] J. Scott, *Corporations, Classes and Capitalism* (London, 1979) provides a lucid review of the literature. The work of Maurice Zeitlin – much of it now collected in his *The Large Corporation and Contemporary Classes* (Oxford, 1989) – is seminal.

group'.[37] Horace Mann's report in the 1851 religious census made the same point and commented that religious observance had come to be regarded as 'a purely middle-class propriety or luxury'.[38] If religious congregations in the towns and cities of early-nineteenth-century England were rarely in any straightforward sense 'middle class' nevertheless the middle class were overwhelmingly affiliated to organised religion. Why? Membership of an urban congregation – whether Anglican, Nonconformist, or Methodist – was an insignia of middle-class status and served a number of important social functions. It brought the middle-class family into a wider community. Chapels of all denominations provided a range of formal and informal social networks for their membership. Here they found 'sociability' and a marriage market that could be carefully supervised. Here too, especially among dissenting groups, they found business contacts and mutual support in economic affairs. In the circumstances of the law of unlimited liability co-religionists often provided much-needed capital in a context of mutual trust and cooperation. At the same time the social values propounded within churches and chapels gave ideological legitimacy to particular patterns of domination and sub-ordination within middle-class social life: the domination of male over female, parents over children, masters and mistresses over servants. Membership of a religious congregation was an active commitment to a whole social project – the role of Christian influence in consolidating order, respect for property and authority, respect-ability, honesty and hard work.[39]

It was important for middle-class formation, however, that there were social institutions which transcended the always potentially divisive boundaries of the religious sect – that, in other words, a secular public sphere was constructed. In Manchester, for example, there were three main religious congregations in the first half of the eighteenth century: the old Collegiate Church representing High Church Toryism; St Anne's, a somewhat Whiggish Anglicanism; and the Dissenting Cross Street Chapel, which originated in seventeenth-century Presbyterianism. Relations between the merchants, pro-fessionals and tradesmen belonging to the first and third were frequently bitter and political antagonisms were often fought out in the rhetoric of the English Civil War ('Down with the Rump' and so

---

[37] H. Heartwell, 'Characteristics of Manchester', *North of England Magazine* (1842): 169.

[38] *Religious Census, P.P. 1852–3*, LXXXIX, clix.

[39] See J. Seed, 'Theologies of power: Unitarianism and the social relations of religious discourse, 1800–50', In R.J. Morris, op. cit. pp. 130–42.

on). However, in the second half of the century, as the town grew rapidly, there was a proliferation of new churches. There were ten Anglican churches in the town by 1800, several Methodist groups and many new Dissenting chapels – two Congregationalist, two Baptist, one Unitarian and one Scottish Presbyterian among them. This weakened the impact of sectarian animosities in early-nineteenth-century Manchester though the opposition of Church and Dissent, here as elsewhere, persisted. More important was the gradual emergence of a secular public sphere through the setting up of bodies such as the Subscription Library, the Literary and Philosophical Society, the Royal Manchester Institution, the Assembly Rooms, the Billiard Club, the Union Club, and so on. Such organisations were very diverse in their purposes but all were important in providing spaces for social association outside the narrow circles of immediate business associates, co-religionists and family. The role of the Manchester Institution in generating social cooperation among the fairly isolated elements of the town's middle class was noted at its inception in 1823:

> An Institution such as this, would . . . serve as a point of union for the enlightened and liberal part of this widely scattered and in some respects, unconnected population . . . many people who might otherwise have continued strangers to each other, would thus be brought into harmonious cooperation.[40]

Such cooperation, it was further noted, would be effective in 'removing prejudice' and 'softening the asperity of party feeling'. The Manchester Institution, then, was conceived as an organisation which would break down not only social distance, but also sectarian and political tensions among the middle class of the town.

Equally important was the way these institutions built recognisable social boundaries. Religious bodies, even if the majority of the working class were not active participants, were socially diverse. Wealthy merchants and manufacturers, bankers and physicians, gathered for religious worship alongside shopkeepers, warehousemen, small masters, even a scattering of artisans. Within most congregations it was usually the case that an elite of male grandees was predominant. Their pew rents provided the bulk of the funds for the congregation's survival and they generally had considerable power institutionally as trustees, church officers, etc. Within the social life of the church social demarcations were fairly precise. Nevertheless the rhetoric of Christianity and the reality of internal power relations

---

[40] Cited in J. Seed, 'Commerce and the liberal arts: the political economy of art in Manchester, 1775–1860', in J. Wolff and J. Seed, op. cit., p. 67.

meant that churches could rarely be socially exclusive. There were no such limitations on many of the new secular associations which were organised from the later years of the eighteenth century. The key mechanism for limiting social access was the market. Exclusion was based on the price of entry. How many shopkeepers, clerks, much less handlooom weavers or mule spinners in Manchester could find in 1823 twenty-five guineas to become a Life Governor of the Manchester Institution, or even an annual fee of two guineas, to procure the privileges of membership? Other organisations asserted their exclusiveness by applying social criteria. The Billiard Club, established in 1795, was restricted to eighty-five members, who paid an entrance fee of five guineas and an annual subscription of two guineas. The club had both Tory and reforming members but access was through a secret ballot and the key criterion was social standing. John Harland recalled:

> To be a member of this club was, it would seem, the only way to rank and station; and to such a length had this notion been carried, that we well remember it being understood that if a man was not a member of the Billiard Room he was not only not in society, but unfit for society . . . Men of fortune and education, and professional men of any pretensions, never had any difficulty in becoming members.[41]

The Assembly Rooms drew a sharp line between wholesalers and retailers and the latter were excluded from access to their regular balls. A local magazine reported in 1822: 'The son of a respectable silversmith and jeweller having polluted this house of Lords by his presence, was ejected from it unceremoniously, because his father retailed his wares'.[42] One of the reasons for the decline of the Assemblies in the 1830s and 1840s was, according to Harland, anxieties about social mixing: 'the necessarily mixed character of Manchester society . . . led to partnerships in the ball-room not always deemed desirable, especially by prudent mammas'.[43] These kinds of exclusiveness were important in early-nineteenth-century towns in demarcating social boundaries, consolidating the inner circles of middle-class sociability, filtering out individuals and families that failed to match the criteria of middle-class status.

The ensemble of cultural institutions constructed by the middle class in major urban centres between the 1780s and 1840s was

---

[41] J. Harland, 'Collecteana relating to Manchester and its neighbourhood, at various periods', *Chetham Society* 72 (1867): vol. II, 50.

[42] *The Scrap Book: A Manchester Weekly Publication* (1822): 75.

[43] J. Harland, op. cit., pp. 44–5.

extremely complex. It embraced trade associations and Chambers of Commerce, educational agencies of all kinds, hospitals and medical charities, cultural and scientific associations, new administrative bodies such as Commissions for Street Improvement, private dining or sports clubs, and not forgetting the freemasons. Some were socially exclusive, confined to a distinct and recognisable elite of property-owners. Others were more open – even in some cases set up precisely to integrate subordinate social groups within the town's cultural life. But all served to establish the intellectual and moral leadership of the middle class and all played an important role in group formation. At the same time there was systematic undermining of incipient working-class organisation – the use of law, of direct intimidation and repression, of all kinds of informal social and economic pressures to disable strategies of working-class formation. It would be wrong of course to see this as some kind of social conspiracy, identifying these organisations, radiating out into civil society, as part of a master plan. There was no central control panel, no central institution where the middle class was embodied and its inner structure revealed; just as there was no inner discourse where the consciousness of the middle class was revealed as an unmediated and transcendent class subject – not even political economy. Rather there was a multiplicity of initiatives and responses to specific problems which, in town after town, created a dense network of institutions and social connections – public and private – through which the middle class took shape. In other words, the social relations of production grounded in economic life were not the only objective determinants of class formation. All kinds of other relations, especially as crystallised in a range of public and private institutions, created out of the 'middling sort' the middle class of nineteenth-century England.

Much of central importance has been omitted here – in particular the question of politics and the British state. Attention has been confined to identifying the middle class as a social formation. I have argued against conceptions of that class as merely a static or abstract aggregate of individual occupations or wealth-holders. What is then central is the specific composition of social relations. This is a matter of focusing on the external relations between capital and labour, between those who buy and those who sell labour power. Equally important are internal social relations among the propertied, realised in the form of organisations such as the family, the Church and a range of private, semi-public and public institutions. In both instances the specificity of context is crucial; which middle class, in what particular local or regional economy, shaped by what kinds of relations to other social classes, at what specific historical moment? Class, then, is not a matter only of this or that aspect of a group – size of income, type of occupation, life-style or whatever – but a shifting totality of social relations. If the middle class resists a simple abstract definition this is not because it is a vacuous term but because class was, and is, in its very essence historical. Schumpeter once remarked that 'class resembles a hotel or an omnibus, always full, but always of different people';[44] perhaps we need to add, sometimes including, generation after generation, many of the same people. How were those continuities orchestrated? How were those changes in personnel managed so as to reproduce the social ascendancy of a propertied minority and the rule of capital?

Acknowledgements

Michael Bush, Simon Gunn and Keith Nield made useful comments on an earlier draft of this chapter.

[44] J.A. Schumpeter, *Imperialism and Social Classes* (New York, 1951), p. 165.

CHAPTER EIGHT

Tenant right and the peasantries of Europe under the old regime

M.L. Bush

University of Manchester

Although sometimes presented as one, the peasantry was not an order *per se* because no peasant rights were enjoyed simply by virtue of being a peasant.[1] This even applied to countries with a peasant estate in parliament, since these estates represented only the freeholders and Crown tenants, the rest of the peasantry enjoying no more than an indirect representation through their landlords: that is in the noble and clerical estates. Unlike the clergy and nobility, the peasantry had no legal definition; the treatises produced to delineate the society of orders simply lumped the peasantry with the other groups that were without either noble or clerical status, terming this heterogeneous mass the commonalty or the third estate. But its failure to qualify as an order does not designate it a class. Central to the peasant community under the old regime were the tenant rights of the manorial system, the social effects of which renders the presentation of the peasantry as a class as inadequate as its presentation as an order. Promoted by these rights, conflicts of interest existed within the peasant community while the relationship between peasant and lord was not necessarily one of class.

Some peasants under the old regime held allods. As landowners they were completely free of lordship. Although marginalised in the course of the Middle Ages, they remained plentiful in the parts of early modern Europe where the manorial system was weakly developed: in Scandinavia, Friesland, the Midi, Castile, the alpine states of

---

[1] For a presentation of the peasantry as an order, see J. Blum, *The End of the Old Order in Rural Europe* (Princeton, 1978), pp. 4–5. The one exception was the Russian peasantry which by the nineteenth century was regarded as the fourth estate (see S. Becker, *Nobility and Privilege in Late Imperial Russia* (Dekalb, IU., 1985), pp. 14–18.

Vorarlberg and Tyrol, and in the Swiss cantons. None the less, by 1500 the typical European peasant was a tenant of Crown, Church or private landlord. But, in many cases, he was a peculiar kind of tenant with a hybrid holding which, while technically a tenancy, possessed some of the proprietary rights of the allod.

No matter whether peasants rented from the Crown, the Church or the private landlord, their land was normally subjected to some variant of the manorial system. This system was a conjunction of lord and tenant rights.[2] The manor itself was usually a combination of tenure and demesne. The lord's property rights awarded him full ownership of the demesne but only final ownership of the tenures. The vital distinction between demesne and tenure created two types of tenant, since lords rented out their demesnes as well as directly working them. A demesne tenancy was quite different from a tenure. The demesne tenant, in fact, was a leaseholder in the modern sense. The relationship between him and his landlord was determined by a contract which specified the rent due and the length of the lease. Typically the lease was short-term(1-3-6-9 years) and rack-rented, that is subject to revision when the lease expired. If not a rack-rent, it was a share-cropping arrangement which guaranteed the lord a proportion of the crop.

In sharp contrast, the tenure-holder was far from being a mere tenant. This was because attached to the tenure were four proprietary rights. The first of these rights enabled the holder to transmit the tenure to his offspring or to dispose of it, entirely by sale or superficially through subletting. The second allowed him to pay his lord a fixed rent. This rent was not temporarily set by agreement in the manner of a lease but fixed for ever more, in accordance with custom rather than any notion of an economic rent. The third proprietary right allowed the tenure-holder the use of the uncultivated parts of the manor: the waste, the pasture traditionally reserved for plough animals, the grainfields and hayfields immediately after the harvest, the land left fallow, the grass verges of the paths leading from the village to the open fields and of the village inroads leading to the highway. Such common rights appertained both to the grazing of animals and to estovers, that is the collection of firewood, bracken, herbs, berries, nuts, mushrooms and nettles. Demesne tenants and mere cottagers could also claim rights of common, but not so indisputably or so extensively as the tenure-holders. The fourth right qualified members of the village to participate in its management.

[2] M.L. Bush, *Noble Privilege* (Manchester, 1983), ch. VI.

137

The holding of a tenure usually entitled a peasant to attend a manorial court or village assembly. In fact, the membership of these two institutions was frequently confined to the lord, his officials and the tenure-holders. The latter, as jurors and as the elected officials of these assemblies, tried cases, revised regulations and issued instructions for the maintenance of ditches and ponds, hedgerows and fences, ways and buildings, and were empowered to preserve the common from overuse. These rights, along with those of the manorial lord, were officially recorded in the manor court records where conveyances and the fines imposed for infringement of manorial rules were registered. Alternatively they were set down in custumals (*Weistümer* or *urbaria*), which were statements of accepted custom and utterly binding even when, as in the case of serfs, the law awarded the lord of the manor ownership of the inhabitants of his estate along with their possessions and children. For the tenant with substantial property rights was a feature of the unfree as well as of the free peasantries. The case made by John Hatcher for the existence of extensive villein rights in thirteenth-century England can also be made for the enserfed (*untertan*) peasants of eighteenth-century central and eastern Europe.[3]

Tenant rights were no safeguard against peasant hardship. This was partly because the peasantry was normally subjected to the triple yoke of state, Church and landlord. Tapping the surplus of peasant production was not simply rents and dues but also government taxes and church tithes. For this reason the strength of tenant right was no guarantee against exploitation. It simply ensured that the source of exploitation was government taxes rather than manorial exactions, as, for example, in late sixteenth-century Castile and in parts of seventeenth-century France.[4] Moreover, peasant hardship did not simply result from exploitation. It often stemmed from a shortage of resources which owed less to high rents and taxes than to rapid population growth, as in the sixteenth and late eighteenth centuries, or to frequent crop failures. In eighteenth-century France, for example, one year in every six witnessed a general famine.[5] For these

---

[3] J. Hatcher, 'English serfdom and villeinage: towards a reassessment', *Past and Present* 90 (1981): 3–39. For modern serfdom, see below.

[4] For Castile: see D.E. Vassberg, *Land and Society in Golden Age Castile* (Cambridge, 1984), pp. 219–22 and 225. For France: see P. Goubert, *The French Peasantry in the Seventeenth Century* (Cambridge, 1986), pp. 203–4.

[5] Blum, *End of the Old Order*, p. 147. For the dire effects of famine in nineteenth-century Russia, see. S.L. Hoch, *Serfdom and Social Control in Russia* (Chicago, 1986), pp. 51–6.

reasons, peasants could suffer extreme impoverishment in spite of their rights. Peasants, well endowed with proprietary and common rights, could be easily pauperised: on a short-term basis by famine, and, in the long term, as population growth outstripped the supply of land and produce and as governments developed punitive tax systems which, while highly sophisticated in featuring regular direct taxes and taxes on sales, remained very primitive in granting fiscal immunity to the wealthy. In this manner the tax burden was placed on the peasant's back, as were the military demands for the conscription and billeting of troops.

In spite of their property rights, then, peasants tended to be far from prosperous. However, the existence of tenant rights meant that the manorial system could benefit peasant as well as lord: so much so that, under the old regime, lords struggled to throw off what was a serious encumbrance to their estate management. Tenant rights were an especial problem to lords in periods of high inflation as fixed rents caused the devaluation of landed incomes, and as security of tenure and common rights impeded an obvious solution to the problem which was to extend the cultivated demesne and thus subject a greater share of the estate either to direct operation or to economic rents and sharecropping. In the course of the early modern period lords struggled to overcome the hindrance of tenant right, essentially by developing the demesne. The outcome was the promotion of a form of serfdom in central and eastern Europe which legally awarded the lord extensive opportunities to exploit his peasants through the manorial system. In the rest of Europe, the outcome was the promotion of leasehold at the expense of tenures and waste. Neither the introduction of serfdom nor the extension of leasehold were necessarily attempts to abolish the peasantry itself. Although serfdom and leasehold were forms of commercialism, both were capable of operating through a peasant mode of production. With one or two exceptions – notably southern England and northern France – reforms in estate management in early modern Europe represented an onslaught not upon peasant farming but merely upon the rights conferred by the manorial system. How successful was this onslaught upon tenant right?

That the serfs of the second serfdom had rights has been long recognised. In view of them Knapp and Gruenberg in the nineteenth century objected to terming this form of serfdom *Leibeigenschaft* since the serfs of the Habsburg and Hohenzollern empires, although technically unfree, were not slaves. They proposed the term *Untertänigkeit* as more appropriate. However, the rights they identified as distinguishing serfs from slaves were legal ones, not those ensconced in custom, and so the impression given was that, as tenants, serfs had little protection against their lords.[6] The second serfdom, like the first, reduced the peasantry's access to public justice, denied them the freedoms to move, to change occupation and to marry without the permission of their lord, and placed them under the obligation of weekly labour services, but, none the less, left them with the basic rights of common, rents fixed by custom, and therefore prone to reduction in periods of inflation, and hereditary possession of their farms. Their village communes could also survive as assemblies of tenure-holders equipped with the authority to appoint local officials and the power to negotiate with the lord over the terms of tenancy and service. The close association of direct demesne farming (*Gutsherrschaft*) with the second serfdom introduced a weight of labour services, chiefly in the form of week work on the lord's fields; but this was established not simply by decree but by a process of bargaining. The outcome was that, in ceding labour services and in accepting the imposition of a greater range of dues, the tenure-holders were allowed to retain important rights.[7] As a result of concessions made and bargains reached the traditional distinction between demesne and tenure tenancies was preserved.

To illustrate the development: in Bohemia a system of real rather than personal serfdom – *Gutsuntertänigkeit* rather than *Erbuntertänigkeit* – developed between 1487 and 1627 when legislation sanctioned a state of unfreedom in which the peasant was bound to the soil and was liable to labour services 'whenever the lord so orders' simply by virtue of being a tenant. As a result, the emphyteutical tenures, made predominant in the thirteenth century by a process of German settlement, were terminated but not through absorption into the demesne and conversion into leaseholds. Two basic types of peasant therefore existed in the early modern period: the *Rustikalisten* (tenure) and the *Dominikalisten* (demesne) tenantry. The former held their farms by hereditary right and in accordance with custom. They even

---

[6] See E.M. Link, *The Emancipation of the Austrian Peasant, 1740–1748* (New York, 1949), p. 22. In the 1950s J. Blum made the point that whereas in the law the lord 'could demand what obligations he wanted' of his serfs, 'in actuality it was a general rule for these obligations to be fixed and even minutely defined by custom' ('The rise of serfdom in Eastern Europe', *American Historical Review* 62 (1957): 808).

[7] For Bohemia and Prussia, see below. For Hungary: B.K. Kiraly, 'Neo-serfdom in Hungary', *Slavic Review* 34 (1975): 272–3 and n. 16. For Austria: H. Rebel, *Peasant Classes* (Princeton, 1983), pp. 157–60. For Poland: A. Kaminsky, 'Neo-serfdom in Poland-Lithuania', *Slavic Review* 34 (1975): 267. For Russia: A. Kahan, *The Plow, the Hammer and the Knout* (Chicago, 1985), pp. 66 and 68.

had the right of disposal, on condition that they secured a *Losbrief* (letter of discharge) from the lord and found a new tenant whom the lord could accept. Furthermore, they could fortify their proprietary rights by paying the *Kaufschilling*, thus becoming an *eingekaufter Bauer* and acquiring the security of an emphyteut. Whether or not *eingekaufter*, the rustical tenants could be evicted only if found guilty of neglecting the farm and for failing to pay at least two-thirds of the rent. Paying the rent was relatively easy because of its lowness. Accounting for this were the labour services required of the same tenants and the fact that, because of their direct farming activities, the lords were not heavily dependent upon rents: for example, by the start of the eighteenth century 69 per cent of their landed income was drawn from the demesne and realised by the sale of grain, livestock and beer. Much less favoured were the demesne tenants, holding short-term rackrented leases and inclined to become cottagers simply because of the amount of demesne required for direct cultivation.[8]

In Bohemia the lord's dependence on labour services preserved the tenure. The substantial holding capable of maintaining a ploughteam was as important to the lord's commercial activities as the directly operated demesne.[9] This was just as true of Brandenburg-Prussia where a system of *Untertänigkeit* developed from the late fifteenth century and was confirmed by the Recess of 1653. The system was not uniform. Serfdom in East Prussia tended, as in Poland, Hungary and Russia, to be based on hereditary personal subjection (*Erbuntertänigkeit*), whereas in much of Brandenburg it represented, in the Bohemian or Austrian mode, a subjection to the estate (*Gutsuntertänigkeit*). As in Bohemia, serfdom terminated, without totally transforming, a system of emphyteusis that again had been established by German settlement in the thirteenth century. Right of migration was lost; weekly labour services were established; proprietary rights, in the eyes of the law, were totally vested in the lord. But, yet again, a distinction was preserved between demesne leaseholders (*Zeitpachtbauern*) and tenure-holders (*Lassbauern* or *Erbpächter* or *Erbzinsleute*), the former on terminal leases with revisable rents and holdings which were extremely limited in size by the amount of demesne required for

---

[8] W.E. Wright, *Serf, Seigneur and Sovereign: Agrarian Reforms in Eighteenth-century Bohemia* (Minneapolis, 1966), pp. 14–18; R.J. Kerner, *Bohemia in the Eighteenth Century* (New York, 1932), p. 274; K. Mejdricka, 'L'état du régime féodale à la veille de son abolition et les conditions de sa suppression en Bohême', *L'Abolition de la féodalité* (Paris, 1971), vol. I, p. 398; A. Klima, 'Agrarian class structure and economic development in pre-industrial Bohemia', *Past and Present* 85 (1979): 59.

[9] Klima, op. cit., p. 56.

direct farming: the latter on substantial tenures which were, in keeping with custom, hereditary and who had received, in return for increased labour services, a freezing or lowering of rents as well as a confirmation of their tenurial security and grazing rights. As with the Bohemian lords, this arrangement was acceptable to the Junkers because of the extent of their demesne receipts and because their farming depended upon serf labour services which included the obligatory provision of ploughteams.[10]

A measure of the efficacy of tenant rights in protecting the peasant interest lies in the survival of the well-off serf. Thus, in eighteenth-century Bohemia: whereas 36 per cent of peasant holdings were held by cottagers with fewer than four acres, 24 per cent were held by peasants with at least twenty acres. These substantial peasants, with hereditary possession of their farms, low rents and the resources to hire labour to fulfil their demesne labour services, and who were invaluable to the lord because of his dependence upon their plough-teams, were strongly placed to retain much of the surplus product of their own farms either for the benefit of their families or for the government.[11] Thus, on the face of it the serf, as the subject and chattel of his lord and on account of his obligation to provide unpaid weekly labour services, would appear to be more open to exploitation than a wage-labourer. But this was not necessarily the case. The substantial serf, operating a largish holding which had commercial possibilities and therefore able to acquit his labour services either with hired labour or through commutation (which like other payments to the lord tended to get frozen by custom) was not a Bohemian peculiarity. In fact, he was a prominent feature of most of the servile peasantries of central and eastern Europe.[12] Reflecting the presence of the well-to-do serf was the standard size of a full holding: over forty acres in Poland; nineteen acres in Brandenburg; sixty-one acres in Bohemia; thirty-four acres in Hungary; at least forty-five acres in East Prussia.[13]

[10] For serfdom in the Prussian monarchy: Shearer Davis Bowman, 'Planters and Junkers', PhD California (1986), p. 133; H. Harnisch, 'Peasants and markets', in R.J. Evans and W. R. Lee (eds.) *The German Peasantry* (London, 1986), pp. 42 and 45; W.W. Hagen, 'How mighty the Junkers? Peasant rents and seigneurial profits in sixteenth-century Brandenburg', *Past and Present* 108 (1985): 83–5, 94, 104–5 and 113–16. For the various forms of serfdom: Blum, *End of the Old Order*, pp. 35–41.

[11] Klima, op. cit., pp. 54 and 56.

[12] W. Kula, *An Economic Theory of the Feudal system: towards a Model of the Polish Economy, 1500–1800* (London, 1976), pp. 64–5; Kaminsky, op. cit., 263–4; Harnisch, op. cit., p. 46; Rebel, op. cit., p. 58.

[13] See Blum, *End of the Old Order*, p. 96; Harnisch, op. cit., p. 46.

Restraining the impact of serfdom was its failure to captivate the whole of the peasantry. Throughout the lands of the second serfdom peasants survived who, as freeholders or as free tenants, were cushioned against its effect. Thus, under the Hohenzollerns there were the *Köllmer* of East Prussia – essentially state tenants. In 1798 they held 21 per cent of all peasant holdings in the province. In addition, there were the *Erbleute* of western Brandenburg who were tenants of private landlords but, unlike serfs, possessed legally recognised proprietary rights. In eighteenth-century Poland 20–30 per cent of peasant holdings were held by freemen, some of them poor nobles but many, runaways whom lords had enticed to settle upon their estates in return for a small, fixed quitrent. In late eighteenth-century Hungary 13.5 per cent of the population were free peasants, many of them living completely free of lordship in autonomous villages. In 1750 0.5 per cent of farm land in Bohemia was peasant freehold. In eighteenth-century Russia, the peasants who had escaped enserfment were collectively termed state peasants. In 1800 they formed 39 per cent of the male peasantry, and 52 per cent on the eve of emancipation. Their obligations were to the state alone. Consisting of the soul tax and a quitrent, overall they were considerably lighter than those of the serfs.[14]

Serfdom in modern Europe was never a static or uniform system. Moreover, a long time could elapse before it established an oppressive grip. This is evident in a comparison of sixteenth- with seventeenth-century Bohemia or of seventeenth- with eighteenth-century Russia.[15] What is more, in practice it could undergo a process of alleviation long before its final abolition either as a result of government intervention or because lords softened their demands in order to curtail peasant flight, especially in periods of high mortality, or to safeguard against peasant revolt. Thus, forms of serfdom persisted in western Europe throughout the early modern period, but contained by custom and memories of peasant militancy, they meant for peasants certainly liability to a greater range of exactions than were

[14] General: Blum, op. cit., pp. 29–33. Hohenzollern lands: Harnisch, op. cit., p. 41; Hagen, op. cit., p. 106; Blum, op. cit., p. 29. Hungary: K. Benda, 'Le régime féodal en Hongrie à la fin du XVIIIe siècle', *L'Abolition de la féodalité*, vol. I, p. 414, and A.C. Janos, *The Politics of Backwardness in Hungary* (Princeton, 1982), pp. 21–2. Bohemia: Klima, op. cit., p. 53. Russia: J. Blum, *Lord and Peasant in Russia* (Princeton, 1961), pp. 475–6 and 485. Poland: Blum, *End of the Old Order*, p. 32.

[15] Bohemia: Mejdricka, op. cit., pp. 393–7 and W.E. Wright, 'Neo-serfdom in Bohemia', *Slavic Review* 34 (1975): 242–7. Russia: E. Melton, 'Serfdom and the peasant economy in Russia, 1780–1861', PhD Columbia University (1984), pp. 62 and 64; Blum, *Lord and Peasant*, pp. 423 and 428–9.

owed by free peasants but also advantageous property rights created by customarily frozen dues and hereditary tenancies coupled with a freedom from weekly labour services that derived from the lord's policy of leasing rather than directly farming the demesne. Although enserfed by their tenancies, the tenure-holders enjoyed property rights which were totally denied the legally free demesne lessees.[16]

Whereas in early modern eastern Europe the solution to the problem of tenant right was demesne farming, in the early modern west it was demesne leasing. By the start of the modern period this practice was well-founded; then, under the stimulus of the sixteenth-century price revolution, it underwent a considerable extension.[17] It depended upon two devices, the money lease and the share-cropping contract, and opened up two possibilities: one of making the demesne economically viable and a sufficient compensation for the custom-bound tenures; the other, of destroying traditional tenant rights by incorporating tenures into the demesne, thus converting them into tenancies which, in being short in term and based upon a rent in kind or upon a revisable money payment, freed the landlord of the restrictions associated with the tenure. Essentially, the lease was a capitalist arrangement, introducing to the countryside a form of rentier capitalism in the case of money rents and a form of merchant capitalism in the case of share-cropping. Both could be highly exploitative. The degree of exploitation, however, depended upon whether the tenant was a commercial farmer or a mere peasant. A conjunction of capitalist rent with capitalist farming, for example, created no real problem for either party. An equitable sharing of the surplus occurred between landlord and tenant. The only victims were the tenant's employees, the wage labourers. A recipe for extreme exploitation, however, was the conjunction of landlord capitalism and subsistence farming. Given the peasant's limited cash resources this was often associated with the share-cropping contract: the *métayage, mezzadria* or *aparceria*.

The extension of leasehold upon an estate represented the enlargement of the cultivated demesne at the expense of tenures or waste. The tenures underwent conversion to leasehold following their inclusion into the demesne through forfeiture, normally the result of the tenant's failure to fulfil his obligations to the lord, or reversion in the

---

[16] T.C.W. Blanning, *The French Revolution in Germany* (Oxford, 1983), pp. 22–3.

[17] For its medieval development: G. Duby, *Rural Economy and Country Life in the Medieval West* (London, 1968), p. 257, and P.J. Jones, 'From manor to mezzadria: a Tuscan case-study in the medieval origins of modern agrarian society', in N. Rubinstein (ed.) *Florentine Studies* (London, 1968), ch. 5.

event of the extinction of the tenant's family, or a buying out of the tenant. In curtailing the amount of land protected by proprietary tenant rights, and also the amount of land to which rights of common applied, the extension of leasehold could be an even more serious threat to the traditional rights of the peasantry than the introduction of serfdom.

By 1600 leasehold was predominant in Lombardy, Tuscany, the Veneto and Romagna: the result of the demesne swallowing up the tenures and converting them into short term, money-rent leases or *mezzadrias*. The process was well under way in the Middle Ages: so much so that P.J. Jones can claim that in Tuscany the spread of leasehold had mostly erased the classical manor by 1300. The tendency in northern Italy was to let the plain in large farms on cash rents and the hill zone in small farms on share-cropping terms. Peasants with proprietorial land rights survived only in the mountains. But frequently the two leasehold systems interlocked, with the large tenant directly farming the better land and subletting the poorer land on sharecropping contracts. Eventually a similar leasehold system gained a grip on the deep south. By the late eighteenth century most Sicilian estates were run on *gabella* contracts, the *gabelloto*, a tenant of the landowner, sometimes farming but often subletting to peasant sharecroppers.[18]

The victim of this development was the emphyteutical tenure and its attached rights. Likewise in Castile: by the mid-sixteenth century the *censo enfiteutico* – a perpetual tenancy subjected to a non-economic rent – had fallen out of favour with the landlords, largely because it proved a financial embarrassment in a period of rapid inflation. The policy thereafter was to replace it with either the short-term rack rent lease or the sharecropping *aparceria* which had awarded the lord one-fifth of the crop in the late Middle Ages and one-third to one-half in the early modern period.[19] In both England and France the tenure (copyhold; *censive*) came under attack from leasehold in the course of the sixteenth and seventeenth centuries as estate management favoured tenancies which could be adjusted in accordance with the state of the economy. On the eve of the Revolution at least half of the

---

[18] Northern Italy: A. De Maddalena, 'Rural Europe, 1500–1750', in C.M. Cipolla (ed.) *The Fontana Economic History of Europe* (London, 1974), vol. II, p. 298; Jones, op. cit., pp. 212–27; K. R. Greenfield, *Economics and Liberalism in the Risorgimento: a Study of Nationalism in Lombardy, 1814–1848* (Baltimore, 1965), pp. 10–15 and 19–23; F. Braudel, *Civilisation and Capitalism* (London, 1982), vol. II, pp. 289–91. Southern Italy: D. Mack Smith, *A History of Sicily* (London, 1968), pp. 278–80.

[19] Vassberg, op. cit., pp. 93–5 and 212–13.

cultivated land in France was leasehold. In the north it featured economic rents extracted from commercial farms; in the south, it featured *métayage*. In England the leasehold was the typical tenancy by 1800, short in term and rack-rented and often let to commercial farmers. Completely absent, however, was the share-cropping contract.[20]

In creating a competitive market for tenancies, leasehold could lead to the engrossment of farms and the replacement of peasant farming by large-scale commercial farming. But this was not so when the prevalent lease was the share-cropping contract. In this situation leasing upheld the peasantry but deprived it of the emphyteutical rights that had attached to the tenures, thus exposing it to landlord exploitation. The extension of leasehold was as significant an agrarian development as demesne farming in early modern Europe. It just happened to affect different parts. Like *Gutsherrschaft* it worked against traditional tenant rights but, in many cases, failed to eliminate them or render them meaningless. Attached to some leases was the sitting tenant's customary option to renew the lease.[21] On some money leases the rent was beneficial, in the manner of the tenure, and it was left to the landlord to compensate by means of casualties.[22] With share-cropping contracts it was often accepted that the produce exacted by the landlord should remain a fixed proportion of the yield rather than a fixed amount. Moreover, if proprietary rights were eroded through the substitution of leaseholds for tenures, rights of common often remained, if gradually attenuated by the extension of cultivation at the expense of the waste and the practice of enclosure. Furthermore, demesne leasing reduced the amount of tenure land but this happened very slowly since tenures could not be arbitrarily annexed and, lightly burdened with dues, their holders had little difficulty in acquitting their manorial obligations and little incentive to sell out. At the Revolution almost as much land was held in France by *censitaires* as by leasehold-ers; and in England the tenure's durability is attested by the manuals

---

[20] France: M. Bloch, *French Rural Society* (London, 1966), pp. 145–6; G. Bois, *The Crisis of Feudalism* (Cambridge, 1984), pp. 242–3 and 258; L. Merle, *La Métairie et l' évolution agraire de la Gâtine poitevine de la fin du moyen âge à la Révolution* (Paris, 1958), pp. 50ff; R. Mousnier, *The Institutions of France under Absolute Monarchy* (Chicago, 1979), vol. I, pp. 502–3; Goubert, op. cit., pp. 30–4; and also see n. 23 (France). England: M.L. Bush, *The English Aristocracy* (Manchester, 1984), pp. 180–1, and C. Clay, 'Landlords and estate management in England', in J. Thirsk (ed.) *The Agrarian History of England and Wales* (Cambridge, 1985), V (ii), ch. 14 (CI).

[21] Bloch, op. cit., pp. 179–80; Blum, *End of the Old Order*, p. 101.

[22] E.g. L. Stone, *Crisis of the Aristocracy* (Oxford, 1965), pp. 309–22.

on copyhold published in the nineteenth century and by the four copyhold enfranchisement statutes enacted between 1841 and 1922.[23]

The outcome of the landlord's onslaught upon the tenures was the creation of a variety of peasant tenancies: some well-endowed with tenant rights, others, meanly furnished. For the peasant the most favourable tenancy was the tenure held of the Crown: hence the Spanish proverb 'On seigneurial lands, almond and cherry; on royal lands, walnuts and mulberry'. The second most favourable tenancy, from the peasant's point of view, was the manorial tenure, held either of a private landowner or of the church. The most unfavourable tenancy, simply because it was poorly equipped with tenant right and most exposed to capitalism, was the demesne leasehold. These generalisations on good and bad tenancies apply equally well to serf as to free peasantries.[24]

For the peasantry the specific value of their surviving proprietary rights depended upon circumstance. Thus, the real value of the fixed rent was determined by the lord's capacity to compensate for it by making other exactions of the tenantry. Within the manorial system were two types of payment: on the one hand, regular dues – chiefly the rent, commutation charges and gifts owed at certain times of the year – and, on the other, the casualties.[25] The latter exactions were payable only in certain situations: for example, when a serf wished to marry or leave the estate, a licence fee fell due; or when a tenure was transferred from father to son, or from one family to another through sale or exchange, a similar payment was necessary, in return for which the lord's authorisation could be assumed. Whereas the regular dues tended to become fixed by a notion of custom, the casualties could be arbitrary. Because of the latter, it was possible for a lord to exploit his tenants in spite of their right to an unchanging rent and hereditary possession. Furthermore, the lord's ability to

---

[23] France: G. Lefebvre proposed between 20 and 70 per cent, dependent upon region, producing a mean of 46 per cent ('Repartition de la propriété et de l'exploitation foncière à la fin de l'ancien régime' in *Etudes sur la Révolution Française* (Paris, 1954), pp. 205 and appendix I). T. Skocpol proposed a proportion of one-third (*States and Social Revolutions* (Cambridge, 1979), pp. 118 and 156; as does P.M. Jones in his *The Peasantry in the French Revolution* (Cambridge, 1988), p. 7. That ownership means largely tenure-holding rather than allod-holding, see Lefebvre, op. cit., p. 204. England: e.g. J. Scriven, *A Treatise on Copyholds, Freeholds and Tenures of Ancient Demesne* (London, 1st edn. 1823; 7th edn. 1896); C. Watkins, *A Treatise on Copyholds* (London, 1st edn. 1797–9; 4th edn. 1825) and L. Shelford, *The Law of Copyholds* (London, 1853). Also see C.S. Orwin and E.H. Whetham, *A History of British Agriculture, 1846–1914* (London, 1964), pp. 186–7.

[24] Vassberg, op. cit., p. 98; Blum, *End of the Old Order*, pp. 98–104.

[25] Bush, *Noble Privilege*, ch. VI (1).

raise casualties could work against the tenant's security of tenure. On the face of it, the hereditary rights seemed to solve one basic peasant problem that naturally arose in a society where ownership of the land did not normally reside with the peasantry. How was a peasant family to remain connected with the land? Put another way, how was a peasant family to retain its peasant status? The peasant answer was as follows: by having an automatic right to inherit land, which in the final analysis, belonged to someone else. This solution, however, became less foolproof when the lord was free to raise the casualties as high as he liked since it gave him not only compensation for the fixed rent but also the opportunity to contrive a confiscation of the tenures. In this respect, then, the value of the tenant's proprietary rights very much depended upon the lord's policy towards casualties. When the casualties were restricted, either by the force of custom or by a concept of what was reasonable and by the willingness of peasants to defend their rights with militancy or litigation, a peasant's proprietary tenant rights became a considerable asset especially in periods of high inflation, such as in the sixteenth and late eighteenth centuries. They also acquired a special value in societies subjected to capitalist rent or capitalist farming, or in societies where rapid population growth gave the landlords a greater chance of raising their landed revenues. Essentially they confined capitalistic practices to what was defined as the demesne. The rest of the estate remained a peasant world in which low rents were not an expression of goodlordship but of tenant right, and the tenures were the family heirlooms of the peasantry.

Peasants realised the benefits of proprietary tenant right partly by subletting and sale. When the dues exacted fell well below the economic value of a tenure, the occupying peasant was strongly placed to make a profit through subletting on an economic rent or through selling his proprietorial rights to the lord or another peasant. To realise these advantages, however, a peasant family needed to have more land than was necessary for its own subsistence or had to be willing to undergo conversion from a tenurial to a demesne tenant. Furthermore, especially in periods of rapid population growth, the well-off serf drew considerable gain from his proprietary rights since his labour services ensured that the rent was uneconomic and the rights of common generous, while the opportunity to hire cheap labour freed him from the burden of performing the labour services. However, the principal assets of proprietary tenant rights were freedom from having to compete in a land market and the ability to retain a larger share of the surplus than an economic rent would have allowed. Socially, tenant rights could render their beneficiaries independent of their lord's paternalism.

As for the remaining tenant rights, the commoning rights came under attack frequently in the early modern period: where fallowing was abandoned, where the area of cultivation was extended at the expense of forest and waste, and where stubble-grazing rights were denied by enclosure. The significant periods for the shrinkage of common rights were not only the times of rapid population growth, as in the sixteenth and late eighteenth centuries. It also occurred in the interim in connection with the development of alternate and convertible husbandry. In addition, common rights were devalued through overuse and exhaustion. This was partly caused by growth in the rural population and an increased dependence upon the common as farms were subdivided and as the development of rural industries enlarged the cottager element in the countryside. But it was also due to the overstocking of the common by lords and those to whom they leased their rights, as they exploited their rights of common grazing for a commercial purpose.[26]

None the less, throughout the early modern period rights of common survived, allowing peasant communities vital access to free wood, food and fodder. This was because wastes remained considerable and peasant farming remained stuck in the rut of two or three field systems which ensured that each year either one-third or one-half of the cultivated land was left fallow. Peasant subsistence often rested not simply upon the cultivation of the smallholding but upon what J.N. Schwerz termed 'the nomadic economy', a reference not to transhumance but to the peasant dependence on making use of things held in common.[27] This was especially true of small peasants; but common rights were appreciated by the whole community for allowing rent-free grazing and the collection of firewood and timber. Unlike the tenurial rights, which were confined to certain privileged families, common rights, in some form or other, were available to most of the rural community, including cottagers and leaseholders.[28]

---

[26] Blum, *End of the Old Order*, p. 125; P. Kriedte, *Peasants, Landlords and Merchant Capitalists* (Leamington Spa, 1983), pp. 106–11; D.W. Sabean, *Power in the Blood* (Cambridge, 1984), p. 203; J. Mooser, 'Property and wood theft: agrarian capitalism and social conflict in rural society . . .', in R.G. Moeller (ed.) *Peasants and Lords in Modern Germany* (Boston, 1986), ch. 2; W.W. Hagen, 'The Junkers' faithless servants . . .' in R.J. Evans and W. R. Lee (eds.) *The German Peasantry* (London, 1986), ch. 3; Bloch, *French Rural Society*, pp. 183–8.

[27] In his *Beschreibung der Landwirtschaft in Westfalen und Rheinpreussen* (Stuttgart, 1836), as quoted by Mooser, op. cit., p. 64 (n. 29).

[28] E.g. Sabean, op. cit., p. 203.

In enabling peasants to retain their surplus production and to control both capital and labour, tenant rights were a safeguard against class exploitation. But this protection clearly did not extend to all peasants. Without it were the leaseholders; and with relatively little protection were serfs subjected to the obligation of week work. For the leaseholders the source of exploitation was not simply the estate owner but also the peasants whose tenant rights had persuaded them to sublet in order to reap the advantage that lay in the difference between tenurial and economic rents. And one important consequence of tenant right was to create a class system within the peasant community.

Working against a high level of social differentiation within the peasantry were systems of community landholding, such as were found in the black earth regions of Great Russia where the land available to the serf community for cultivation was distributed to the member families according to need, with each husband and wife team (*tiaglo*) awarded the same amount of ploughland.[29] This system was by no means peculiar to Russia, but elsewhere it was highly unusual. In much of Europe the cultivated land was held not by the community but by individual families. If anything, the size of their holdings was reduced rather than increased through family enlargement since this could lead to a subdivision of the family holding. Furthermore, peasant families acquired additional land not through a system of regulated redistribution but through their initiative in renting more land, or in purchasing tenures, or in clearing the waste. Because of this basic difference, it is inappropriate to apply Chayanov's generalisations, which were based on a study of repartitional community land tenure, to the rest of *ancien régime* Europe.[30] It is also misleading to accept Lenin's belief that a high level of social differentiation was a simple consequence of the peasant community's submission to capitalism and its consequent dissolution.[31] Social differentiation was a regular feature of peasant communities. It sprang naturally from the existence of tenant rights.

In a peasant society position was primarily determined by landedness. The peasant family that lost its land forfeited its status. The landholders regarded themselves as superior to the mere cottagers and the completely unhoused, that is those living within the community

---

[29] Hoch, *Serfdom and Social Control in Russia*, pp. 15–16; Melton, op. cit., p. 83; Blum, *End of the Old Order*, pp. 123–4.

[30] See D. Thorner's introduction to A.V. Chayanov's *Theory of Peasant Economy* (Homewood, 1966), ed. D. Thorner, B. Kerblay and R.E.F. Smith.

[31] Lenin, *The Development of Capitalism in Russia* (Moscow, 1974), pp. 173–4.

as lodgers or servants. Then, within the corpus of landed families, the peasantry proper, a hierarchy was determined by the sufficiency of the landholding. A landholding with its own ploughteam awarded its occupier a higher status than one without; a landed family capable of subsisting without the need to sell its labour was seen as intrinsically superior to one with a holding that could not provide this degree of independence. In addition, certain functions imparted status by virtue of their social importance and connotation of wealth. The first was landlordship. In subletting their property, peasant families acquired a special status because the action indicated an excess of land in their possession and implied a subscription to aristocratic values. A second status-bearing function was office-holding. Since the village officials were chosen from the more substantial landholders, this upheld the connection between status and land. The other status-imparting functions were innkeeping, milling, haulage and money-lending.[32] How did this system of stratification stem from tenant right?

A major source of social differentiation was the manner in which tenant right was inherited. Often, the tenure was impartible. With tenant right conferred upon one son only, the practice of inheritance was a major cause of low status, creating vulnerable leasehold farmers, landless cottagers as well as lodgers and live-in servants.[33] Furthermore, the rights of fixed rent and of inheritance made the tenures that more capable of sufficiency. They also created opportunities to accumulate a surplus, which a family could use either to purchase waggons, horses and milling rights or to develop a money-lending business. Unless they were farming portions of demesne for a commercial purpose, leaseholders were less well placed to accumulate capital and the status that it could buy. Tenant right was also closely associated with status because the difference between the tenurial rent and an economic rent encouraged peasants to set up as landlords. Impartible inheritance rights, moreover, encouraged subletting by sustaining a sibling demand for tenancy. The same rights also provided peasants with the means and opportunity to take lodgers and to employ live-in servants. From the system of tenant right came

[32] Rebel's analysis has a general application: see his *Peasant Classes*, chs 3 and 4. Also see Blum, *End of the Old Order*, pp. 97 and 109; W.I. Thomas and F. Znanieki, *The Polish Peasant in Europe and America* (2nd edn., New York, 1958) vol. I, pp. 117–18 and 162; O.E. Handlin, *The Uprooted* (Boston, 1951), ch. 1; J.C. Miller, 'The nobility in Polish Renaissance society, 1548–1571', PhD Indiana University (1977), pp. 177–9; *Sliavic Review* 34 (1975): 249, 265–6 and 274–5. For a medieval overview, see R. Hilton, *Bond Men Made Free* (London, 1973), pp. 32–4 and 37.

[33] E.g. Rebel, op. cit., pp. 146 and 162–3; Blum, *End of the Old Order*, p. 96, and E. Le Roi Ladurie, 'Peasants', in *New Cambridge Modern History*, vol. XIII, pp. 119–20.

the surplus income that allowed the payment of wages and the surplus population of siblings which required some form of employment and accommodation in order to remain part of its native community. In these ways, tenant right ensured that a peasant community should be marked by a high degree of social differentiation.

Within peasant communities was a concealed proletariat of siblings, landless and dependent upon wages or equipped with holdings which were too small to keep their occupants out of the labour market. This proletariat was not created, only enlarged, by population growth or the spread of rural industries. Its development was integral to the peasant world, a natural consequence of the social system. Moreover, the original source of its exploitation was not the external forces of capitalism or aristocracy but an elite of peasants operating through high rents and low wages while protected themselves by tenant right.[34]

As for the tenure-holders, they were not simply a social elite since they had a ruling function. The government of the community resided with them. It was they who dominated village assemblies and village offices, often by virtue of their tenant rights since participation in the assemblies and office-holding was often reserved for the occupants of the tenures. In this world cottars, demesne tenants, houseless servants and lodgers were expected to be represented by their landlords and masters.[35]

Such a wide range of social differentiation naturally created tension and conflict within the peasant community: a conflict intensified in the closing stages of the manorial system as rural industries, demesne leasing and population growth created a society in which the majority possessed no more than commoning rights which the tenure-holders were often driven to deny in order to safeguard the common from overuse and exhaustion. This situation, however, only brought conflict to a head. Deeply imbedded within the traditional village, and a consequence of its social diversity, was a basic friction, a conflict of interest between capital and labour, which was kept under only by kinship ties and a limited class consciousness.[36]

The manorial system is often seen as an exploitative machine, very much geared to serving the lord's interest. But the existence and value

---

[34] Rebel, op. cit., pp. 162–3 and 278. For an increase, heavily reliant on proto-industry and especially evident in the eighteenth century: Hagen, op. cit., p. 91; Harnisch, op. cit., p. 46; Mooser, op. cit., p. 55; Sabean, op. cit., pp. 9–10; Klima, op. cit., p. 54; Kriedte, op. cit., p. 137.

[35] Blum, op. cit., p. 109; Rebel, op. cit., p. 164.

[36] Blum, op. cit., p. 113; Sabean, op. cit., p. 163; Rebel, op. cit., pp. 162–3 and 278.

of tenant rights awarded the beneficiaries good cause for promoting its preservation, while giving lords of the manor a good reason for securing its abolition. None the less, throughout the early modern period the lords tolerated it, partly because manors were 'local centres of political authority' (Weber) and a mark of true nobility, and partly because they could make ends meet by exploiting the demesne – in the west through the medium of the leasehold and in the east by means of *Gutsherrschaft*. As we have seen, however, at certain times they could not let it be. Certain circumstances drove them to infringe tenurial custom. Notably in periods of high inflation, lords were pressed to seek a redefinition of their manorial rights so as either to promote demesne farming or to prevent the devaluation of the income drawn from the tenures. Alternatively, they were driven to seek commercial profit at the expense of commoning rights by overstocking the common, selling timber, enclosing the demesne or abolishing the fallow. And peasants resisted, not only by revolt but also by means of legal actions in the royal courts, extensive pilfering, flight, feigned stupidity, drunkenness, footdragging and by using various devices of intimidation such as arson, *tapage*, houghing and pseudonomy. The serfs of eastern Europe may have lost access to the royal courts but this simply removed one means of action. Serfs involved in demesne production were in a strong position to express their disapproval by stealing demesne produce and by performing their labour services in a dilatory manner.[37] In *Gutsherrschaft* societies a marked contrast existed between the inefficiency of demesne production, the result of footdragging in the performance of *robot*, and the high efficiency of tenure farming. Likewise in certain circumstances, especially when tenants were in short supply, peasants would seek to alter the manorial system in their own interest by challenging the payment of certain dues or by refusing to pay them. This happened in the late medieval west.[38] Then, in the sixteenth century, with the recovery of the population, attempts to alter manorial rights were the work of lords seeking to restore what had been lost as well as to counter the effects of inflation.

Because it usually centred upon the issue of tenant right, the conflict between peasants and lords was very much a constitutional one. In 1887 G.F. Knapp coined the term *Agrarverfassung*, or estate polity.

---

[37] E.g. Hoch, op. cit., pp. 11, 183–4 and 165; Kiraly, op. cit., p. 278. For forms of non-rebellious protest in the west, see O. Hufton, 'Attitudes towards authority in eighteenth-century Languedoc', *Social History* 3 (1978): 281–302.

[38] E.g. C. Dyer, 'A redistribution of incomes in fifteenth-century England', *Past and Present* 39 (1969): 11–33.

The concept of the estate as a state is a helpful one, especially if it is conceived as a system of peasant protection as well as of serf oppression. So is its implication that the conflict between lord and tenant could be a constitutional defence of rights and prerogatives, rather than simply taking the form of a direct and primitive struggle to appropriate or retain the surplus.

In the conflict, landlords understandably sought to narrow the difference between what custom permitted and what could be regarded as a fair return on rented land; peasants understandably resisted, not necessarily to protect themselves from gross exploitation but to uphold their rights. Peasant resistance, then, was a defence of custom, but it was not always an attempt to conserve the tradition. Peasant demands could be innovatory. Just as a political struggle in defence of ancient liberties could seek to impose novel restrictions upon the royal prerogative, so a social struggle in defence of tenant right could seek a novel curtailment of the lord's authority. Kett's rebellion of 1549 produced a petition which sought to terminate certain rights enjoyed by the lord of the manor as well as to safeguard the rights of the tenants. Likewise peasant litigation in eighteenth-century France sought to deny the seigneurs the enjoyment of certain traditional rights – on the grounds that, having lost their original purpose, they were no longer justifiable – as well as to assert the rights of the peasant community.[39] Peasant resistance, therefore, was a mixture of innovation and conservation, a practical attempt to make the system serve the peasant interest through ensuring that the traditional tenant rights were neither devalued nor terminated. At the same time it was not radical. An adjustment of the system, not its demolition, was the substance of the peasants' demands.

In obliging lords to infringe custom and peasant, to defend it, tenant rights helped to generate and maintain a tension in rural societies which was not necessarily connected with exploitation and which did not persuade peasants to advocate that the manorial system be scrapped. And yet it was scrapped – dramatically between the mid-eighteenth and the mid-nineteenth centuries. The process was started paradoxically by governments who decided to pursue a policy of peasant protection in the belief that, for fiscal and military reasons, powerful states needed a prosperous peasantry. This helped to create an ideology which condemned serfdom, and the demesne farming

---

[39] For Kett, see the twenty-nine articles, especially articles 3, 11, 13, 16, 17 and 29 (S.K. Land, *Kett's Rebellion* (Ipswich, 1977), pp. 63–6). For France, see H.L. Root, 'Challenging the seigneurie', *Journal of Modern History* 57 (1985): 652.

associated with it, but not the manorial system, and which basically sought to give legal recognition to tenant rights which previously had been authorised by custom alone.[40] For lords, this step intensified the inconvenience of the manorial system and gave them even less incentive to support its preservation. Abolition of the manorial system was an act of government; but it occurred in such a way as to offend neither of the two beneficiaries since the lords were compensated for their loss of rights with redemption payments, and sometimes an extension of demesne and an appropriation of common land, while the peasant elite had their tenant right converted into full ownership.[41] The catalyst for the final abolition of the manor was revolution and a coinciding spate of peasant unrest which, in largely focusing upon manorial abuses, convinced revolutionary and counter-revolutionary governments that emancipation would quieten rural unrest and enlist popular support.[42]

The term 'peasant emancipation' is a misnomer. The only peasant beneficiaries were the elite of tenure-holders who were already protected by proprietorial rights and who, in return for complete freedom from lordship, were obliged to cede their access rights to the lord's forests and pastures and to make heavy redemption payments. As for the rest of the peasantry – the demesne leaseholders and the sublessees of the tenures – they gained nothing and often lost their rights of common.[43] Furthermore, since the emancipation was accompanied by rapid population growth, the new freeholders were quickly impoverished by the subdivision of farms and increasingly obliged to work for low wages. The demand for land, morever, that population growth created obliged peasants to lease from the nobility at economic rents. The shortage of land for peasant farming was exacerbated by the development of capitalist farming, promoted by the cheap labour resulting from the population explosion and by the demand for food that resulted from urbanisation. In the circumstances of emancipation and landhunger, landlords acquired a firmer control of the tenantry than they had enjoyed under the manorial system, one resting upon

---

[40] For the seventeenth century, see J. De Vries, *The Economy of Europe in an Age of Crisis, 1600–1750* (Cambridge, 1976), pp. 61–2. For the eighteenth century, see P.G.M. Dickson, *Finance and Government under Maria Theresa, 1740–1780* (Oxford, 1987), pp. 126–7; W.W. Hagen, 'The Junkers' faithless servants', in R.J. Evans and W. R. Lee (eds.) *The German Peasantry* (London, 1986), pp. 83–6; Blum, *End of the Old Order*, ch. 16.

[41] Blum, *End of the Old Order*, ch. 17.

[42] Bush, *Noble Privilege*, pp. 171–5.

[43] Blum, *End of the Old Order*, pp. 391–7.

their unassailable right to determine the duration of the tenancy and to revise the rent when the lease expired.

A new world was thus created, one far different from the old when tenant rights had controlled much of the land and commercial farming, in largely taking the form of share-cropping and *Gutsherrschaft*, had operated through the medium of a peasantry rather than wage-labour. In this new world a more conventional class relationship could develop between peasant and lord. Nothing could have been more harmonious than the relationship that existed between large commercial farmers and their landlords; but, no longer cushioned by rights, short of land, prone to cheap wage-labour and with their way of life and very existence threatened by a process of proletarianisation, peasantries in the course of the nineteenth and twentieth centuries acquired a unifying militancy which declared itself in revolt, the formation of peasant parties and a new radicalisation which stemmed from land hunger and promises of land redistribution.[44]

The image of the European peasantries in the early modern period has been distorted by a number of broad generalisations. Some were generated by social anthropologists, notably Redfield, Kroeber and Wolf, who, in seeking to distinguish peasants from primitive cultivators, emphasised the former's exploitation by landlords or tax officials.[45] Others were generated by Chayanov's attempts to distinguish between peasant and capitalist societies and the emphasis he consequently placed upon the lack of social differentiation within a peasant community where variations in the size of landholdings were presented as no more than a flexible consequence of family needs.[46] Further distortion was caused by Blum's tendency to perceive the manor in eastern European terms. This was encapsulated in his often repeated phrase 'the servile lands' and its application to the whole of early modern Europe. In tending to present the peasantry in class terms, as a group reduced to wretchedness by landlord exploitation, he is prone to accept at face value the ideology of peasant emancipation which was developed in the late eighteenth and early nineteenth centuries by absolute monarchs, seeking to increase their tax revenues, and revolutionaries seeking popular support for the overthrow of the

[44] See M. Hildermeier, 'Agrarian social protest, populism and economic development', *Social History* 4 (1979): 319–32.
[45] See R. Redfield, *Peasant Society and Culture* (Englewood Cliffs, 1966), p. 131; E. Wolf, *Peasants* (Englewood Cliffs, 1966), ch. 1.
[46] See n. 30.

old order.[47] Finally the recent past and present, in which peasantries, notably of the Third World, have been impoverished or extinguished by a combination of rapid population growth, rentier capitalism and the withdrawal of land from peasant cultivation through the spread of capitalist farming, has further reduced our ability to comprehend the state and nature of the old regime peasantries, mainly through creating the paradigm of a peasantry ruthlessly exploited and threatened with extinction. The outcome of these distortions is a picture of the early modern peasant as 'necessarily an underdog', prone to the extremes of impoverishment from which landlord paternalism could offer the only protection and under a constant threat of marginalisation and destruction.[48]

To remedy the distortion, the image of serfdom needs serious revision; the social differentiation integral to the peasant community requires emphasis and elaboration. In addition, the concept of peasant hardship has to be presented less simply in terms of landlord exploitation and more complicatedly in terms of demographic change, crop failure, government demands (taxation, conscription and billeting) and the ways in which peasants exploited each other through low wages, high rents and money-lending. Finally, to explain more satisfactorily the relationship between lord and peasant, the concept of *Agrarverfassung* should be revived and used alongside that of class. In view of their social ramifications, the tenant rights authorised by the manorial system provide a basic starting-point for this revision.

[47] Blum, *End of the Old Order*, pp. 3, 34 and 192–3; Blum, 'From servitude to freedom', in J. Blum (ed.) *Our Forgotten Past* (London, 1982), pp. 64–5.

[48] S.J. Watts, *A Social History of Western Europe, 1450–1720* (London, 1984), p. 105; C. Lis and H. Soly, *Poverty and Capitalism in Pre-Industrial Europe* (Brighton, 1979), chs 3 and 4.

CHAPTER NINE

Deferential bitterness: the social outlook of the rural proletariat in eighteenth- and nineteenth-century England and Wales

K.D.M. Snell

University of Leicester

The 'rural proletariat' usually has very different connotations from a 'peasantry'. However, in many parts of eighteenth- and nineteenth-century Britain these two agrarian classes were closely connected. The predominance of small tenant farms and owner–occupiers in many areas – particularly in the pastoral west and north, where many rural inhabitants worked just occasionally and seasonally for wages, or before stocking their own farm – and the ways in which some independence could be gained from commons and waste, meant that an entirely wage-dependent, socially isolated, rural proletariat was regionally rare.[1] Partly for this reason, contemporaries often used the word 'peasant'. It is found in the titles of classics of contemporary rural writing, and in most such cases 'peasant' meant the wage-dependent poor.[2] In the nineteenth century it was not often used to describe anyone of erstwhile yeoman standing or higher. In England

[1] See M. Reed, 'The peasantry of nineteenth-century England: a neglected class', *History Workshop* 18 (1984): 53–76, and his 'Nineteenth-century rural England: a case for peasant studies', *Journal of Peasant Studies* 14 (1986): 78–99.

[2] W.S. Gilly, *The Peasantry of the Border* (London, 1842); F.G. Heath, *The English Peasantry* (London, 1874); R. Heath, *The English Peasant* (London, 1893); R.M. Garnier, *Annals of the British Peasantry* (London, 1895); A. Jessop, *England's Peasantry and Other Essays* (London, 1914); J.W. Robertson Scott, *The Dying Peasant and the Future of His Sons* (London, 1926). Or see R.L. Gales, *The Vanished Country Folk, and Other Studies in Arcady* (London, 1914), p. 20, or R.M. Dorson, *The British Folklorists: A History* (London, 1968), p. 83, citing William Thoms, for typical uses of the word. It was often also used to denote a small farmer. See e.g. the implied definition in W. Davis, *Hints to Philanthropists* (Bath, 1821), p. 95. For further discussion, see J.V. Beckett, 'The peasant in England: a case of terminological confusion?', *Agricultural History Review* 32 (1984): 113–23.

the word had pejorative implications because of its association with the Irish or French peasantry; but it also ironically carried the unarticulated sense, reassuring to some, that the rural poor were perhaps not so dispossessed of land, self-reliance and other supposedly traditional attributes as many made out.

Another term commonly found was the 'labouring poor'. In a country context – the term was also urban – this comprised those who worked with their hands in rural labour, or in rural artisan crafts, as well as commoners and squatters, or the various groups of peripatetic poor, including the migrant Irish, but probably excluding the tinkers and gypsies: those especially prone to dependency upon poor relief at some point in their lives, and this could include small farmers. One can also find in rural areas that English stigmatic notion of the 'classes' of 'ratepayers' and 'the poor', a divide emphasised in the 1870s as a way of cutting poor relief, the transfer payment being the crucial criterion. 'The poor' of course had long-term usage. Of these various terms, the 'labouring poor' (which might include ratepayers) was probably most prevalent to describe the workers which concern us here. In many ways 'labouring poor' is historically preferable to the anachronistic 'rural proletariat': it captures better the idiosyncrasies of wage labour, without presupposing an emphasis on the *wage* as the defining feature of the broad occupational group; it is also largely free of theoretical presupposition. In relation to a *community* issue like class, it is more appropriate than the term 'rural proletariat', given the largely male connotations of the latter. The 'labouring poor' is less amenable to comparative discussion though, being a British term with its heyday around the turn of the eighteenth century. I shall use 'rural proletariat' and 'labouring poor' synonymously here, with a preference for the latter.

As this preamble suggests, it is the variety of occupational and regional experience which needs first to be stressed. For this above all makes it difficult to generalise about the social sentiments of the class. The predicament of a loyal worker on a large Rutland or Vale of Belvoir estate, in a closed village, under a landlord with a paternalistic self-image, could differ markedly from that of a labourer say in Castle Acre, or another such open, over-populated and heavily pauperised settlement. Or again, the isolated situation and social connections of a labourer in the Fens would differ from that of his counterpart in a Midlands semi-industrial village, mixing with miners, or framework knitters and the coterie of associated trades. The work ethic and labour consciousness of a worker on a large corn-producing Norfolk farm would set his experience aside markedly from that of a farm worker in say Carmarthenshire or Radnorshire, where one would expect a farm's servants or labourer to be outnumbered by members of the farmer's family, even if that labourer was not himself one of the farmer's kin.[3] In west Wales, one could expect small farmer and labourer to attend the same chapel, to share the same grievances against landlords over tenancies, to stress their mutual Welshness against English and Anglican landlords. There would have been the traditional divisions by age and married status between farm servants and labourers; yearly hiring would still continue well into the nineteenth century, often even for married labour; small farms would be abundant with their occupiers blurring into the same class as labourers; employment was comparatively secure because of service contracts, or because so often it was self-employment.[4] Rebecca was a revolt of small farmers backed by labourers – not of the latter *per se*.

In East Anglia by contrast, rural antagonism was predominantly landlord/farmer/clergyman versus labourer. Here, by the 1830s, wage-dependent labourers would outnumber farmers by nearly ten to one, and the likelihood was far greater that they would attend different denominational services to their masters, that sectarian animosity would add to the many other composted bones of class contention. These included unemployment, farm machinery, enclosure and issues of access to land, the game laws, extremely low wages, tied cottage insecurity, the operation of the poor law, or the way local charities were administered by the Anglican clergy. This west–east comparison opens another dimension. The participation of women in agricultural work was itself influenced by region, largely by whether one lived in the west or north, or in the south and east. Women considerably outnumbered men in west Wales – the opposite was true in rural eastern England – and this indicates their fuller role

[3] Labour-farmer ratios in Wales around 1851 would commonly be in the region of 2:1. K.D.M. Snell, *Annals of the Labouring Poor: Social Change and Agrarian England, 1660–1900* (Cambridge, 1985), p. 97. And see there the high proportion of labour which was farm-servant – very much higher than in England. For the numbers of farms with and without labour in England, by county, see E.A. Wrigley, 'Men on the land and men in the countryside: employment in agriculture in early-nineteenth-century England', in L. Bonfield, R. Smith and K. Wrightson (eds) *The World We Have Gained: Histories of Population and Social Structure* (Oxford, 1986), pp. 310–11.
[4] In the nineteenth century, 'the social history of rural Wales resolved itself almost exclusively into a struggle between the landowners and their tenants', wrote D. Williams, *The Rebecca Riots: A Study in Agrarian Discontent* (Cardiff, 1955), p. 68. Such a statement could not possibly be made about rural England. As he says, in south-west Wales, 'there was no great social gulf between the farmer and his labourers as there was, for example, in south-east England' (ibid., p. 109).

in Welsh agriculture. Perhaps one should also note the sexual difference in the names Rebecca and Captain Swing; although of course Rebecca also made clear biblical reference.[5] The possible distinctiveness of some female rural social sentiments is not an issue I shall explore here, as the evidence is slim. For the most part, these do not seem to run counter to divisions based on social status and class.

Because of such diversity, one might expect superficial, apparent or real 'class' sentiments to vary considerably. Perhaps this explains some historiographical differences. The views of a faithful gamekeeper mediated through a squire's diary (if such could be found) might well diverge from those of most village inhabitants expressed in their own words, let alone from poachers discussing the New Poor Law in a village beer shop. There were undoubtedly loyal workers dedicated to certain estates and to some of the landed gentry. Furthermore, the Duke of Rutland never lacked for a gang of thugs to beat up Bible-carrying Primitive Methodist preachers when they strayed into the Vale of Belvoir. Brutal behaviour like this shows loyalty of a sort, I suppose, even if only for beer and cash. Such men under the immediate aegis of the Duke of Rutland might even have shared F.M.L. Thompson's view that 'the landed aristocracy has done great service', that they did indeed 'serve as the respected symbol of order and continuity in a changing world' – although even they would have seen through this questionable language of 'service' to describe landed power.[6]

Some labourers might also have approved Alan Armstrong's dismissal of widespread rural protest – like the 'Bread or Blood' riots of 1816, the Captain Swing unrest of 1830–1, or the ferocious troubles of the 1840s or 1870s – as 'particularly colourful and apparently significant episodes or events', 'capable of being explained to a large extent by short-period influences'. Perhaps they would have agreed with him that such events are largely irrelevant for an assessment of rural social relations.[7] In fact, Armstrong attests that 'never very far from the minds of many farmworkers at any time during the nineteenth and twentieth centuries was a sense of identity with the

[5] This apparent sexual contrast seems to be documented in contemporary illustrations of the two movements. However, the actions of 'Rebecca' were probably dominated by men, even if often dressed in women's clothes.

[6] F.M.L. Thompson, *English Landed Society in the Nineteenth Century* (London, 1963), p. 345.

[7] A. Armstrong, *Farmworkers* (Frome, 1988), p. 12, and his 'The influence of demographic factors on the position of the agricultural labourer in England and Wales, *c.* 1750–1914', *Agricultural History Review* 29 (1981): 71.

interests of their employers'.[8] Such is the reassuring tenor of conservative agrarian historiography, backed up in this case with plenty of cartoons from *Punch*. An argument like this can certainly be made in the very different period since the Second World War, as by Howard Newby.[9] However, it seems superficial with reference to large areas of the country in the late eighteenth and nineteenth centuries. The evidence is dramatically contrary to it. As we shall see, there is little justification for the notion that feelings revealed during protest movements were in some way unrepresentative: that they were colourful and lightly sporadic, due simply to short-term influences, mere aberrations atypical of the usual harmonious social outlook agreeably shared by all.

One should allow the labouring poor to speak for themselves, or be spoken for by those with close knowledge of them. In doing this we need to isolate those social sentiments and causes which drew such heterogeneous and regionally fragmented workers together; we can then weigh these against those issues which divided the rural proletariat within itself: ties of locality and place, local forms of xenophobia, work practices and employment priorities. The main problem is evidential. We are dealing with one of the most illiterate, subdued, silent, maligned and shadowy classes in nineteenth-century society, despite the fact that in 1851 these workers made up the largest single class of employed people in England and Wales, larger even than servants.[10] The language of abuse and debasement used to describe them was to be an important reactive element in their consciousness and identity, in their aspirations for recognition and esteem, whether through dissenting religion, friendly societies, the rural unions or politics. For country-dweller or farm worker my *Thesaurus* heads off into the litany of contemporary terms which speaks much for the way this class was perceived by those outside and above it: Hodge, swain, gaffer, peasant, boor, churl, bog-trotter, yokel, hind, chaw-bacon, clod, clodhopper, hayseed, hick, bumpkin, Tony Lumpkin, hillbilly, village idiot – 'see ninny'. The terms could be expanded considerably with historical reference to the various regional names

[8] Armstrong, *Farmworkers*, p. 15. 'The concept of "class"', he remarks, is 'not to the taste of all historians', ibid., p. 13. It was nevertheless widely used by contemporaries.

[9] H. Newby, *The Deferential Worker* (London, 1977: Harmondsworth, 1979 edn), pp. 360–3. See also his *Green and Pleasant Land?* (Harmondsworth, 1979), and the concluding chapters of his *Country Life* (London, 1987).

[10] Agricultural labour was about two-fifths of the working population in 1750, about one-third in 1811, and one-fifth in 1851. The fraction then fell much further.

used; they carry the same or a more hostile signification. Contemporary expression oscillates between such words of bovine and comic connotation, matching the images of *Punch*, and a language of the secret, insidious unknowable rural poor, which would break out especially during the frequent periods of unrest, arson or unionism. In pictorial terms too, there were the juxtapositions of figures by a bemused Rowlandson and the secretive, sullen, opaque images of Morland, whose pauper-cloaked labourers avert their morose faces from the viewer, and whose body language tells of a closed, discomforting and nearly impenetrable social world within the labouring, poaching, travelling or family group.[11] This was by necessity of circumstance a class with the potentiality of many faces, sometimes almost theatrical, perfecting deference in their own interests; but this was a face which could alter at other times to greater frankness, whether between themselves, during moments of conflict, or retrospectively as personal memory.

Many commented on this problem of understanding, of reaching under the stereotype of Hodge. Wordsworth's pastoral flights of fancy were occasionally disturbed by some yokel, one of those creatures that seemed to him to be 'like a caterpillar sheathed in ice': a figure however which harmonised naturally with the sublime and silent landscape he (like many others) required. Holdenby commented that there was always the 'mysterious barrier of "Ay, ay", "may be", "likely enough", with which the labourer hedges himself in'.[12] 'When you accost him,' wrote the *Morning Chronicle*'s correspondent on the rural districts,

> if he is not insolent – which he seldom is – he is timid and shrinking, his whole manner showing that he feels himself at a distance from you greater than should separate any two classes of men. He is often doubtful when you address, and suspicious when you question him; he is seemingly oppressed with the interview whilst it lasts, and obviously relieved when it is over.[13]

Unlike some historians, Holdenby was not long in penetrating further, and his conclusion was this:

> It is the idea of a legitimate prey, the right to make some folk disgorge, the suggestion of a just reprisal . . . It is often the same spirit, too, which

---

[11] On Morland, see J. Barrell, *The Dark Side of the Landscape: The Rural Poor in English Painting, 1730–1840* (Cambridge, 1980), pp. 89–130. On Rowlandson, see Barrell's 'The private comedy of Thomas Rowlandson', *Art History* 6 (1983): 423–41.

[12] C. Holdenby, *The Folk of the Furrow* (London, 1913), p. 7.

[13] *Morning Chronicle*, 1 December 1849.

initiates poaching rather than the actual material gain. There is a satisfaction in carrying the war right into the enemy's country. I know so well the attitude in which the villagers touch their hats to the gentry while they are in their employ. The salute is thrown in with the service, but it ceases with the latter.[14]

The salute was also of course manipulative, and in their obvious self-interest. As far as Fred Kitchen was concerned,

The only important person was the gentleman farmer who farmed the Manor House. He was one of the fussily important sort, and alderman and Justice of the Peace. If you wanted a favour of him, all you had to do was to pump hard on the handles at each end of his name. If you omitted the handles you drew no water from his well.[15]

In Charles Kingsley's novel *Yeast*, when Lancelot wishes to go with Tregarva into the village wake, to hear the real views of the poor expressed among themselves, Tregarva tells him, 'Well, sir, we will go to-night. You are not ashamed of putting on a smock-frock? For if you go as a gentleman, you will hear no more of them than a hawk does of a covey of partridges'.[16] 'There are a fluent few,' wrote R.L. Gales, 'but for the most part their speech is very guarded and cautious when dealing with members of the better classes . . . As they grow older they become enigmatic, sybilline, oracular'.[17] Cynicism was also expressed about deference to the clergy. In Robertson Scott's view,

The country clergy have from most of their labourer parishioners the hat-touching of rural social usage. But the secret indifference is not a little contemptuous . . . In the fireside judgement of the mass of agricultural labouring families, the average parson is witless and lazy, a self-satisfied drone, who, by the advantage of his social position, has secured a soft job, to which he hangs on.[18]

One finds this view of what one person called the 'teeth-clenching days' expressed in various ways in all the agricultural labourers' autobiographies. Here is Arthur Tweedy's account, from a region which was not notable for its rural social hostilities:

Whenever we met the squire or anyone else who thought himself a step above the farmers' joskins (a derogatory term used in the North Riding

---

[14] Holdenby, *The Folk of the Furrow*, pp. 26–7.

[15] F. Kitchen, *Brother to the Ox* (Letchworth, 1942, 1945 edn), pp. 134–5.

[16] C. Kingsley, *Yeast* (London, 1902 edn), p. 152.

[17] R.L. Gales, *The Vanished Country Folk, and Other Studies in Arcady* (London, 1914), p. 14.

[18] Anon [J.W. Robertson Scott], *England's Green and Pleasant Land* (London, 1925, 1931 edn), p. 90.

for farm lads) we had to 'Sir' them and raise our caps and the ladies and girls had to curtsy. If you did not you were very smartly rebuked. I have seen women hide behind a hedge because they hated to humble down in this way. I remember asking my father why we should address them as 'Sir' and he replied 'Sir, my boy, is only the nickname for a fool'.[19]

And, talking about hiding behind hedges, let us not forget Lady Chatterley:

'What do I care about my ladyship! I hate it really. I feel people are jeering every time they say it. And they are, they are! Even you jeer when you say it'. 'Me!' For the first time [Mellors] looked straight at her, and into her eyes.[20]

Deference, in other words, cannot be taken at more than its face value and semblance; for that, after all, is all labourers intended of it. Nor is it really worthwhile throwing up a theoretical smokescreen around the word, if this obscures the feelings at stake. Deferential attitudes become a manner, one side of an habitual double-faced outlook, a form of self-presentation. They were buttoned in as a necessity for survival, insisted upon by vulnerable parents from an early age, parents who despaired at gross and often capricious landed power, who felt themselves without the slightest influence to change a seemingly immutable social structure. However, we shall see that deference often covered a deep-rooted sense of grievance, of social bitterness, which had to be censored because of the very precarious circumstances of livelihood. Arthur Tweedy spoke of workers terrified of being sacked.[21] Such grievance has eased in the twentieth century. But it previously had many reasons to persist.

To what was this animosity due? During and by the end of the Napoleonic Wars, many commentators were remarking on the passing away of older social relationships, to which they looked back with nostalgia, and for which the 'moral economy' is probably the best current phrase. We will not find equivalent statements so voluminously expressed ever again, however one may wish to qualify them: this was not simply a recurring generational tendency to bemoan a more harmonious rural past. Cobbett, Clare, Crabbe, Bloomfield, Eden, Ebenezer Elliott, David Davies, Arthur Young, and the many others speaking of this period are well known. There were earlier voices, like Goldsmith's, but they were less noticeable,

---

[19] A. Tweedy, 'Recollections of a farm worker', *Bulletin of the Cleveland and Teeside Local Historical Society* 21 (1973): 3.

[20] D.H. Lawrence, *Lady Chatterley's Lover* (1928, Harmondsworth, 1975), p. 129.

[21] Tweedy, op. cit., p. 6. The same point is constantly made in F.E. Green, *The Tyranny of the Countryside* (London, 1913).

and the issues they raised later became more prominent. There was first the decline of farm service – the hiring of unmarried people to live in with the farmer. This change occurred from the 1780s in the south and east, and owed much to rising prices, the pretensions of a richer farmer class, and an abundance of labour which could be hired on a shorter-term basis when needed. Shorter periods of employment without yearly contracts guarded against settlements and extra expenditure from parish rates. This was one factor intensifying social segregation. It occurred during the parliamentary enclosure period, itself marked by the building of new farms away from nuclear villages, and by continued engrossing of farms. The consequences for the labouring poor included less security of employment, and difficulties over settlement at a time when it was increasingly important that they be eligible for poor relief in a convenient place. It was now far less likely that they would be able to save up to stock a small farm of their own, and so ended one of the traditional prudential checks on early marriage. Cobbett's view is well known, and illustrates also a household economic basis for the 'moral economy':

> Everything about this farmhouse was formerly the scene of *plain manners* and *plentiful living* . . . But all appeared to be in a state of decay and nearly of *disuse*. There appeared to have been hardly any *family* in that house, where formerly there were, in all probability, from ten to fifteen men, boys and maids: and, which was the worse of all, there was a *parlour*! Aye, and a *carpet* and *bell-pull* too! . . . and there was the mahogany table, and the fine chairs, and the fine glass . . . And, there were the decanters, the glasses, the 'dinner-set' of crockery ware, and all just in the true stock-jobber style . . . This Squire Charington's father used, I dare say, to sit at the head of the oak table with his men, say grace to them, and cut up the meat and the pudding . . . all lived well . . . [But] that long table could not share in the work of the decanters and the dinner-set. Therefore, it became almost untenanted; the labourers retreated to hovels, called cottages; and, instead of board and lodging, they got money; so little of it as to enable the employer to drink wine; but then, that he might not reduce them to *quite starvation*, they were enabled to come to him, in the *King's name*, and demand food as *paupers*.[22]

There are elements of nostalgia here, but the same change can be quantified with some exactitude using settlement records, which also record time and again the adverse reaction to it.[23] There were other abundant complaints from farm labourers themselves, as in John

---

[22] W. Cobbett, *Rural Rides* (1830, Harmondsworth, 1975), p. 228.
[23] On the decline of service and its social effects, see my *Annals of the Labouring Poor* (Cambridge, 1985), ch. 2. One should not of course embellish the social relationships of living-in employment, and harsh or negligent treatment could occur under it.

Clare or Bloomfield's poetry, or from this Dorset man interviewed by the ex-farm worker Alexander Somerville:

> Ah! you be a precious lot o' hard screws on a poor man, the whole lot of
> you be . . . I see you ha' got a good coat on your back, and a face that
> don't look like an empty belly; there be no hunger looking out atween
> your ribs I'll swear. You be either a farmer or somebody else that lives on
> somebody else. May be you be a lord for aught I know on; or a squire; or
> a parson, dang it – you be a parson perhaps! One thing I see, you ben't
> one of them as works fourteen hours a day, to feed lords, and squires,
> and parsons, and farmers; dang the farmers, they be the worst of the lot
> of ye . . . I dare say you be one of them as has your daughter . . . playing
> the piano on a Saturday night to drown the noise of them brutes of
> labouring men what come to get their wages through a hole in the wall;
> what cannot be allowed to set foot within a farmer's house now-a-days;
> what must be paid through an opening in the partition, lest they defile the
> house of a master what gets rich as they get poor; a master what must get
> his daughter to play music lest the voice of a hard-working man be heard
> through the hole in the wall! Ah! it be enough to drive men mad; it ha'
> made men think on things they would never ha' thought on.[24]

The ending of farm service in the south was a significant contributory factor to class distrust. Its continuation in the north and west was frequently said by contemporaries to be a background reason for something approaching a north–south divide in the character of rural class relations. Furthermore, the persisting custom of living-in in America and Canada (related there to conditions of labour shortage) was often mentioned by emigrants as conducing to more favourable social relations than they had ever experienced in England.[25]

During the same period, after the mid-eighteenth century, the parliamentary enclosure movement was another factor aggravating social ill-feeling. The bitterness and hostility of the labouring poor to enclosure was notorious. 'I should *like* to see they woods all go up in flames!', said an elderly labourer to George Sturt, pointing at the enclosure which had once been open common, where 'you could go where you mind to. Now 'tis all fenced in, and if you looks over the fence they'll lock ye up. And they en't got no more *right* to it, Mr Bourne, than you and me have!'[26] On the question of equity, this

---

[24] A. Somerville, *The Whistler at the Plough* (Manchester, 1852, repr. London, 1989); p. 42.

[25] See e.g. the discussion of emigrants' letters in Snell, *Annals of the Labouring Poor*, introduction.

[26] G. Sturt, *Change in the Village* (London, 1912), p. 73. See my *Annals of the Labouring Poor*, ch. 4 for the effects of enclosure. See also the reappraisal by J.M. Neeson, 'Parliamentary enclosure and the disappearance of the English peasantry', *Research in Economic History* Suppl. 5 (1989): 89–120.

view prevailed. The loss of a multitude of common and wasteland rights through enclosure, the completely inadequate recompense (acknowledged by many from higher classes), the consequent deterioration in material standards of living, and the enforcement of tighter labour discipline and restrictive moral codes as labourers found their chances of semi-independence eroded – all these contributed to the enduring sense among the labouring poor that enclosure had dispossessed them of a heritage which was theirs by right.

Robertson Scott later summed up feelings in his ironically titled *England's Green and Pleasant Land*:

> More and more intelligent working people, with more and more
> backing, are minded to have a different countryside from the countryside
> they now put up with. What they see in their beautiful church building is
> – salvage. Their land is gone. Their common is gone. Their fuel rights
> are gone. All these things that belonged to them were mostly stolen from
> them – if not in one way, then in another; at any rate they were lost,
> undeservedly.[27]

The enclosure movement was largely over by the 1820s. But this theme endured long after, informing the demands of the agricultural unions, the agitation for allotments and smallholdings,[28] in some cases for land nationalisation and radical change in the way land was held and owned. The *Morning Chronicle*'s rural correspondent in 1850 was

> astonished at the extent to which I have found Socialist doctrines
> prevailing among the rural poor . . . its principles have made their way
> amongst them to a considerable extent – their progress being promoted,
> if it was not originated, by the daily contemplation of their own wretched
> lot . . . they contend that they have 'a right to live, and to live
> comfortably, as well as the best of them', and they . . . reason with
> themselves that they cannot do this until land is treated not as a property,
> but as a trust . . . They are becoming more and more imbued with these
> sentiments, and many of them will tell you so.[29]

Stanhope in 1875 complained of 'the mischievous doctrine of community of land' which was frequently held by rural labourers.[30]

---

[27] Anon [Robertson Scott], *England's Green and Pleasant Land*, p. 209. And see Somerville, *The Whistler at the Plough*, p. 103: 'We have always proceeded on the principle of teaching our rural population to respect property by taking all property from them'.

[28] Which bore only limited fruit in the 1887 Allotments Act, and the 1892 Smallholdings Act. The results of the latter in particular were negligible.

[29] *Morning Chronicle*, 7 November 1849, reprinted on 1 January 1850.

[30] E. Stanhope, 'The agricultural labourers of England', *Edinburgh Review* 141 (1875): 143.

Baldwyn Leighton, for all his sympathy, was clearly worried by the prospect of what he called agrarian 'communism'; and looked to forms of rural cooperation and guild-type organisation as the option to this.[31] In 1874 the *Labourer's Union Chronicle*, the rural workers' paper, adopted the subtitle: 'An Independent Advocate of the British Toilers Rights to Free Land, Freedom from Priestcraft, and from the Tyranny of Capital'.[32] 'Land, land: that was all we were thinking about and talking about', wrote Joseph Arch later.[33] It is evident from his own discussion that they were thinking about much else besides, especially wages, emigration, cottage conditions and the like; but the importance of this rancorous issue for the beliefs and social outlook of the labouring poor cannot be underestimated.

The other major factor behind the growth of rural class hostility was the New Poor Law. The hatred and fear of this institution, and everything it stood for in social coercion and the repressive enforcement of a lop-sided political economy, runs like a mental wound through the writing and documentation left by nineteenth-century rural labourers. George Edwards, Alexander Somerville, George and James Loveless, John Buckmaster, Josiah Sage, Joseph Arch, James Hawker, let alone sympathetic commentators from a different class like George Sturt, Richard Jefferies, George Crewe, Reverend Maberly, Flora Thompson, Rider Haggard, Rowntree and the many others, provide some of the most bitter and scathing prose one can ever read in their attacks on the New Poor Law. The views on the social repercussions of this law were well summed up by George Crewe: 'Those who mix with the lower classes,' he wrote in 1843 (mainly about the rural work-force),

> who obtain their confidence, and hear their opinions freely and
> unhesitatingly spoken, know how rapid and great the change is, which
> has taken place in their mind towards the higher classes – in the last three

---

[31] Sir Baldwyn Leighton, *The Farm Labourer in 1872* (London, 1872), p. 16.

[32] This was the paper of the NALU, edited by J.E. Matthew Vincent. It adopted this subtitle in 1874.

[33] J. Arch, *The Autobiography of Joseph Arch* (London, 1898, 1966 edn), p. 129. On the way labourers prized land, see e.g. A. Young, *An Inquiry into the Propriety of Applying Wastes to the Better Maintenance and Support of the Poor, with Instances of the Great Effects which have attended their Acquisition of Property, in Keeping them from the Parish* (Bury St Edmunds, 1801), pp. 23–5; Sir B. Leighton, *The Farm Labourer in 1872* (London, 1872), p. 14: 'They value land more than wages'; J. Rae, 'Why have the yeomanry perished?, *Contemporary Review* 44 (1883): 561–3; E. Stanhope, 'The agricultural labourers of England', *Edinburgh Review* 141 (1875): 139; D.C. Barnett, 'Allotments and the problems of rural poverty, 1780–1840', in E.L. Jones and G.E. Mingay (eds) *Land, Labour and Population in the Industrial Revolution* (London, 1967), pp. 167ff.

or four years especially: and they must also be fully aware, that of all the various causes thus operating to promote strife and division, the New Poor Law has been the most powerful.[34]

The Poor Law guardians were now to become the main recipients of rural incendiarism and animal maiming. As Somerville and many others described, the labourers look upon 'the guardians and justices, as their natural enemies, on whose property they may make war, on whose haystacks, and stables, and barnfuls of grain, they do make war – fearful, savage, wasteful war'.[35] There was no easing of the antagonism over this law for the remainder of the nineteenth century: the 'return to the principles of 1834' in the 1870s aggravated this issue still further.[36]

There were further factors which contributed to the gradual change from a rural society of subtle, complex ladder-like stratification, of tolerably amenable ranks and orders below high-gentry level, based upon a general and evolving moral economy (anchored in Tudor legislation), to one in the south and Midlands of simpler and more static conceptions of station, and clear-cut lines of hostile class division. These factors included the attitude of the Anglican Church to rural dissent, the prominence of clerical magistrates, the issue of parliamentary reform, anti-tithe agitation, the game laws and the harshened penal code, changes in Poor Law and settlement administration even before 1834, considerable reductions in material living standards in the south after about 1780, exceptionally squalid housing, unemployment and the use of threshing machinery, the Corn Laws and the Anti-Corn Law League (the latter active and persuasive among labourers, as Buckmaster or Somerville testify), and the franchise issue.[37] It is probably true to say that, on these issues, the rural proletariat was very largely united in view, but with differing regional perspectives and emphases. Certainly from the mid-nineteenth century, people as diverse as Richard Jefferies, or the *Morning Chronicle*'s rural correspondent, or J. Stratton were talking about the 'public opinion' among farm labourers, and making firm generalisa-

[34] Sir G. Crewe, *A Word For the Poor, and Against the Present Poor Law* (Derby, 1843), p. 20.
[35] Somerville, *Whistler at the Plough*, pp. 128–9. He also argued that only a small proportion of rural fires were reported, for fear that the crime would become even more contagious.
[36] D. Thomson, 'The decline of social security: falling state support for the elderly since early Victorian times', *Ageing and Society* 4 (1984): 451–82.
[37] Somerville, *Whistler at the Plough*, and J. Buckmaster, *A Village Politician* (nd, Horsham, 1982 edn). Rural labourers finally gained the vote in 1884.

tion as to its nature.[38] This was not in any way a pre-political class. There was almost universal resentment of enclosure and reduced access to land, the New Poor Law, and adverse changes in employment practice, whether in Wales,[39] Norfolk or the North Riding – as also of the game laws, low wages, and the operative versions of political economy. Of the latter, its fundamental tenets and its Malthusian bias were never accepted by the labouring poor, for many social, moral and biblical reasons. However, threshing machinery was not a significant issue in many northern districts, like Northumberland or Durham, where it was less of a threat to employment. In the more turbulent parts of Wales in the first half of the nineteenth century, it was not contentious simply because it had rarely been introduced.[40] In northern England, money wages were less of an issue than in the south, and in the north-east the main conflict over employment practices came relatively late and for regionally specific reasons.[41]

One of the most revealing avenues open is to discuss the language and imagery of the labouring poor. In the anonymous or emigrant letters written by them a deep social resentment emerges, usually directed at specific employers, but with even the more sympathetic among the employer class suffering by association.[42] This becomes more generalised but often as strongly worded in the agricultural autobiographies. One of the most pervasive features of this language was its biblical and religious reference, and indeed we will find the Bible referred to by the poor far more frequently than it ever is in the diaries of the Reverends Woodforde, Kilvert, Holland or Skinner.[43]

---

[38] See e.g. R. Jefferies, *Hodge and His Masters* (London, 1880, 1949 edn), p. 232; the *Morning Chronicle*, 16 January 1850, on northern labourers being 'thorough-going liberals in politics and Puritans in religion'; J.Y. Stratton, 'Farm labourers, their friendly societies, and the Poor Law', *Journal of the Royal Agricultural Society* VI (1870): 94. For the political views of the agricultural proletariat, see R. Wells, 'Rural rebels in southern England in the 1830s', in C. Elmsley and J. Walvin (eds) *Artisans, Peasants and Proletarians, 1760–1860: Essays Presented to Gwyn A. Williams* (London, 1985), pp. 124–65.

[39] In Wales, however, parliamentary enclosure was slight, late and expanded cultivation into waste land, allowing further settlement. It did not displace employment, population or even common rights to the same extent as in parts of England, and was probably less unpopular for this reason.

[40] See Williams, *The Rebecca Riots*, p. 74.

[41] J.P.D. Dunbabin, *Rural Discontent in Nineteenth-Century Britain* (London, 1974).

[42] See E.P. Thompson, 'The crime of anonymity', in D. Hay *et al.* (eds) *Albion's Fatal Tree: Crime and Society in Eighteenth-century England*, (London, 1975); Snell, *Annals of the Labouring Poor*, introduction.

[43] Rev. James Woodforde, *The Diary of a Country Parson, 1758–1802* (Oxford, 1979); Rev. Francis Kilvert, *Kilvert's Diary, 1870–1879* (Harmondsworth, 1980); William

The study of biblical exegesis among the labouring poor, in relation to the social order and to work, is almost wholly undeveloped. One awaits the redeployment of a well-trained theologian to rural social history. In the meanwhile, let me make some start on this; parts of the discussion henceforth may read like the transcript of a Primitive Methodist rural camp meeting – as we 'get into the power', as their preachers used to say.

Here is an extended quotation from one of the best known agricultural labourers of his time, illustrating how class hostility was enunciated in biblical language. 'Good God,' wrote George Loveless from Tolpuddle in 1837,

> what hypocrisy and deceit . . . the most cruel, the most unjust, the most atrocious deeds are committed and carried on under the cloak of religion! If I had not learnt what religion meant, such practices [as transportation, or the New Poor Law] would make me detest and abhor the very name. And yet, strange as it may appear, those hypocrites who pretend to be so scrupulous, that rather than submit to have their most holy religion endangered, they would starve hard-working, honest husbands and fathers, and who have solemnly pronounced, 'What God hath joined together, let no man put asunder', are some of the first to separate man and wife, to send some to banishment, and others to poor-law prisons; to oppress the fatherless and widow. From all such religion as this, 'Good Lord deliver us!' . . . It is indelibly fixed in my mind, that labour is ill-rewarded in consequence of a few tyrannizing over the millions; and that through their oppression thousands are now working in chains on the roads, abused by the overseers . . . and punished by the flagellator; young, and once strong, able men, now emaciated and worn almost to skeletons . . . the groans and cries of the labourers ere long will bring down vengeance on the heads of those who have been, and are still, the authors of so much misery. I believe that nothing will ever be done to relieve the distress of the working classes, unless they take it into their own hands . . . How long will it be, ere they [the great men of England] will cease to grind to the dust, trample under foot, and tread down as the mire of the streets, the hard-working and industrious labourer? How long will it be ere they will cease to 'join house to house, and field to field, until there is no place'; to oppress the hireling in his wages, and to keep back by fraud that to which he is so justly entitled? When will they attempt to raise the working man to that scale in society to which he can lay claim from his utility? Never – no never, will (with a few honourable exceptions) the rich and the great devise means to alleviate the distress, and remove the misery felt by the working men of England. What then is to be done? Why, the labouring classes must do it themselves, or it will

Holland, *Paupers and Pig Killers; the Diary of William Holland, a Somerset Parson, 1799–1818* (Gloucester, 1984); Rev. John Skinner, *Journal of a Somerset Rector, 1803–1834* (Oxford, 1985 edn).

for ever be left undone; the laws of reason and justice demands their doing it. Labour is the poor man's property, from which all protection is withheld. Has not then the working man as much right to preserve and protect his labour as the rich man has his capital?

But I am told that the working man ought to remain still and let their cause work its way – 'that God in his good time will bring it about for him'. However, this is not my creed; I believe that God works by means and men, and that he expects every man who feels an interest in the subject to take an active part in bringing about and hastening on so important a period. Under such an impression, I would call upon every working man in England, and especially the agricultural labourers, who appear to be the lowest, degraded and the least active, to shake off that supineness and indifference to their interests, which leaves them in the situation of slaves, for no longer can they live by the sweat of their brow . . . the working classes of Britain . . . will accomplish their own salvation.[44]

This passage is worth citing at length, as it captures many aspects of the thinking of Loveless's class, often repeated elsewhere. It is by no means exceptional for its biblical and religious features – more florid and persistent biblical language can be found emanating from the National Agricultural Labourers' Union (NALU) or the Amalgamated Labour League. Even so, it contains at least six biblical references that are easily recognisable, and probably more.[45] One also sees the influence of the Book of Common Prayer – 'Good Lord deliver us'. The rhetoric itself is immediately biblical: the recurring 'How long will it be . . .' for example, that was to become part of the phenomenal charismatic repertoire of some rural union leaders. Some phrases are almost direct quotation: 'to oppress the fatherless and widow'; or to 'join house to house, and field to field, until there is no place', taken from Isaiah: 'Woe unto them that join house to house, that lay field to field, till there be no place'; this was a recurring passage with agricultural workers and unionists throughout the nineteenth century, with its obvious attack on engrossing.[46] It was also used to similar effect in Wales. And its succeeding passage in Isaiah had its appeal too, with its talk of

many houses shall be desolate, even great and fair, without inhabitant . . . And the harp, and the viol, the tabret, the pipe, and wine, are in their feasts: but they regard not the work of the LORD, neither consider the

[44] G. Loveless, *The Victims of Whiggery* (London, 1837), pp. 25–6, 31–2.

[45] Zechariah 7:10; Isaiah 5:8; Isaiah 10:6: James 5:4; Malachi 3:5; Genesis 3:19.

[46] Buckmaster, *A Village Politican*, p. 40, recalled that 'The landlords and some of the farmers were prayed for by name. Cursed is he who removeth his neighbour's landmark, and oppresseth the poor and needy, and joineth land to land, and stoppeth footpaths; these sentences always met with hearty amens'.

operation of his hands. Therefore my people are gone into captivity . . . their honourable men are famished, and their multitude dried up with thirst. Therefore hell hath enlarged herself, and opened her mouth without measure . . . their glory . . . and their pomp . . . shall descend into it. And the mean man shall be brought down, and the mighty man shall be humbled . . . Therefore as the fire devoureth the stubble, and the flame consumeth the chaff, so their root shall be as rottenness, and their blossom shall go up as dust.[47]

Another recurring theme was that of the subjected children of Israel, needing to be led, and of deliverance and the Promised Land. Thus Joseph Arch – by the time we reached Wellesbourne:

I mounted an old pig-stool, and in the flickering light of the lanterns I saw the earnest upturned faces of these poor brothers of mine – faces gaunt with hunger and pinched with want – all looking towards me and ready to listen to the words, that would fall from my lips. These white slaves of England stood there with the darkness all about them, like the Children of Israel waiting for someone to lead them out of the land of Egypt.[48]

As a delegate put it to an 1870s union meeting, 'Sir, this be a blessed day: this ere Union be the Moses to lead us poor men up out o' Egypt'.[49] (And note the habit of deference, even here.) There were plenty who took Arch to be that Moses, including himself, leading the way to 'temporal salvation', as the common phrase was.[50]

During the ferocious lock-out of 1874 the National Union published a card consisting of Old Testament texts to encourage followers. The contents illustrate how a literal biblical interpretation was used, and indicate further the social sentiments of the class:

From the farm labourers of Christian England to their arch-enemies, Ellicott,[51] Stradbroke, Rutland, Bristol, Walsingham, North, Salisbury and company.

'Behold the hire of the labourers who have reaped your fields which is of you kept back by fraud, crieth: and the cries of them which have reaped are entered into the ears of the Lord Sabaoth.' 'Ye have lived in pleasure on the earth and have been wanton, ye have condemned and killed the just.' 'I will come near to you to judgement, and I will be a swift witness against those that oppress the hireling in his wages, saith the Lord.' 'Hear, O ye heads of Jacob, and ye princes of the house of Israel. Is it not for you to know judgement, who hate the good and love the evil?'

---

[47] Isaiah 5:8–24.
[48] Arch, *Autobiography*, p. 43.
[49] Cited in Newby, *Deferential Worker*, p. 67.
[50] See N. Scotland, *Methodism and the Revolt of the Field: A Study of the Methodist Contribution to Trade Unionism in East Anglia, 1872–96* (Gloucester, 1981), p. 35.
[51] The Bishop of Gloucester and Bristol.

'Hear this, O ye that swallow up the needy, even to make the poor of the land to fail, that ye may buy the poor for silver, and the needy for a pair of shoes.' 'Forasmuch, therefore, as your treading is upon the poor, and ye shall take from him burdens of wheat, ye have built houses of hewn stone, but ye shall not dwell in them; ye have planted pleasant vineyards, but ye shall not drink of them. For I know your manifold transgressions, and your mighty sins, afflicting the just, taking bribes, and turning aside the poor from their right.' 'Woe unto him that buildeth his house by unrighteousness and his chambers by wrong, that useth his neighbour's services without wages, and giveth him not for his work.' . . . 'Moreover the profit of the earth is for all.'[52]

In the context of the labourer-farmer dispute at hand, it was natural that citations mentioning wages would figure prominently. Many other passages were of 'the labourer is worthy of his hire' type; most speak of social injustice, greed, embezzlement of land, cruelty to the poor and needy. Most are from the Old Testament. However, there appear to be differences in the passages chosen by the rural proletariat and those picked by some other occupational groups, and it may be that the rural labourers' choices were less radical. We know that in the Midlands farm labourers lived in the same villages as industrial workers, like framework knitters or miners; they often took up frame work, and the framework knitters in large numbers joined rural poaching gangs.[53] There must have been considerable interaction between them and agricultural labourers. As far as one can tell, however, the extreme radicalism of biblical reference among the framework knitters did not as a general rule spread to the farm labourers, unless one considers the above quotations very radical. Even so, one is probably in a different biblical referential world among the depressed village hosiery workers, with their biblical language of secret oaths and violent upheaval, like for example the commonly used Ninety-Fourth Psalm:

O Lord God, to whom vengeance belongeth . . . shew thyself . . . Lord, how long shall the wicked, how long shall the wicked triumph? How long shall they utter and speak hard things? and all the workers of iniquity boast themselves? They break in pieces thy people, O Lord, and afflict thine heritage. They slay the widow and the stranger, they murder the fatherless . . . Who will rise up for me against the evildoers? . . . who will stand up for me against the workers of iniquity?

Or there was the passage from Ezekiel:

---

[52] Cited in Scotland, *Methodism and the Revolt of the Field*, p. 93.
[53] See e.g. *Select Committee on the Framework Knitters Petition*, V (1845), pp. 11 and 55.

> And thou, profane wicked prince of Israel, whose day is come, when
> iniquity shall have an end. Thus saith the lord GOD; Remove the
> diadem, and take off the crown . . . exalt him that is low, and abase him
> that is high. I will overturn, overturn, overturn it: and it shall be no more
> . . . The sword, the sword is drawn: for the slaughter it is furbished.[54]

Secularisation clearly diminished the language of radicalism, and its
cathartic potential, even if it allowed it to be more clearly focused.
Parts of even these passages were certainly used by agricultural
labourers, but selectively, and as far as I am aware not the more
radical and violent sentences. Class conflict in the rural south was
intense, more so than in northern country areas, and it periodically
flared into the open buttressed by historically backward looking
notions of a moral economy, and biblical literalism. Yet its major
collective and public expressions were usually moderate and orderly.
This was largely true of price riots, the 'Bread or Blood' agitation,
Swing, the 1870s, or 1923. Arch was careful to safeguard the NALU
from any charges of violence. Even when violence was used in a
personal, surreptitious form, with the frequent vicious animal maiming, arson or occasional property destruction, it was not usually
directed against the individual person. In this it differed from the
situation found in the 'peasant' smallholding regions of Ireland, where
issues of access to land and tenant right were often associated with
more openly violent means.[55] Private attacks on Poor Law Guardians
and relieving officers were exceptions to this in England and Wales.
Following my title, I shall not discuss rural protest actions, questions
of agency, or the institutional forms of agricultural unionism and
other such organisation. These extremely important and revealing
manifestations of class attitudes have been very well dealt with by
others, and in a way which supports my argument. Even putting
aside such actions, however, one is still struck by the evidence of
prevailing social discord, and an accompanying language of incipient
conflict. This is especially true of the south and east from the early
nineteenth century. The condemnation of large farmers and landlords
– the latter described as the parasitic or burglar class[56] – was so
frequently made, even by teetotal Primitive Methodists priding

---

[54] Ezekiel, 22:25–8. For brief discussion of the biblical radicalism of textile workers
and perhaps miners, see E.P. Thompson, *The Making of the English Working Class*
(London, 1963, Harmondsworth, 1975 edn), pp. 431, 559–60.

[55] On Ireland, S. Clark and J.S. Donnelly (eds) *Irish Peasants: Violence and Political
Unrest, 1780–1914* (Manchester, 1983); also my forthcoming edition of A. Somerville,
Letters from Ireland During the Famine of 1847 (1992).

[56] E.g. by Buckmaster, *Village Politician*, pp. 168–9.

themselves on their respectability, that the claim that farm labourers always had a strong sense of identity with and loyalty to their employers seems insupportable. Class as a sentiment and a concept was certainly not irrelevant to the countryside. The term was also abundantly used at the time to describe the agricultural workers as a group, as one of the constituent parts of the 'working classes', and then, by the 1830s and 1840s, of the 'working class'.[57]

In all the lowland areas, by the mid-nineteenth century, a strong sense of occupational and labour identity was apparent. There was also marked occupational endogamy within labouring families. This was less apparent in upland small-farm regions, with their often closer ties of farmers and workers. However, aspects like these coincided with attitudes tending to fragment the labouring poor: considerable attachment to place, and local exclusivity and xenophobia; a longer-term suspicion towards outsiders reinforced by the same economic insecurities which had fostered social ill will; and a conservative insistence upon welfare expedients based on the parish, which were held to as an historically tested resort.

These last factors added to the problems arising from the isolating nature of work, and minimised the propensity of this class to combine together. They had important implications for local social relations. The immediate labour market was the parish, in which married labourers usually looked for most of their work. Parochial settlement contributed to this. Priority in employment commonly went to those who were legally settled, for otherwise they might become a burden on the parish rates.[58] In practice this was often true until the Union Chargeability Act and the irremovability legislation of the mid-nineteenth century. Unlike many trades, there was no institutionalised rural tramping system. Accepted migrant labour for many seasonal purposes, the mobility especially of unmarried farm

---

[57] See Armstrong, *Farmworkers*, p. 15, for a denial of differences of class identity. He is unable to provide serious documentation for this. The same claim for an identity of interests between farmers and farm labourers was made by Edmund Burke, *Thoughts and Details on Scarcity* (London, 1795, 1800 edn), p. 10: 'In the case of the farmer and the labourer, their interests are always the same'. Outside trivial idealisations of Victorian pastoralia (e.g. Mary Mitford, *Our Village* (nd, Oxford, 1982 edn), pp. 1ff), this view is not often found. The use of the plural term 'working classes' in the first few decades of the nineteenth century is often mentioned – see e.g. G. Himmelfarb, *The Idea of Poverty* (London, 1984), pp. 15–16, 291ff. The most illuminating discussion was A. Briggs, 'The language of "Class" in early nineteenth-century England', in A. Briggs and J. Saville (eds) *Essays in Labour History* (London, 1960). On artistic attempts to deny the existence of class in the countryside, see Barrell, *The Dark Side of the Landscape.*

[58] I shall discuss this further in a future book on belonging and settlement.

servants, widespread non-resident poor relief, or the limited use of settlement certificates, were among the means which helped to obviate any stay-at-home incentives of parish settlement. Population turnover was certainly extensive. However, one can hardly read John Clare, Fred Kitchen, Thomas Bewick, and many others without becoming aware of an intense attachment to place, due to many factors beyond legal settlement, which was strongly complained about by political economists.[59] Workers' nicknames often went back for generations, building upon the fathers' and grandfathers' names.[60] It required local continuity in areas which were small-scale, even if beyond the parish, and certain types of local occupational communities, for this to occur.

The parish remained also a strong cultural focus among the labouring poor into the later nineteenth century. There were long-established reasons for this. Not only was the parish the effective unit for taxation, the administration of poor relief, payments in kind, and so on. It also made its impact through a multiplicity of local seasonal customs, the parochial festive calendar and its sources of patronage, the observance of the parish Saint's day, the friendly society festival, the various doleing and charity-based handouts endowed and unique to separate parishes, or the parish bounds perambulations at Rogationtide.[61] These were often reinforced by long-enduring local inter-parochial hostilities, which could ensure that one came to a muddy near-end if one stepped foot in the wrong direction without gang support. Such practices focused attention inwards, on the parish itself, rather than outwards, towards an identification with the general agricultural labouring class. This was one reason why class division was perceived in immediate terms, why social resentment was often literally parochial. It was intense for all that, if by 'class' one means an implicitly or explicitly conflictual sense of 'them' and 'us', based on hierarchic social and economic divisions. Some of the seasonal events, like Plough Monday, even legitimised their expression, at a specific time of the year, when deference would indeed crack up; although even then there were always the *disguises* of Hallowe'en, the

[59] See J. Barrell, *The Idea of Landscape and the Sense of Place, 1730–1840: An Approach to the Poetry of John Clare* (Cambridge, 1972); his 'Geographies of Hardy's Wessex', *Journal of Historical Geography* VIII (1982); Snell, *Annals of the Labouring Poor*, pp. 337–40.

[60] R. Heath, *The English Peasant* (London, 1893, Wakefield, 1978 edn), p. 96.

[61] For an account of one relic of parish perambulations, see C. Cox, 'Parish boundary markers and the decline of parish authority: a nineteenth-century Gloucestershire study', *Local Historian* 18 (1988): 58–64.

muddened, black-corked faces of the plough bullocks, stots or jacks, taking it out on certain people's gardens, porches and front doors.[62]

Accounts of this parochial sense of place abound. 'I went to the pub to meet the young men. They never talk ideas, it is always people with them. The church is the vicar – that kind of thing. They seem, well, hemmed in by the village itself.'[63] So we are told in Ronald Blythe's *Akenfield*. We have seen that there is much evidence for the circulation of ideas, particularly biblical ones, in an earlier period. But something of this *personalising* of class, defining it with regard to certain individuals, interpreting and recognising their behaviour in class terms, had long been apparent: in the anonymous letters, in the animal maiming, in arson attacks, in the issues of parish relief, maladministration of charities, in the building of Primitive Methodist, Baptist or Bible Christian chapels, in the defence of the commons and the condemnation of enclosure – itself usually a parochial occurrence, albeit tied to the wider and more remote system of rulership. The miniature welfare and governing systems of the parish were a quite sufficient background against which class feelings could develop; one can see this clearly in the bitter language of John Clare's lengthy poem 'The Parish: a Satire'.[64] Or there were the concerns of M.K. Ashby's father, centred on political matters within the village itself.[65] Or one recalls the frequent conflicts over representation on parish councils, with labourers pitted against farmers, 'every one considering it a fight between the farmer and the labourer', as one person put it. The Parish Councils were fought over much more hotly by labourers than were the Rural District Councils.[66] Later, one thinks of the Burston school strike. The early unions were themselves highly localised: hence for example the *Tolpuddle* martyrs.[67] The NALU and the Amalgamated Labour League both brought together a host of very small local associations. Other labour disputes were often lightning strikes by particular harvest gangs, poised at an advantageous seasonal moment – gangs comprising, like some of their Irish counterparts, very frequently just men from a certain village. These gangs would migrate in search of further work; that was

[62] Plough Monday was the first Monday after 6 January. For discussion see e.g. C. Hole, *A Dictionary of British Folk Customs* (London, 1978, Aylesbury, 1984 edn), pp. 238–9, 287, 297.

[63] R. Blythe, *Akenfield* (London, 1969, Harmondsworth, 1977 edn), p. 115.

[64] See J.W. Tibble and A. Tibble (eds), *John Clare, Selected Poems* (London, 1965).

[65] See M.K. Ashby, *Joseph Ashby of Tysoe, 1859–1919* (Cambridge, 1961).

[66] See R. Heath, 'The rural revolution', *Contemporary Review* (February 1895): 182–200.

[67] See J. Marlowe, *The Tolpuddle Martyrs* (London, 1971).

when other forms of conflict, based on insider–outsider position, could occur. It was not only at the county level that insults and hostile stereotypes abounded: the phenomenon was deeply ingrained parochially, giving rise to the dense variety of local proverbial insults, folkloric stories about the stupidity, cupidity, venality and so on of people from certain parishes. 'There is a nationality in districts as well as in countries,' wrote Robert Chambers,

> nay, the people living on different sides of a streamlet, or of the same hill, sometimes entertain prejudices against each other, not less virulent than those of the inhabitants of the different sides of the British Channel or the Pyrenees. This has given rise . . . to an infinite number of phrases, expressive of vituperation, obloquy, or contempt, which are applied to the inhabitants of various places by those whose lot it is to reside in the immediate vicinity.[68]

This local xenophobia seems often to have been strong, coupled as it was to a parochial sense of place, of belonging, the sense of local rights which entitled one to precedence over outsiders – as well as needing to be defended against larger farmers and gentry. In the rural context, the persistence of such xenophobia was inevitable when labour was in such abundant supply, when unemployment, cottage provision, difficulties in securing the means for marriage (let alone securing the disillusioned outmigrating women), were such problems.[69]

Wages were also a matter of local custom: both the money wage paid, and the very diverse payments in kind which often accompanied it. It was almost impossible for any national organisation to negotiate fixed increases or weekly sums, because of the disparate local hiring and payment systems in operation.[70] Work skills and practices too (as well as the dialect to describe them) were very localised, almost deliberately so, in part one suspects to exclude outsiders. There were for example a multitude of local billhook or shepherds' crook designs, adapted to the varied work practices of disparate regions.[71] And one will look in vain for standardised dress across different areas in nineteenth-century rural photographs. There were an abundance of

---

[68] Quoted in R.M. Dorson, *The British Folklorists: A History* (London, 1968), p. 131.

[69] See M. Strathern, *Kinship at the Core* (Cambridge, 1981); J. Robin, *Elmdon: Continuity and Change in a North-West Essex Village, 1861–1964* (Cambridge, 1980).

[70] E.H. Hunt, *Regional Wage Differentials in Britain, 1850–1914* (Oxford, 1973), pp. 19ff.

[71] J. Geraint Jenkins, *Life and Tradition in Rural Wales* (London, 1976), pp. 30–1, 52–3, 87; R. Brigden, *Agricultural Hand Tools* (Aylesbury, 1983), pp. 7–8; A. Ingram, *Shepherding Tools and Customs* (Aylesbury, 1977).

different hats, smocks, gaiters, waistcoats, and so on, which can often locate the photograph to a particular district. This was quite unlike the cloth-cap and suit of the urban working class in the inter-war period.

One may point also to the range of variously skilled farm proletarian occupations, the incidence of which also varied geographically: agricultural or farm labourer, carter, castrator, cattle man, clerk-bailiff, cottager, drover, farm servant, gardener, groom, ground keeper, horseman, pigman, husbandman, market gardener's labourer, seedsman, nurseryman, poultryman or woman, dairy maid and the different types of female farm servants, shepherd, steward or under-steward, sawyer, ploughman, or woodman – these are some which avoid more esoteric regional names. They often had their own distinctive occupational and regional insignia (manifest for example at hiring fairs, as described by Hardy, whose account of Gabriel Oak also showed the possible fluidity between them),[72] setting them apart to some extent from the others, as well as from the many other wholly or partially wage-dependent occupations of the labouring poor. Many of these occupations felt identity with others in the same line of skill locally. They also felt superior or inferior to other categories of country workmen, and tried to protect their skill status. The gradings and distinctions within the class, and the regional differences which existed, raise problems for discussion of the nature of social consciousness among the rural proletariat. However, people in most of these occupations would certainly have identified more with farmworkers than with large farmers or landlords.

The localised xenophobia of labouring parish society, and the divisions within the work-force, limit any argument for a full class consciousness of the agricultural proletariat. This geographical and occupational variety is a more significant limitation on class than any generalised sense of an agricultural interest, which embraced all rural classes in some mythical togetherness. That so-called agricultural interest has been emphasised by some historians who are sceptical of class differences; yet it existed predominantly in the minds and landlord propaganda of those with high political involvement. For the most relevant periods, especially the 1840s, it did not include the unenfranchised rural workers. The case remains to be made – with proper evidence from the class concerned – for rural workers in the eighteenth or nineteenth centuries seeing themselves as part of an

---

[72] Thomas Hardy, *Far From the Madding Crowd* (London, 1874).

agricultural interest, sharing an identity with landlords and farmers.[73] In 1884 Bisset cited a rural aristocrat using the term 'the whole agricultural interest'. He added:

> By the word *whole* here prefixed to agricultural interest, the noble lord makes the usual assumption that the agricultural interest comprehended the farmers and the labourers in the same sense as it comprehended the landlords – certainly a strong assumption, since an opinion has prevailed somewhat extensively that rent and profits, and rent and wages do not vary in a direct but in an inverse ratio.

His mocking tone with regard to this concept was well justified.[74] Farm labourers as a body did not even support that most quintessential concern of the agricultural interest: Corn Law protectionism. They were much more sympathetic to arguments like Alexander Somerville's, that artificially inflated prices were an immoral expedient to secure high rents for a parasitic class, at the expense of agricultural investment, longer-term leases, high employment and their own real wages.[75]

One should draw attention to diversity among the labouring poor. But overall this is probably a minor qualification. On the important social issues, there was near unity of sentiment. So let me end on a note of moral-force anti-pastoral, by recalling parts of the ballad in Charles Kingsley's *Yeast*. Although we move away from the language of the poor themselves, Kingsley captures well their class sentiments; his ballad is extremely close in feeling to the interviews reported from the south-west by Somerville. His candour made him very unpopular in many polite circles, and led the subscription-conscious editor of *Fraser's Magazine* (which was popular among the rural gentry) to grind the instalments of *Yeast* to a hurried and discrete end.[76] Contrary to all Kingsley's interests, he stressed how the pessimistic evidence in parliamentary Blue Books was supported by his own experience of rural life. There are no water babies here, no pre-political poor in evidence:

---

[73] The notion is much used by Armstrong, *Farmworkers*, e.g. pp. 15, 28, 58, 85, 132, 251; yet he is unable to justify it in the manner requested here. He admits that in the 1890s it 'came to nothing' (p. 132).

[74] A. Bisset, *Notes on the Anti-Corn Law Struggle* (1884), p. 157.

[75] Somerville, *Whistler at the Plough*; and see A. Prentice, *History of the Anti-Corn Law League* (London, 1853, 2nd edn. 1968), pp. 381–2, quoting from a labourers' meeting against the Corn Laws.

[76] On the problems Kingsley had with *Yeast*, see B. Colloms, *Charles Kingsley* (London, 1975), pp. 98–109.

The social outlook of the rural proletariat in England and Wales

A poacher's widow sat sighing
On the side of the white chalk bank,
Where under the gloomy fir-woods
One spot in the ley throve rank.

She watched a long tuft of clover,
Where rabbit or hare never ran;
For its black sour haulm covered over
The blood of a murdered man.

She thought of the dark plantation,
And the hares and her husband's blood,
And the voice of her indignation
Rose up to the throne of God.

I am long past wailing and whining –
I have wept too much in my life:
I've had twenty years of pining
As an English labourer's wife.

A labourer in Christian England,
Where they cant of a Saviour's name,
And yet waste men's lives like the vermin's
For a few more brace of game.

There's blood on your new foreign shrubs, squire;
There's blood on your pointer's feet;
There's blood on the game you sell, squire,
And there's blood on the game you eat!

You have sold the labouring man, squire,
Body and soul to shame,
To pay for your seat in the House, squire,
And to pay for the feed of your game.

You made him a poacher yourself, squire,
When you'd give neither work nor meat;
And your barley-fed hares robbed the garden
At our starving children's feet;

When packed in one reeking chamber,
Man, maid, mother, and little ones lay;
While the rain pattered in on the rotting bride-bed,
And the walls let in the day;

When we lay in the burning fever
On the mud of the cold clay floor,
Till you parted us all for three months, squire,
At the cursed workhouse door.

We quarrelled like brutes, and who wonders?
What self-respect could we keep,
Worse housed than your hacks and your pointers,
Worse fed than your hogs and your sheep?

Our daughters with base-born babies
Have wandered away in their shame;
If your misses had slept, squire, where they did,
Your misses might do the same.

Can your lady patch hearts that are breaking
With handfuls of coals and rice,
Or by dealing out flannel and sheeting
A little below cost price?

You may tire of the gaol and the workhouse,
And take to allotments and schools,
But you've run up a debt that will never
Be repaid us by penny-club rules . . .

She looked at the tuft of clover,
And wept till her heart grew light;
And at last, when her passion was over,
Went wandering into the night.[77]

Finally wandering, one should add, like the countless farm workers, who with very good cause, turned their backs on the countryside during this period, taking their experience of rural class relations with them.[78]

Acknowledgements

I am grateful to Huw Beynon, Michael Bush, Andrew Charlesworth, Robert Colls, Barry Reay and David Wise for their comments.

[77] C. Kingsley, *Yeast*, (London, 1851, 1902 edn), pp. 147–9.
[78] See M. Chase, *The People's Farm: English Radical Agrarianism, 1775–1840* (Oxford, 1988).

CHAPTER TEN
Order, class and the urban poor

Stuart Woolf

European University Institute and Essex University

'Social order' and 'class' are unfashionable terms nowadays. They have little place in the brave new world that trumpets its rupture with the past, in beliefs as much as in practices. As always, the appearance belies the substance, for the critique of order and class in their more reified forms had been gaining impetus for some time before the 1960s. It is evident that they may be too broad as social categories for many purposes of historical analysis (or may be deployed in too clumsy or mechanistic a manner). But to dismiss them as useless or systematically distortive is equally unsatisfactory. For order and class reflect, in different periods and places, with varying degrees of intensity, significant and at times dominant modes of thought, revealed through the discourse of language, comportment, symbols and rituals. It is a truism that any order or class – all three of the 'estates', for example, or the middle or working classes – will encompass a wide range of economic conditions and social status. But such disparities do not negate the subjective identification of the individual group with an order or class. Indeed, it is tempting to argue that those whose economic fragility made their membership of an order or class most precarious – such as the *hobereaux* of eighteenth-century France or the penniless clerks of Victorian England – were the most vociferous in its affirmation. Gramsci (also out of fashion nowadays), with his concept of hegemony, can still offer powerful insights into the capacity of concepts such as order and class to retain allegiance, even against the evidence of apparent reality, over long periods in different historical contexts.

As always with social categories, the difficulties in discussing the composition of an order or a class become the more apparent the closer one approaches its confines. No historian would deny that a seventeenth-century duke belonged to the noble estate or an ordained canon to the ecclesiastical order, as there is no contradiction between their discourse and our observation of the reality of their circumstances. What is meant by membership of an order appears to be unequivocal in the language of those who claimed to belong to a privileged body. But the evidence of contemporary practice is far more ambiguous. The tonsured cleric in sixteenth-century France, for example, could claim to belong to the ecclesiastical order, with all the legal privileges of benefit of clergy, while to all effects and purposes remaining a layman. The rich peasant or successful merchant consolidated his local reputation as a landowning *coq de village* when the less successful and poorer members of the village community began to refer to him as 'esquire', *seigneur* or even *nobile*. Through stealthy encroachment or improper appropriation of a title, a status, a life-style, through exploitation of symbolic practices, a layman could become a clergyman, an unprivileged subject could claim status as a noble. By the convocation of the French estates general in 1788, it proved difficult and painful in the extreme to define who had the right to sit in the noble estate, according to criteria which had become anachronistic through their disuse since the last convocation of 1614.

For the historian, as for the contemporary, it is difficult to mark the point at which the practice justified the discourse, when an acquired identity as a gentleman or *seigneur* was sufficiently accepted by the surrounding society that its transmission and inheritance became a reality. Where is the line drawn and the boundary of the order sealed off? It is evident that analogous problems are raised about class, as, for example, in the slightly tired debate about where to place artisans and shopkeepers.

Such questions are far from inappropriate in a discussion of the poor, where the ambiguities between practice and discourse have always been marked. In essence, the contrast between the two can be described as one between economic practice and social perception. Poverty was a recurrent economic reality experienced by a large proportion of the labouring classes in all European societies in all periods. To be poor did not mean being different from others, precisely because poverty was such a normal condition. To be described as being poor, on the other hand, was perceived as something distinctive by all parties.

Jeremy Bentham captured admirably the economic reality of poverty as the condition of the life course and family cycle of the vast majority of the population:

> Poverty is the state of everyone who, in order to obtain *subsistence*, is
> forced to have recourse to *labour*. Indigence is the state of him who, being
> destitute of property . . . is at the same time either *unable to labour*, or
> unable, even for labour, to procure the supply of which he happens thus
> to be in want.[1]

By the eighteenth-century, if not earlier, contemporaries certainly
understood this symbiotic relationship between poverty and the life
pattern of the 'most numerous and useful class', whether rural or
urban, peasants or practitioners of the mechanical arts. All individuals
and families without material reserves, such as property or savings,
were dependent on manual work for their subsistence, and hence
were vulnerable to and almost always experienced Bentham's indigence at some point in their life. Patrick Joyce has written recently of
the variety of historical meanings of work.[2] It would be as valid to
discuss the historical meanings of being out of work. For access to
the labour market was the crucial frontier. To be on the wrong side
of that frontier made (and makes) poverty inescapable, albeit at
differing levels of indigence and destitution, dependent on family
circumstances, the length of the period of unemployment, institutional arrangements, the solidarity of local social relations, and so
on.

Precisely because poverty was a recurrent condition, it is possible
to classify and quantify the poor, as Gutton and Pullan have done, in
structural and conjunctural, or concentric circles of poverty, ranging
from the 4–8 per cent core of urban populations in early modern
Europe to the 50–70 per cent at times of trade stoppages.[3] Both cause
and consequence of poverty, the average household size of property-
less labouring families, especially but not exclusively in the cities, was
small, with late age at marriage, high rates of infant mortality or
abandonment, and early departure of children from the household.
Such demographic facts, combined with the structural dependence of
wage levels on age and gender, ensured recurrent pressure on
subsistence levels. With low wages for children and the aged, with
women paid far less than their male peers, even able-bodied parents
at the height of their earning capacities in their thirties and forties
easily fell into difficulties because of the burden of dependent infants

---

[1] Quoted in J.R. Poynter, *Society and Pauperism: English Ideas on Poor Relief. 1795–1834* (London, 1969), p. 119.

[2] P. Joyce (ed.) *The Historical Meanings of Work* (Cambridge, 1987).

[3] J.P. Gutton, *La Société et les pauvres: l'exemple de la généralité de Lyon 1534–1789* (Paris, 1971), p. 53; B.S. Pullan, 'Poveri, mendicanti e vagabondi (secoli XIV–XVII)', in *Storia d'Italia. Annali. I. Dal Feudalesimo al Capitalismo* (Turin, 1978), pp. 988–97.

and grandparents. Individuals and families moreover were more likely to slide into a condition of poverty during longer or shorter periods of unemployment or underemployment. And such economic poverty was a fact of life not just in the pre-industrial period, but – as Keyssar has recently documented for Massachusetts[4] – also in fully industrialised societies.

How relevant are such well-established facts about the reality of poverty and the causes of pauperisation to discussions of order and class?

The doyen of theorists of orders, the jurist Charles Loyseau, writing in the early seventeenth-century, represented the third estate in hierarchical manner in his *Traité des ordres et simples dignitez*. His main concern was to rank the social categories with which he was familiar, such as men of letters, financiers, lawyers and merchants. Beneath them were what we can describe as the labouring classes. As William Sewell has argued, the essential criterion Loyseau employed was the dichotomy between what he called 'art' and 'labour'.[5] Art, by which were understood activities requiring intelligence, skill, training and rules, was associated with honour; labour, with its connotations of fatigue, lack of skills and rules, carried overtones of degradation. Within the corpus of mechanical arts, the ranking was dependent on the degree of manual input. At the very bottom was unskilled labour: 'And for all the more reason those who exercise neither crafts nor commerce, and who gain their livelihood with the labour of their arms . . . are the vilest of the *menu peuple*. For there is no occupation so bad as no occupation at all'.[6] A mere labourer could earn, but precisely because he was unable to demonstrate any training or skill, he was regarded as without a trade, an occupation. He was, as Sewell notes, customarily regarded as *sans état* (not belonging to an estate). We can add, he might also be *sans aveu* (without a guarantor), which was a worse and potentially more dangerous condition, as inability to produce oral of written evidence of one's identity meant suspicion, sometimes leading to accusation, expulsion or imprisonment.

It would be ingenuous to accept Loyseau's treatise as a description

---

[4] A. Keyssar, *Out of Work: The First Century of Unemployment in Massachusetts* (Cambridge, 1986).

[5] W.H. Sewell, *Work and Revolution in France: The Language of Labor from the Old Regime to 1848* (Cambridge, 1980), pp. 22–5.

[6] Quoted in Sewell, *Work and Revolution*, p. 24. Loyseau's *Traité* was first published in 1610.

of the real world. But few would dispute that it constituted a particularly informative example of how contemporaries perceived *ancien régime* society as corporately structured. Like the day-labourers, everyone outside a corporation – such as a trade guild or a confraternity – was considered to be of lower social status.

The crucial quality at the basis of all classifications of corporate membership and hierarchy within the third estate was 'skill', however defined. Skill in the twentieth-century sense of the practice of formally learned technical knowledge and expertise in a stage in the process of production was not always the case in the *ancien régime*, where the technical skills might be (and usually were) of an extremely elementary nature. More relevant (and in this respect similar to the present day) was the professional or publicly acknowledged qualification, which provided legitimate title to property in skills – often the only property of labouring men. Skill, as Sonenscher, Kaplan and Rule have recently argued, was an attribute of the worker, as much as (indeed usually more than) the quality of the work.[7] For our purposes, it is important to note that possession of a skill acted as the fundamental distinction in at least three respects. In economic terms, it determined wage levels, usually with a sharp divide between the skilled and unskilled. In terms of social relations, it defined status. In terms of social reproduction, it acted as a highly selective filter, impeding passage to a superior level of skill except for the small minority favoured by birth, marriage or protection.

The corollary was that those without a skill, or outside corporate organisation, were economically condemned to low levels of earnings, with recurrent falls into a condition of indigence. Equally, they were considered as socially inferior, the breeding ground of the poor, dependent on assistance and potentially dangerous.

There are always many ways of interpreting the past: I would suggest that in these *ancien régime* societies whose self-perception placed such stress on corporate organisation, the profundity of the divide between skill and lack of skill offers a key to understanding the insistent concern of those without skills, or whose skills were at risk, to create or consolidate their own associative structures. The tendency towards endogamous remarriage of widows in specific groups of

---

[7] M. Sonenscher, 'Mythical work: workshop production and the *compagnonnages* of eighteenth-century France', in Joyce (ed.) *Historical Meanings*; S.L. Kaplan, 'Social classification and representation in the corporate world of eighteenth-century France: Turgot's "Carnival"', in S.L. Kaplan and C.J. Koepp (eds) *Work in France* (Ithaca-London, 1986); J. Rule, 'The property of skill in the period of manufacture', in Joyce (ed.), *Historical Meanings*.

specialised workers, such as wine-producers in the countryside or some artisan trades in the towns, can be explained as a means of retaining identity or effective (as distinct from legal) membership in the corporate structure. The *compagnonnages*, recently discussed by Sonenscher, with their rituals, ceremonies and procedures derived from those of the trade confraternities and law courts, were structured as a means of access to the labour and product markets of the skilled by those who were excluded. Among the 'inferior' occupational groups of labourers, some were more effective than others in organising themselves as a closed shop – like the water carriers or the notorious dock-workers of all great cities. The handicapped, crippled and blind people of Rome not only set themselves up as a formally structured association of beggars, but also were so recognised. The underworld of vagabonds, cheats and thieves was always portrayed as organised in sophisticated, hierarchical corporative structures, from Teseo Pini in the late fifteenth century to Balzac or Dickens in the nineteenth century. Mutual aid societies replicated in many respects the assistential-religious functions of the guilds and confraternities of earlier periods.

Such examples can be interpreted as indicative of a widespread need to achieve a corporate identity. They range across a broad spectrum of the social structures of the *ancien régime*, from groups with recognised skills to the outcasts. In this, they are faithful to the reality of these societies. For even in towns where the guilds and confraternities were most developed and during periods of their greatest power, the majority of the population always lived outside or at the margins of such corporative structures. The rural migrants, the casually employed, the domestic servants, the outworkers employed by the guilds, not to speak of most women and children, were excluded. Hence, as individuals or as families or as a group, where possible they tried to negotiate social recognition by utilisation of informal networks, such as kin or neighbourhood, or formalised associations, like *compagnonnages*. We know very little about the mechanisms of such transactions or their interrelationships. How effective, for example, was the protection provided in reality (as distinct from the statutes) for dependent members of a family whose head belonged to a guild? Should membership of a *compagnonnage*, peripatetic by definition, be understood as a definitive alternative to the potential network of a domiciled family? Even if the family itself is conceived of as an associative structure mediating aid to its individual members, it seems evident that it was an inadequate substitute for the formal corporate organisation for those without skills or in danger of losing their property in skill. Unless the barrier could be passed and social recognition obtained, with all its associated benefits of access to the labour market, the excluded would remain poor and transmit their poverty across generations. In societies enveloped in the social language of corporations, institutional imitation (whether realistic or parodic) would appear to have been regarded as a necessary prerequisite.

Such imitation, if a necessary prerequisite, was usually inadequate. In economies with structural imbalances between labour supply and regular employment, the ability of individuals to forge a social identity depended not just on their participation and position within some acknowledged network, but on a variety of other contexts: within some, they could assert their place (such as through demonstrations of physical prowess or adaptability to work conditions), over others they were wholly without control (such as cyclical trade interruptions, bad weather or illness).

Hitherto my discussion has related to the social location of the unskilled and to their expedients to counter absence of recognition by others. But at the level of individual and family, the economic realities of changing markets and processes of production could also remove the apparently greater security of those with property in skill, and recurrently did so. Shifts in market demand and changes in the organisation or technology of production periodically weakened or destroyed the protection attributed to guilds or similar corporations. Throughout western and central Europe, at one or another moment, members of recognised guilds or trade associations fell into a condition of material poverty, caused not only by the dilution or deskilling to which the historians of early industrialisation point, but also for instance by international competition. The artisans responded by defensive attempts to protect their livelihood: seventeenth-century Venetian artisans contemporaneously belonged to more than one guild; early-nineteenth-century English skilled workers insisted on custom or restriction of entry into the trade.[8]

The contrast between economic reality and perception of social identity is revealed perhaps more clearly in the case of the skilled workers in decline. The social vocabulary that expressed the contradiction between practice and discourse is evident in the language and concept of the 'shamefaced poor', a terminology ('*pauvres honteux*', '*poveri vergognosi*', etc.) to be found in every western society. The fact that such a category should have been invented and that it aroused

[8] R.T. Rapp, *Industry and Economic Decline in Seventeenth-Century Venice* (Cambridge, Mass., 1976); Rule, 'Property of skill'; R. Gray, 'The language of factory reform in Britain *c.* 1830–1860', in Joyce (ed.) *Historical Meanings*.

widespread debate and organisational efforts in the early modern period suggests how social labels can influence social behaviour. (Traces have survived into the twentieth century in the various charities for decayed gentlefolk.) The shamefaced, particularly in the sixteenth and seventeenth centuries, generated a vast contemporary literature, which subsequently has caused considerable confusion and mystification through concentrating attention on spectacular examples of lapsed gentility, like poor nobles or Shakespeare's merchant Antonio of Venice. In reality, at least by the eighteenth century, craftsmen and tradesmen constituted a substantial majority of those identified and assisted as the shamefaced poor.

It is significant that, over many centuries, European urban society should have considered this particular category of poor so important as to merit the creation of special institutional arrangements outside the guilds and confraternities. For the extremely discreet provision of assistance for the shamefaced was designed specifically to protect the social identity of those whose skills or position were considered to provide a superior rank in the ordering of society by hiding the reality of their economic distress from the community. Nor is it surprising, given the inextricable economic and social interdependence between family, community and market, that an important identifying sign of such poverty, which justified assistance, was visible consumption. Clothing, perhaps more than food, was symbolic of status. It might vary in quality and luxury according to the grade of social relationships, but precisely because of its visibility outside (and even within) the home, clothing was emblematic of the determination to hide the evidence of poverty.

As well as an economic reality, poverty, then, must equally be understood as a social construct, which was seen as such both by the poor and the non-poor. Poverty has always incorporated a cluster of values, which have varied over time, but have always conditioned social responses. It is for these reasons that welfare specialists have long insisted that poverty must be understood as a relative concept, relative that is to the expectations of the particular society.

In the present century, because of the explicit recognition of the intrinsic link between employment and avoidance of poverty, the language of the debate (and the welfare provisions that have come out of it) has been structured around the concept of the right to work.[9]

[9] J.A. Garraty, *Unemployment in History: Economic Thought and Public Policy* (New York, 1978).

192

While moral and religious affirmations of such a belief can be traced over many centuries, in socio-political terms the idea is relatively recent, and historically identifiable with the French Revolution. The right to work, *liberté de travail*, was seen by the early revolutionaries as a problem of government: deregulation of the market, it was assumed, would resolve the material problem of poverty by making it possible for all to work. But, as Fernand Tanghe has pointed out, [10] this did not imply a subjective right of the individual to employment (*droit de travail*), a claim made only with the 1848 revolution. At the individual and family level, employment remained a private concern, not the responsibility of the public authorities, except in the occasional, highly limited and temporary form of public works during moments of particularly widespread unemployment. But recognition that unemployment was not necessarily evidence of moral failures (such as idleness or sin) always implied the obligation of some form of assistance, whether charity or (over the past century) welfare.

Charity can be defined as the institutionalisation of the social construct of poverty. It was regulated by a symbolic dialogue of comportment tacitly accepted by both sides. Its basis was insecurity, the necessary condition to create a material dependence on others. The social relationships that provided the context of charity were regulated through a broad spectrum of rules affecting both institutions and individuals, all of which incorporated three specific assumptions. The first is the invasion of privacy. Individuals applying for assistance (except for the shamefaced) were forced to do so publicly, whether in person (such as physical presence at the soup kitchen) or in writing (filling in a form); and their applications were subject to controls by extraneous parties to ensure the correspondence of the physical and moral condition of the pauper and his family to the social and cultural expectations of the donors or their institutional representatives. The second assumption was a model of comportment, which combined deference, respect and gratitude. Finally specific forms of comportment were discouraged and usually repressed, because they put at risk, through their very extremism, the previous two assumptions. Thus both vagrancy and tramping, on the one hand, and unregulated begging and Christian alms, on the other, were unacceptable because they denied the condition of individual identification that was at the core of the charitable nexus.

Over many centuries charity usually functioned effectively. The

---

[10] F. Tanghe, *Sociale Grondrechten tussen Armoede en Mensenrechten* (Antwerp, 1986–7).

explanation of this somewhat surprising fact needs to be sought in the operation of cultural norms and their limits, whether these be related to order or class. It can be argued cogently that to derive the definition of the poor from the operations of charitable and relief institutions is too restrictive. In terms of historical analysis, it subordinates the poor within the constraints of an excessively consensual model of society, whereas the economic realities of poverty point towards a broader concept of the poor as opposed to the rich, which allows for notions of solidarity.

I would not wish to argue against the historical reality of solidarity or of conflict, both of which underlay forms of social consciousness. 'The labouring poor' was a term of universal currency not only as a description of economic reality, but also as a perception of the condition that identified and contrasted the majority of society to the 'others', the rich. Working people felt close to the poor precisely because poverty was a condition they had experienced or anticipated. It is difficult to explain in other terms the repeated gestures of solidarity, such as the protection of beggars from arrest, the fixing of popular prices in food riots and the multiple other acts and signs interpretable as recognition of a common lot.

Nevertheless the evidence of solidarity needs to be read alongside the defensive attitudes frequently adopted by working people towards the poor. The constant redefinition and revaluation of skills and work, the use of tradition and custom as means of excluding labourers and all those regarded as without property in skill, point to a separateness not only from the employers but also from the poor. The two attitudes, if superficially contradictory, were both coherent and not incompatible, as they depended on context and objective. But given the coexistence among the labouring poor of feelings of both solidarity and exclusion, it is important to consider the role of charity in counter-balancing solidarity. At least two levels can be identified. In practical terms, the institutional forms through which assistance was structured, by their very stress on individuals and families, separated the assisted poor from their peers. It would be interesting to know whether those on relief were among the demonstrators at moments of conflict, such as bread riots. At a broader, more ideological level, it can be argued that the values deemed by the elites central to the orderly functioning of society – the desirability of independence of the family, good behaviour, deference – were appropriated and put to their own uses by individuals and whole groups within the ranks of the labouring classes. Among the assisted poor, the rules of charity enjoined at least passive acceptance of such values. By the nineteenth century, if not earlier, independence, status and respectability were so deeply incorporated into the values of the skilled workers that they were explicitly opposed to the equally middle-class value of charity.

What, then, of shame? That shame cannot be separated from the social construct of poverty is evident in the term and concept of the shamefaced poor. The quality of shame lies in its association with public knowledge. The ample literature on the values of independence upheld by the working-class family of the later nineteenth century confirms the antipathy towards charity which was premissed in the sense of shame that derived from a publicly known dependence on institutional assistance. Historians agree about the appropriation by the labour aristocracy of some of the values of middle-class society (among others, status distinctions such as clothing, thrift, respectability), although they have tended to stress those elements that mark the distinctive individuality of the skilled workers, like refusal of deference. Common to capitalists and workers was respect for work, which in an age-old social vocabulary was contrasted to idleness (*fainéantise, ozio*). The *droit au travail* of Louis Blanc in 1848 already carried with it the corollary of the humiliation of dependence on poor relief. Blanc's socialism incorporated a strand of anticlericalism (critical also of Catholic charity) that ran deep in the French democratic tradition. But in Protestant societies like England or Scotland, where anticlericalism was not an issue, the shame of such dependence was still deepened by a sense of guilt.

Nevertheless, it is rash to assume that the values of the labour aristocracy in a limited and relatively short time-span were valid for all the labouring poor over far longer periods. It is reasonable to affirm that at some levels among the poor shame was always associated with charity, because of the religious-moral connotations of social rank. In this sense it was the direct consequence of the social construction of poverty by the non-poor. But the very breadth and depth of the category of the poor, deriving economically from its close identification with the labouring classes, and the vulnerability of those with property in skill or with limited material property, argues against any conclusion about social cohesion or homogeneity of values and comportment. Historians of labour increasingly question an undifferentiated working class based on the identification of class with solidarity and explore the varied, often contradictory sources and location of consciousness and codes of behaviour. Attitudes towards charity among the equally vast category of the poor similarly require more critical and open investigation.

Rather than assume that relief was always tainted with shame, it would be more profitable to enquire whether individuals and families, in their responses to conditions of poverty, made conscious use of charity as one of a range of resources. How individuals viewed charity may well have altered over their life course, partly because their objective needs changed. It is also plausible that attitudes were transformed as a result of direct personal experiences with charitable institutions, creating a sense of shame where initially none existed. Nevertheless, if charity implied shame for some, for others it needs to be viewed as a due anticipated and utilised in family strategies. To students of the moral community, expectation of relief and assistance as of right in particular circumstances will not sound novel. In this sense, the uses of charity need to be studied like other available networks (such as kin, neighbourhood, community, religion, etc.), bearing in mind the complexity and ambiguity of behaviour codes and practices of mutuality and solidarity habitually attributed to such networks.

It is evident that such an approach is fraught with difficulties. Take, for example, the language of the poor and its implications. Only in the late nineteenth century did the practice of individual case-studies by voluntary charities and subsequently state intervention generate detailed written evidence on a substantial scale that incorporated self-descriptions by the poor. Until then, statements about attitudes towards charity – even when noticed by the poor – are filtered through the language of the non-poor. Even when the poor leave a record, their language may be chosen to conform with the expectations of those whose assistance they seek. Deference, as Snell pointed out, may hide social bitterness.[11] I would suggest that the appropriate comportment demanded for recourse to charity – public expression of respect, gratitude, and also shame – may likewise have masked a more pragmatic approach by the individual and family.

Because of their deliberately generalised purpose, my propositions about the poor have treated the long period from the sixteenth to the nineteenth century as a continuum. To conclude, a remark seems appropriate about the relationship of the poor to the working class as mechanisation, the factory system and urbanisation gained pace in the nineteenth century.

The conflictual environment created by these capitalist developments was well depicted by Thomas Chalmers as early as the 1820s:

[11] See Snell, Chapter 9 in this volume.

In a manufacturing town . . . the poor and the wealthy stand more
disjointed from each other. It is true they often meet, but they meet more
on an arena of contest, than on a field where the patronage and custom of
the one party are met by the gratitude and good will of the other.[12]

Research in recent years has broadened our understanding of the
sources and location of consciousness alternative to the workplace,
such as family, gender, household, community, politics, pubs or
chapels.[13] We now understand far more about how the complexity
and multiplicity of these sources of class consciousness profoundly
modified the values of workers.

One of the consequences of such a structural transformation,
whether rapid as in Lancashire, the Lyonnais or Massachusetts, or
slower as in the Po valley, was to deepen the perception of the
differences between the workers and the poor. Among the elites,
there was concern and widespread international debate about what
was described as the new problem of pauperism (itself a new term of
the 1820s). As the greatest theorist of charity of the nineteenth
century, de Gérando, observed, the problem was not so much new as
more visible, because of its concentration in the factory and urban
context.[14] In any case, it led to a more self-conscious level of social
paternalism: encouragement of savings, church attendance and education with their inculcation of middle-class values.

The sense of their difference from the poor also deepened among
the workers. Arguably, the long-established distinction that skilled
workers defended against labourers – ever less applicable as the
factory system destroyed the old definitions of skill – was transferred
and extended to all workers. The middle-class work ethic, with its
moralistic opposite of idleness and disorder, was now deployed as the
new dividing line, to the extent that workers temporarily out of
employment claimed their separateness from the unemployed. In the
words of a Massachusetts labour newspaper in 1877:[15]

We have used the term dis-employed as more expressive and true . . .
than the ordinary, and more general term un-employed – which includes
not only this class but all who are voluntarily or involuntarily without
employment; the sick and incompetent, the thriftless, the lazy and
vicious, the willing paupers and the professional beggars – all belong to

[12] Quoted in R.J. Morris, 'Introduction' to R.J. Morris (ed.) *Class, Power and Social
Structure in British Nineteenth Century Towns* (Leicester, 1986), p. 6.
[13] For a recent survey, see Joyce (ed.) *Historical Meanings*.
[14] J.B. de Gérando, *De la Bienfaisance Publique* (Brussels, 1839); 'The poor and how
to relieve them' in J.A. Davis and P. Ginsborg (eds) *Politics and Society in the age of
Risorgimento* (Cambridge 1991).
[15] Quoted in Keyssar, *Out of Work*, p. 3.

the comprehensive and motley crowd of the un-employed; and we
protest against the injustice of associating – even in idea – the honest,
industrious workers – who are idle from no fault of their own – with that
same motley crowd.

I have argued elsewhere[16] why the poor did not become part of the
modern working class, remaining separate and as it were insulated
from the development of a class consciousness. Appropriation by the
working class of the social construct of poverty played its role in
ensuring that the poor would remain apart, regarded not as a potential
for class solidarity, but rather as a threat to wages and employment,
in Marx's words, a 'reserve army of labour'.

[16] 'The poor, proto-industrialization and the working class: Italy (sixteenth to
nineteenth centuries)', in S. Woolf, *The Poor in Western Europe in the Eighteenth and
Nineteenth Centuries* (London, 1986).

CHAPTER ELEVEN

A people and a class: industrial workers and the social order in nineteenth-century England

Patrick Joyce

University of Manchester

Surely the matter of class in British history is sealed and settled? However much the presence of class may be debated in the Britain of the 1980s, is not its past sacrosanct? After all, was not Britain the first industrial nation, giving rise to a new industrial proletariat and a new form of 'class consciousness'? This is indeed still the official version, one echoed in the most recent, and ambitious, synoptic account of class formation in Europe and the USA.[1] However, there is room for scepticism, even though this does not here extend to denying altogether the significance of class; and this is apparent in recent work.[2]

Rather, class was one of a number of ways in which contemporaries perceived the social order of which they were a part. These ways could be not only complementary, but also noticeably divergent. Among the most notable was the notion of 'the people', and what follows is an account of this and the social images and identities allied to it. Ways of seeing society differed according to the situation at hand. I shall have little to say here about the experience of work, and the social perceptions derived from and expressed through that experience. There is no doubt that class was more salient here than elsewhere, if defined in the usual sense of the word: namely a set of social categories principally derived from the economic relations of

[1] If not taken as prototypical, the British case is seen as straightforward; see I. Katznelson, 'Working-class formation: constructing cases and comparisons', in I. Katznelson and A.R. Zolberg (eds) *Working-Class Formation: Nineteenth-Century Patterns in Western Europe and the United States* (London, 1986), esp. p. 10.

[2] See W.M. Reddy, *Money and Liberty in Modern Europe: a Critique of Historical Understanding* (Cambridge, 1987); P.N. Furbank, *Unholy Pleasure: The Idea of Social Class* (London, 1985).

capitalist production, prominently concerned with social exclusion and social conflict, and expressed through a vocabulary of social classification in which 'class' terms themselves were actually employed.[3] A rather different route is taken here, since political and artistic rather than economic representations of social attitudes are considered. The focus is Britain, but in fact chiefly England, especially its northern manufacturing districts. If class proves to be a somewhat elusive presence among the workers of these districts – presumably the shock troops of the industrial proletariat – then perhaps it is the case that its significance has more generally been overestimated.

Before looking further at how workers saw society, it is necessary to dwell on what is meant by industrial workers and allied terms such as 'industrial proletariat'. However, it is first necessary to dwell at some further length on how we define class. Class is usually employed in one of two broad senses, the structural and the cultural. In the first sense attention is given to ways in which political, social but chiefly economic arrangements place individuals in different relations of power and with different access to resources. How people come to perceive the situations in which they find themselves is the cultural sense of class – sometimes called class consciousness – though this is not of course usually taken as a necessary concomitant of class or socio-economic position. It is this second sense I am mainly concerned with here.

The term class consciousness has in fact by now acquired a rather antiquated ring, one redolent of a time, not so long ago, when class was seen in terms of uniform, and highly idealised patterns of action and belief: for example, a revolutionary class consciousness or a labourist consciousness. These concepts emanated from earlier forms of Marxism, but were by no means its exclusive preserve.[4] Their superannuation is due to the new historical interest in theories of language, culture and ideology.[5] Instead of monolithic types of consciousness, the latter are resolved into series of different, overlapping and sometimes competing discourses. Above all, what has become evident is the dissolution of the old assurance that a formative

---

[3] For a full account of class in the sphere of labour, and of all the other subjects touched upon in this chapter, see P. Joyce, *Visions of the People: Industrial England and the Question of Class, c. 1848–1914* (Cambridge, 1991).

[4] The wider currency of this labelling is evident in student textbooks, e.g. R. Morris, *Class and Class Consciousness in the Industrial Revolution 1780–1850* (London, 1979). The most recent British textbook, admirable in many other respects, mostly ignores the problems of language and consciousness – D.G. Wright, *Popular Radicalism: the Working-Class Experience, 1780–1880* (London, 1988).

[5] L. Hunt (ed.) *The New Cultural History* (Berkeley, 1989).

bond existed between social structure and culture. Class is seen as a social construct, created differently by different historical actors. Instead of class consciousness we have languages of class, bearers of class meanings which may not be so apparent on the surface. Such languages do not simply reflect social structure, but actively create and enact values.

Suggestive as this approach is, it does seem to me to create certain difficulties. First, it tends to foreclose discussion of the socio-economic condition of workers, which is often taken as a given. Second, it opens the meanings of class to such a multitude of expressions that it renders the term so ambiguous and arbitrary as to be of limited use. Stedman Jones's work has done much to develop this approach, and his re-evaluation of Chartism is a good case of what I mean:[6] the ideology and rhetoric of the movement is seen as a language of class when on the face of it these would seem to concern instead a political subject, the people, rather than an economic one, the working class. The difference matters.

None the less, the approach must be applauded, for encouraging us to address the real meaning of terms, and for avoiding idealised notions of class. It can be seen at work in more recent interpretations of popular radicalism in early-nineteenth-century England, where popular constitutionalism is regarded as a language of class in the sense that radicals are held to have spoken a language of political equality and universal suffrage significantly different from more restricted middle-class notions of political rights.[7] Class is now seen in terms of 'opposed discourses' fighting it out 'within the general unity of a shared code'.[8] For instance, the political subject of the people in Chartism might, as Stedman Jones argues, have class meanings.[9]

But the people, and popular constitutionalism, had other meanings too, and when we pursue these we get a different history. It seems to me that the class label, and the fixation with class meanings, in fact stand in the way of this alternative history. In proposing an economic

[6] G. Stedman Jones, 'Rethinking Chartism', in his *Languages of Class* (Cambridge, 1983).

[7] See the critiques of Stedman Jones's essay, esp. D. Thompson, 'The language of class', *Bulletin of the Society for the Study of Labour History* 52 (1987): 54–7; J. Epstein, 'Rethinking the categories of working-class History', *Labour/Le Travailleur* 18 (1986): 195–208, but see in particular J. Epstein, 'Understanding the cap of liberty: symbolic practice and social conflict in early nineteenth-century England', *Past and Present* 122 (1989): 75–118.

[8] Epstein (1989), op. cit., p. 117.

[9] Stedman Jones, op. cit. pp. 173–4.

definition of class, I am conscious that I run the danger of describing class in an idealised, anachronistic way. None the less, to sever class languages from an economic dimension seems to me to lead to a conceptual elasticity which goes nowhere. Without some definitional exercise of this sort it is exceedingly difficult to know what class is – where it starts and stops, as it were. Is every manifestation of collective discontent by a subordinate group evidence of class? Surely one cannot ascribe class consciousness or a class meaning to the social struggles of subordinate groups merely because they are in struggle? Presumably, in this line of reasoning, ideologies of the extreme right if defined by workers in such a way as to make them their property are evidence of class consciousness?

The result of this academic language game is that the real sources of social identity and political mobilisation are lost to view. In Chartism, the difference between class and populist meanings did in fact matter. The true people might at times be the working people of England, but it is a moot point whether the identity that really counted was a class rather than a populist one. Similarly, popular constitutionalism may be evidence of values significantly different from those of class. Quite simply, the consciousness of a class need not be the consciousness of class. To assume that the values of the social constituencies we choose to call classes can be given a class label merely by dint of association with these constituencies is to open the door to almost any cultural manifestation being interpreted as the expression of class.

These observations bear on the case of the rural proletariat examined elsewhere in this volume.[10] In one sense, Snell is fully justified in applying the terminology of class to the outlook of this proletariat: the amalgam of custom, or moral economy, and popular biblical exegesis which seems to have made up the agricultural workers' language of class expressed fundamental cleavages of interest and identity in the countryside. In smiting his scholarly foes Snell properly dwells on a class division between 'them' and 'us' (imprecise as the distinction was in practice). All this is of course far from an academic game. However, my point would simply be that the use of class, while purposeful in its forensic place, does not get us very far in analysing the popular identities involved. It is indeed but a first step in locating them. In fact, the similarity between the sources of social values among the rural and urban poor is striking, particularly the recourse to custom and religion. There are marked similarities too in

[10] See Snell, Chapter 9 in this volume.

the way in which social outlook was generated in people's immediate, local life, whether the parish or the urban neighbourhood. Ambiguity was, however, the keynote of this localism: class had to start somewhere, and its most propitious ground was the locality, but local experience also involved unities of sentiment that cut across class (the sentiments of insiders against non-local outsiders say, or of a village and town community sense that was not at all restricted to working people).

The consciousness of a class, then, need not be the consciousness of class, but how far can we be certain that it is a class with which we are dealing in the first place? Snell's account notes the elements of division in people's socio-economic position, differences of religion, occupation, gender and so on. I would make more of these than he does (and I would emphasise more the ambiguity of localism). In dealing with nineteenth-century industrial England, this may at first sight seem perverse. However, when one looks closely at the process of industrial change something other than a naked and unadorned proletarian emerges. Versions of social identity are correspondingly complex. Before looking at popular politics a brief consideration of these structural aspects of class is in order.

Recent interpretations of industrialisation question the centrality of large-scale factory production,[11] and with it the notion of a work-force homogenised in condition and outlook. The picture of capitalist industry that has emerged in recent years is fairly familiar,[12] though its ramifications and implications for the social outlook of workers have not been much developed.[13] Very briefly, what has been termed 'combined and uneven development' involved the incorporation rather than the supercession of earlier forms of industrial organisation. For instance, outwork and small workshop production continued to be of great importance, at least as late as the First World War. In supposedly modern forms of industrial organisation (for example in engineering, shipbuilding, even textiles) it is the archaism of arrangements that is striking, particularly the reliance of employers upon the strength, skill and authority of the work-force. The labour process is seen to involve not a linear process of de-skilling – and an homoge-

---

[11] For a review of the literature see D. Cannadine, 'The past and the present in the English Industrial Revolution, 1880–1989', *Past and Present* 103 (1984): 131–72.

[12] Influential accounts have been by R. Samuel, 'The workshop of the world: steam power and hand technology in mid-Victorian Britain', *History Workshop* 3 (1977): 66–72, and C. Sabel and J. Zeitlin, 'Historical alternatives to mass production', *Past and Present* 108 (1985): 133–76.

[13] For a consideration of these implications, expanding on the present paragraphs, see P. Joyce, 'Work', in F.M.L. Thompson (ed.) *The Cambridge Social History of Great Britain 1750–1950*, vol. II (Cambridge, 1991).

nous working class – but a multiplicity of outcomes and much continuity in the worker's experience and outlook. Explorations of capital reveal the paternalist values and strategies of employers, the strength of inter-capitalist competition, and the relatively small-scale and fragmented pattern of industrial ownership. The Victorian, and in many respects the Edwardian economy was irregular and diverse. So too was the nature of the individual occupation and the pattern of the individual's work life.

The consequences of all this are evident in a very diverse and fragmented labour force, one to which the term 'proletarian' applies only with a good deal of qualification. By this term one denotes, among other attributes, work for wages, usually lifelong, and usually manual work. Workers are subject to contract rather than to extra-economic compulsions and traditions.[14] Above all, ownership and control over the means of production are lost. However, the great variety of forms of industrial organisation, and the resulting complexity of the ways in which authority actually worked in industry, involved many situations in which the worker had more to lose than his (or her) chains. As well as a stake in the ownership and control of production (sometimes vestigial to us but not for the workers involved), he (rarely she) also often had a stake in how production should be organised.

The term 'proletarian' simply does not do justice to the range of experience involved, or to the great array of skills and statuses so evident in what, in the singular, is clearly a decidedly tenuous working class. This questioning of the idea of the proletarian (even more necessary in nineteenth-century Europe given the more irregular nature of industrialisation there),[15] is further deepened by new considerations of the relationship between labour and capital. Instead of an overmastering, trans-historical tendency towards conflict – along classical Marxist lines – what is evident is the interdependence of capital and labour, as well as tendencies making for both the dependence and independence of labour.[16] Relations depend upon historical circumstances. Capitalists need to secure consent. The vested interest

[14] For an account of the proletarian condition, see J. Kocka, 'Problems of working-class formation in Germany: the early years, 1800–1875', in I. Katznelson and A.R. Zolberg (eds) op. cit., pp. 281–3.

[15] On the irregular nature of German industrial organisation, and the greatly varied experience and outlook of workers, see Kocka, op. cit., see also the essays on France in the same volume.

[16] The work of Burawoy has been influential, esp. M. Burawoy, *The Politics of Production: Factory Regimes Under Capitalism and Socialism* (London, 1985). For a useful survey; see P. Thompson, *The Nature of Work* (London, 1983).

workers and employers have in co-operation is at least as great as any tendency to conflict.

The upshot of all this for many received ideas about class is evident enough. Just as linear notions of industrialisation seem untenable, so too do linear notions of class development.[17] The socio-economic situation of workers emerges as so ambiguous and fractured that the very notion of class is questioned. Indeed, it may well be that versions of social identity which were themselves socially inclusive and ambiguous, above all that of the people perhaps, may more accurately reflect the economic condition and self-perceptions of workers than the outlook of class. However, pursuing further the relationships between the socio-economic condition of workers, their experience of work, and their perceptions of the social is impossible here. Instead, let me turn to the area of politics, which, given the hetero-geneity of the work-force, may have had more bearing than econ-omics in understanding the uniformities of sentiment uniting workers.

Of fundamental importance in Victorian popular politics was the growth of mass-based political parties. Though Liberalism and Con-servatism might represent workers' interests and exploit class feelings, the popular faith both parties represented was one that sought the transcendence of class in the name of the people and of the nation. The understandings of the social order which political parties both reflected and shaped are a vital place to begin an exploration of the significance of class. This is also apparent in recent work on labour in the USA, where party is seen as not simply reflecting class, religious or ethnic identities.[18] In the ante-bellum period, for instance, party gave voice to these identities but was not subservient to them. Rather, it provided a public identity for people, drawing upon but transcend-ing these affiliations. The same was so in Britain, where political allegiance was compounded of a similarly broad range of loyalties beyond class alone.[19] Politics actively formed social outlooks, particu-larly in situations such as those of Britain and the USA where popular political traditions encountered the franchise early on, and with it parties which sought to accommodate popular values and aspirations.

[17] For further discussion, see P. Joyce, 'Introduction', to P. Joyce (ed.) *The Historical Meanings of Work* (Cambridge, 1987).

[18] A. Bridges, 'Becoming American: the working classes in the United States before the Civil War', in I. Katznelson and A.R. Zolberg (eds) op. cit.

[19] Including the politics of influence and deference. For an account of the broad range of loyalties operative in politics see P. Joyce, *Work, Society and Politics: The Culture of the Factory in Later Victorian England* (Brighton, 1980).

It is this symbiosis of party and popular culture I wish to explore, albeit briefly, concentrating on the majority creed, that of popular Liberalism.

John Bright was perhaps the first to understand what party might mean to the labouring classes. He it was who most effectively made Liberalism a creed. Long ago, John Vincent saw what political historians still so often miss, the emotional and imaginative dimensions of party loyalty.[20] Liberal politics gave its popular constituency a sense of agency in national politics, at once a sense of its own audacity and shrewdness and a chance of service to a higher cause. Gladstone knew well the strength of this sense of service: his (unstoppable) formula for political reform was to equate moral right and moral worth. To deny reform was to deny the morality of the working man.[21] In the Victorian years moral right was often religious right, and the religious dimensions in popular Liberalism were never far to find, particularly in militant Nonconformity. But the aspirations both men articulated went beyond formal religion alone. Moral aspirations and exalted feeling had in fact long dominated the sensibility informing the radical tradition. That sensibility was shaped by the romantic temper of the first half of the century,[22] as well as by popular religious feeling that often had little or no formal religious affiliation.

Popular Liberalism represented a particular distillation of these older elements, giving to them a new moral earnestness in line with the philosophy (and cant) of the age, the belief in reason, progress and improvement. Bright for instance frequently employed religious terminology in his speeches. This went beyond the Nonconformist constituency alone, involving the superiority of the moral law,[23] and presenting the struggle for reform in terms familiar from radical days, those of light against darkness, and good against evil (the unreformed institutions of England were in this demonology literally evil and corrupt).[24] Reform became almost an end in itself, the source from which would flow 'just law' and 'enlightened administration'. More

[20] Vincent's book is still the most revealing account of popular party politics: J. Vincent, *The Formation of the Liberal Party 1857–1966* (London, 1966).

[21] F.B. Smith, *The Making of the Second Reform Bill* (Cambridge, 1966), pp. 30–1.

[22] For an account of popular romanticism in politics, and of all the other aspects of politics touched on in this essay, see Joyce, *Visions of the People*, chs 2 and 3.

[23] J. Bright, *Speeches on Parliamentary Reform by John Bright, revised by himself* . . . (London, 1866), Leeds speech.

[24] J. Bright, *Mr Bright's Speeches* . . . *revised by himself* (London, 1859), Birmingham speech.

than this, ignorance and suffering would lessen, and in Bright's impassioned words, 'Eden would be reared up in the wilderness'.[25]

Gladstone took up Bright's mantle and became the greatest of all exemplars of moral populism. Not quite the gentleman leader – though a good deal of this remained – Gladstone was a new version of leadership, the embodiment of the moral claims of the people's cause, claims newly strengthened by political reform and still insistent. To his popular audiences Gladstone was variously 'conquering hero', 'idol', 'grand old warrior', also the 'woodman' cutting down Disraeli's 'tree of state'. It is impossible to do justice here to his peculiar appeal. The words of Joseph Wilson none the less convey some idea of it.[26] Leader of the north-eastern miners, Wilson was a leading exponent of Liberal-Labour politics. In giving the working classes a stake in the nation, Gladstone had allied them with 'the great social forces which move onwards in their might and majesty', and which were in turn inseparable from the moral elevation and transcendence of the individual. Quoting Mazzini he went on to declare that education was everything, 'the bread of our souls', and the key to understanding both one's political role and one's mission in life. Quoting Mazzini quoting Gladstone, he represented life as a great and noble calling to an elevated destiny in which all the human faculties would at last be unlocked. Though re-directed down moralising paths, the romantic temper of the early nineteenth century was quite evidently at home in Gladstone's England.

Gladstone touched other beliefs too, not least the sense of fair play so widely pervasive in the popular culture of the time, and very near the heart of popular conceptions of justice. As the radical co-operator G.J. Holyoake put it in 1865, the multitude of working people turning out on Tyneside to greet Gladstone had come to witness 'the only English minister who ever gave the people right because it was just they should have it'.[27] The central identity and narrative upon which the Liberal appeal to religion, morality and justice turned concerned an excluded and embattled people in struggle with the forces of privilege and reaction. This people was the rightful heir to the long history of English rights and liberties, and the true English. If the poor or the working people of England must at times be seen as the truest of all the English, then the essential public identity with which Liberalism dealt was not that of a class but of a classless people

[25] J. Bright, *Speeches* (London, 1866), Glasgow speech.
[26] J. Wilson, *Memories of a Labour Leader* (London, 1910, 1980), pp. 218–19.
[27] Vincent, op. cit., p. 230.

and nation. An ideology of the people might articulate class sentiments, and be in this sense a language of class, but it also spoke to other sentiments and identities to which the terms of class do little justice.

For instance, Liberal tactics depended on playing up the sense of insult and exclusion. Working men were seen as true citizens of their country, but in this Liberal flattery of the voter the pride of being a worker was subsidiary to the pride of being a citizen. This pride was widely echoed in Liberalism's popular constituency. For Edmond Beales, leader of the workingmen's Reform League, the people's rights were enshrined in the constitution if only its purity could be realised: statute after statute showed that no laws could be passed without the consent of the whole commonwealth.[28] For Beales, Bright was the man who could maintain all that was best in the constitution, and for Bright the House of Commons was to be the house of the common people, the house it was designed to be, so giving the people back their ancient heritage.[29] At the vast, 200,000-strong Reform meeting at Woodhouse Moor, near Leeds, in 1866,[30] as at other Reform meetings,[31] the notion of the 'battle' or 'struggle' for liberty as something handed down from 'sire to son' was crucial to workingmen's conceptions of reform. What, on this account, seems not to have been crucial was a sense of class conflict, or indeed much of a sense of class at all.

Instead, the emphases of an older political radicalism were still much in evidence: there is the same emphasis on the political sources of oppression, the same exaltation of political liberty, and the same self-conception of the nation as essentially political, rather than social, in character. Not least in evidence was the view of Liberalism as yet one more chapter in the antique struggle for liberty, a view denoting an historical sense that was of course deeply embedded in the radical tradition, especially in popular constitutionalism. Just as the old radicalism was not about class, neither was the new Liberalism, umbilically connected as it in fact was to the radical tradition. Bright's idea of class was clear enough, and it was shared by the great majority of workingmen. What 'we', 'the people', wanted was justice. Whereas justice could not be got from a class, it flowed naturally from a whole people. Class rule had been tried and had failed. This was the class

[28] *Reynolds News*, 9 December 1866, Beales at Birmingham Town Hall.
[29] Vincent, op. cit., p. 217.
[30] *Reynolds News*, 30 September 1866.
[31] See stump speech outside the Manchester Free Trade Hall, *Reynolds News*, 14 October 1866.

rule of the aristocracy and the governing classes. Bringing the rich into communion with the people would assure its end.[32]

Gladstone's doctrine of class was essentially the same as Bright's. By the 1870s he had made the crusade of the masses against the classes the central motif of British popular politics. Popular Liberalism represented the union of the classes against class. It worked with the better selves of the classes, sloughing off the bad and divisive. The terms of class were used only to be dissolved in higher social unities, not least those of humanity and mankind, foci of social identity not examined here but none the less important (for example in the influence of the humanism of that great poet of the worker and the poor, Robert Burns). This reminds us how it is necessary to attend to the meanings class terms had at particular times. For instance, for French as for English workers in the mid-nineteenth century,[33] the terms of an explicit class vocabulary were in fact universalist rather than exclusive in character, derived as their meanings were from Enlightenment thought and the era of eighteenth-century revolution. Moral criteria mattered more than economic ones, and class was usually seen in a negative way, as a reprehensible, selfish denial of the common interests of all people. It was only later, much later in England and perhaps never so fully as in France, that class came fully to have the positive attributes of social exclusiveness, namely solidarity, struggle, and a clear sense of sub- and super-ordination, along with the exaltation of manual labour above other sorts of work.

This history of an ostensible class vocabulary is not however the purpose here. Rather, the suggestion is that behind such a vocabulary operated rather different discourses and identities. This was evident at a local level as well as on the national political stage so far considered. Popular Liberalism was in fact pioneered in the regions, not least in the new industrial districts, the most precocious of which was Lancashire. No cotton town was more precocious, and typical, than Ashton-under-Lyne, bastion of ultra-radical Chartism, citadel of the new Liberal populism, and as near an example of the new industrial proletariat of which Marx and Engels spoke as any town in the nation.

By the 1860s, when not Tory, the politics of this town were permeated by the influence of Bright. For workingmen 'class representation' and 'class legislation' were anathema, and political reform

[32] Bright, *Speeches* (London, 1866), Glasgow City Hall.
[33] W. Sewell, jnr, *Work and Revolution in France: The Language of Labor from the Old Regime to 1848* (Cambridge, 1980), pp. 281–5.

heralded the end of class rule and in its place the reign of 'the universal brotherhood of man' and the realisation of rich and poor as 'one happy family'.[34] Workingmen at reform meetings were prone to emphasise how physical and mental labour went hand in hand.[35] The major categories emphasised in the public political talk of the town were 'people', 'brotherhood' and 'humanity'. In 1867, the ex-Chartist, and new Liberal, Ernest Jones, visited the town to reinforce its native stigmatisation of class rule.[36] If perverted by class, England was still the land or home of the free (it should be noted that it was England that was almost always spoken of in this context, rather than Britain).

If we look beyond the factory districts, to the politics of the radical artisans as exemplified in the hugely popular, ultra-radical Sunday newspaper *Reynolds News*, then we find the same story repeated elsewhere. The political and social understanding *Reynolds* expressed concerned not production and class, but politics and the people. The major social distinction it described was that between rulers and ruled. The chief enemy it identified was not the middle class but the aristocracy. One does not have to look far in this newspaper to discern the longevity and continuing vibrancy of the radical tradition, a tradition it should be added which provided most of the essentials of early British socialism.[37] Though the emphasis here is on the third quarter of the century, it is amply apparent that the Liberal populism of this time was of lasting relevance for subsequent developments in popular politics.

Though the role of parties was of great importance in shaping the character of social outlooks, political appeals always had to work with the grain of popular preconceptions. As the brief account of aspects like religion and cognate moralities will have indicated, popular perceptions of the social order were a product of the broader popular culture beyond politics. Politics, and party, have to be set beside other matters, not the least important of which was the role of the imagination in voicing and in a sense creating social identities.

In terms of popular art, it is the broadside ballad which perhaps best exemplifies the social outlook of the labouring populations. Far from declining in the industrial centres, until at least the 1880s the

---

[34] *Ashton Reporter*, 26 January 1867, Town Hall meeting; also ibid., for February 1867 meetings, and 7 April 1860.
[35] Mottram reform meeting, *Reporter* 26 January 1867, also 7 February 1867 (Stalybridge Meeting).
[36] Ibid., 27 July 1867.
[37] For further consideration see Joyce, *Visions of People*, chs 2 and 3.

ballad continued to be of great moment, and very responsive to the changed circumstances of the time. The trade in ballad sheets was frankly commercial, if primitive in organisation compared to later publishing developments. To sell and survive, the hacks, printers and vendors that made up the trade had to adapt their wares to the presuppositions of their audience. The ballads are an extraordinarily sensitive barometer of events, and of fluctuations in popular taste and manners. At the same time, there were great uniformities of style and content, across regions and over time. These uniformities argue the force of precedent. They also suggest that audience expectation enforced this precedent. In this sense, like much traditional popular art, there was a collective as well as an individual author at work. It is this combination of adaptability and precedent that makes them so revealing.[38]

This account cannot be other than selective, though the collection I mainly draw on has the merit of a definite mooring in place and time, being the contents of a ballad shop in the industrial city of Manchester in 1873.[39] In this collection, as in all the ballads, the sense of a lost golden age is very powerful. This took the forms of 'the good old town', 'the days of yore', 'the fine old English gentleman', but above all that of 'old England'. The paternalism and patriotism of the ballads could be backward-looking and conservative, but more often these sentiments were a stick to measure, and beat, the present, a means of interpreting and dealing with the present rather than of ignoring it. For instance, the glory of old England was often accompanied by a strong sense of rights, rights lost in the past and claimed in the present. The ballads gave ample voice to the popular constitutionalism already noted. In the 1870s ballads still talk of the time-hallowed constitution and the freeborn Englishman. I quote from the first three verses of an older song, but one evidently popular at the time, 'The White Cliffs of Albion':[40]

> On the white cliffs of Albion, as musing I stood,
> Surveying the waves of the rough swelling flood,
> I saw from the surface a female arise,
> And with wings like an angel she mounted the skies.

[38] The English ballads have been subjected to very little detailed historical analysis. For an account, developing the themes of this section, see ibid., ch. 10. The best general account is R. Palmer, *Sounds of History: Songs and Social Comment* (Oxford, 1988).

[39] The Pearson Collection, Manchester Central Reference Library.

[40] Pearson Collection, no. 268.

> Her figure was noble, and comely her mein,
> I looked and knew it was Liberty's Queen;
> With sword in her hand she shouts as she flies
> Ye rulers of Britain be prudent and wise.
>
> For this island I chose, long before you had birth,
> For the seat of my empire, the freest on earth,
> And tho' you have forged them, no chains will she wear,
> Nor ee'r be enslav'd whilst a sword I can bear.

The perspective here is assuredly not that of class, but of the popular radical tradition in which liberty is the goal, Albion her island empire, and the struggle is one between rulers and ruled, not classes.

Most often, however, especially in the ballads of contemporary events, the social distinction that matters is that of rich and poor. Now, one may call this an economic distinction of a class sort, but it is far removed from the sense of working-class consciousness we usually associate with an industrial proletariat, and indeed historically long preceded the emergence of such a proletariat. The first two verses of 'Rich and Poor' convey the flavour:[41]

> I pray give attention and listen to me,
> I'll point out some facts with which you'll agree,
> There's two classes of people the rich and the poor
> Betwixt them there is a great difference I'm sure,
> While they live in splendour you all are aware,
> How the poor man is living they know not or care
> But if you'll attend I've the object in view,
> To show you the difference there is twixt the two.
> So don't be offended at what I shall say
> For good and bad times I have seen in my day.
>
> The rich live in castles with grandeur all round,
> While the poor they are buried a mile under ground
> The rich they have gold and it mouldering in bags
> While the poor of old England are dressed up in rags
> Their daughters can ride out with saddle and whip,
> With flounce down like the sail of a ship,
> The rich they can go out a shooting at noon,
> But the poor can shoot nothing except at the moon.

In ballad explorations of riches and poverty, the rich were known by their external signs, their flaunting of wealth. But external signs indicated the moral interior: the deviousness and hypocrisy so often associated with the getting of wealth are contrasted with the moral, useful and temperate poor. The categories of thought and feeling are moral, rather than situating wrong in political or economic spheres.

---

[41] Ibid., no. 99.

212

At the same time there is an ambiguous attitude to wealth. A scepticism towards the acquisition of wealth is reflected in a strong belief in the innate superiority of the poor (echoing the exaltation of the poor evident in Gladstone's political populism). But there is also a strong sense of the rightness of wealth when it is used to fulfil the obligations of the rich. Right-doing wealth can be accepted. In this regard the following is revealing, the 'Elegy on the Death of Sir Francis Crossley, The Poor Man's Friend'. Crossley was one of the Crossley family of Halifax, very big carpet manufacturers. The first two verses are given:[42]

> You loyal sons of Halifax, what makes thee complain?
> Or, why? in such sorrow relenting,
> Alas! 'tis for one, who is now dead and gone,
> And the people in grief is lamenting.
> That excellent man, the pride of our land,
> Whom every virtue possessed in,
> Is gone to that home, from whence no one can return,
> Sir Francis Crossley, our dear friend, God rest him.
>
> The rich and the poor, all did him adore,
> Admired, beloved, and respected;
> For he's never stood in the way of doing good,
> And nothing by him was neglected,
> For he was respected by the rich and the poor,
> And the poor, long has praised and blest him,
> Now, tears wet each eye, while in sorrow they sigh,
> He is gone, is Sir Francis, God rest him.

However wealth is seen, the accent is on a common underlying humanity. As well as the people, there is a clear sense of people, not only of the dignity of ordinary people (the poor, or the common people), but also of the common identity of all people. The ballads deal in a universal human nature, and give voice to a desire for human fraternity as well as for justice. This accent on fraternity is somewhat removed from what we usually deem the attributes of class. The sources of all this in the popular culture of the time are too diverse to explore here, though again the force of religious feeling is not far to find. For instance, in the 'Dialogue between Mr Gladstone and a Working Man' the belief is that in God's sight people are all alike. This triggers a powerful denunciation of the cruelties of the rich, but also points to the coming time when the rich and poor will unite and act as the brothers they truly are. The song wishes God speed to the

---

[42] Ibid., no. 98.

time when pride and distinction will be no more. The final two responses in the dialogue go as follows:[43]

Working Man

We do not crave for gold,
But all we ask is right,
Of better times we have been told
By men like *you* and *Bright*;
You may be clever, honest men;
Of course we must not doubt it,
We tell you what we want and then,
Like rebles[*sic*] we are routed,
You must not think that we are fools,
Devoid of understanding,
For years gone by we've been your tools,
But now, we are demanding,
The rights of men, who toil each day,
Though not of noble station,
And Justice, demands a fair days pay
To the supportes [*sic*] of your nation.

I trust the time will not be long,
God speed the happy hour,
When pride and distinction will be gone,
Between the rich and poor;
From pride and all such such nonsense [*sic*] part,
From you forever more.
Would it not move the hardest heart,
To see the suffering poor,
Mortals starving day by day,
Midst cold and bitter jeer,
Deserted to their God they pray,
And find relief in tears;
Be kind and never wound a heart,
But heal thy brother's sore,
And when from worldly care we part,
We'll meet to part no more.

In 'Remember the Poor' rich and poor must lie down together in the Second Coming.[44] I give the last two verses here:

But a thaw will ensue when the waters increase,
And the rivers again they will flow,
When the fish from confinement obtain a release,
And in danger the dwellers do go;
When your paths are annoyed by the proud swelling flood
And your bridges are useful no more
When in peace you enjoy everything that is good,
Do not grudge to remember the poor.

[43] Ibid., no. 238.
[44] Ibid., no. 60.

The time it will come when our Saviour on earth
And the world will agree with one voice,
All nations unite to salute the blest morn,
And the whole of the world will rejoice;
When grim death is depriv'd of its hardkilling sting,
And the grave reigns triumphant no more,
Saints, Angels and Men, Hallejuhas will sing,
And the rich must lie down with the Poor.

Lest it be thought that these sentiments were the last gasp of a dying tradition, it needs to be emphasised that they deeply infused the dialect literature of the industrial districts of the north.[45] This literature grew between the 1840s and the First World War to enjoy a huge popularity with factory operatives, and others beyond and within the ranks of manual workers. If we seek for a literature of the new industrial proletariat then this, even more than the ballads, has very strong claims. The industrial worker, particularly the machine operative, is explicitly the subject of the literature, making up its heroes and heroines. Whether it was the literature of a class is, however, another matter.

In the simple sense of its social constituency it has claims, though in its representation of very specific regional and occupational identities it was arguably the literature not of a class but of fragments of a class. In the sense of the meanings it imparted it strongly reflected the experience of the transition from domestic to factory industry, and from village to town. In this sense it expressed the outlook of a class in the making, not of a class made. Most of all, however, while it reflected the views of working people undergoing industrialisation, views which expressed their slant on the world, that slant was far removed from class as socially exclusive, conflictual and economic in character.[46] What was involved was broadly populist in character: 'people' and 'the people', 'rich' and 'poor', were still the dominant ways of seeing. If there was an increasing tendency to define these terms in relation to the attributes of labour, then their social catholicity still remained dominant.

While popular art drew its effect from the wider characteristics of popular culture, it should not be thought that it merely reflected this culture. Instead, it combined cultural elements in particular ways, in the process relegating certain ways of seeing the social order and advancing others. Above all, it forged social images of novel form and enduring effect. Nowhere is this plainer than in the case of the

---

[45] For a good account see M. Vicinus, *The Industrial Muse* (London, 1974), ch. 1.
[46] For a full discussion, see Joyce, *Visions of the People*, Chs. 11, 12.

music hall, and it is to this I shall turn in conclusion. In moving from dialect literature to music hall one turns from a regional to a national audience. Bailey's work on the music hall is both original and pioneering.[47] He has shown how the themes of feast, plenitude and profusion were central to the ethos of halls in their late-century manifestations. These themes reflected new patterns of consumption, and a new accent on leisure in popular culture. The halls celebrated consumption by glorifying style.[48] In the comic art of the 1880s as well,[49] one may see the glorification of 'the good time' (as opposed to 'the good life' of the morally strenuous mid-Victorian period). In the music hall the masters of the good time were the entrepreneur-impresarios.

Bailey dwells on the example of Billy Holland. Holland as impresario symbolised the merits of the market and of competitive self-advancement. He and his like dwelt on the ideas of success and social mobility. Yet these were capitalist entrepreneurs of a strange sort, of the ranks of the gambler and the *parvenu* rather than of respectable wealth. In establishing the idea of the good time, of feast and profusion, they developed notions of themselves and their stars as heroes and servants of the people. Holland was 'the people's caterer' another 'People's William', alongside the greatest of all Williamite heroes of the people, William Gladstone. There is indeed a clear parallel here between the development of notions of the fraternity of pleasure and the growth of democracy attendant upon the Second and Third Reform Acts. Just as the people were the rightful beneficiaries of the democracy of leisure, so too by their virtue had they earned the right of inclusion in the reformed political order. Their rights to inclusion in the social and political order were argued by their twin tribunes, the two Williams.[50]

In the contrast, but also the affinities, between moralistic and hedonistic populism one can see at work the force of art in complementing politics, especially party, in the creation of popular understandings of the social order. One can also see the capacity of images

[47] P. Bailey (ed.) *The Victorian Music Hall: The Business of Pleasure* (Milton Keynes, 1987), and J. Bratton (ed.) *The Victorian Music Hall: Performance and Style* (Milton Keynes, 1987).

[48] P. Bailey, 'Introduction: making sense of music hall', in P. Bailey (ed.) op. cit.; also 'The swell song', in J. Bratton (ed.) op. cit.

[49] P. Bailey, 'Ally Sloper's half holiday: comic art in the 1880s', *History Workshop Journal* 16 (1983): 4–31.

[50] On other, more conservative and Conservative implications of the halls, see G. Stedman Jones, 'The "Cockney" and the nation, 1780–1988', in D. Feldman and G.S. Jones (eds) *Between Neighbourhood and Nation* (London, 1989).

of the people and of populist discourses, to be reproduced in new settings, and in new ways adapted to these settings. This shows the great purchase social images other than those of class have had on English society, also the great longevity of such images. Whatever we term the social outlook of industrial workers after the Victorian period, whether we describe this as class or not, that outlook was itself deeply marked by the inheritance of Victorian populism. This account is only a highly selective version of that phenomenon. It says little or nothing of other sources of social identity and understandings of the social order; areas such as customary practice and belief, the experience of labour and the place of unions, and the role of ideas about culture and history (particularly as these were reproduced in the schoolroom). It only hints at the difficulty of applying oversimplified models of the economy to the understandings of society evident in those areas of popular culture with which there has been time to deal, namely politics and popular art. None the less, however selective the account, it may serve to question the often assumed centrality of class in nineteenth-century England, and perhaps in other places and at other times.

CHAPTER TWELVE
Myths of order and ordering myths

William Doyle
University of Bristol

Peter Burke shows in convincing detail (in Chapter 1 of this volume) how far back the analysis of society in terms of orders goes; but he is entirely right to concentrate on the version of it propounded by Roland Mousnier. For Mousnier's is the version which has influenced historians of our own generation, whether through his own extensive and insistent writings, or those of his numerous pupils and disciples. And since none of the preceding chapters quotes his definition, it might be useful to recapitulate it here. A society of orders, Mousnier contends:

> consists of a hierarchy of degrees . . . distinguished from one another and arranged not according to the wealth of their members and the latter's capacity to consume, and not according to their role in the production of material goods, but according to the esteem, honour and dignity attached by society to social functions that can have no relationship with the production of material goods.[1]

The touchstone is social functions; whereas in a society of castes it is religious purity or impurity, and in a society of classes it is the production of material goods. It is true, Mousnier concedes, that societies purely of one type or another are very rare. Most are in some form of transition. The historian's job is to identify a society's dominant principle of stratification, which is not always easy. But for early modern France, and by implication much of Europe too, there could be no doubt. This was a society of orders; and it only began the transition to a society of classes between about 1750 and 1800.

No historian wishing to work on this period has been able since the 1960s to overlook these claims; those whose field is France can

[1] *Les Hiérarchies sociales de 1450 à nos jours* (Paris, 1969), p. 19.

218

scarcely avoid taking a position about them. My own has always been extremely sceptical.

First of all the notion of an early modern society of orders has always seemed politically tendentious. Mousnier began to elaborate it in response to Boris Porchnev's Marxist analysis of popular uprisings in seventeenth-century France, which depicted them in terms of class struggle.[2] Mousnier seemed more concerned to refute historical Marxism than to advance dispassionate investigation. His later claims that most societies in history have been societies of orders rather than of classes seemed to bear out that this was the basic purpose.[3] Mousnier has never made any secret of his right-wing, authoritarian sympathies, and from certain angles his society of orders recalls the corporative society discerned in the *ancien régime* by pre-war sympathisers with Fascism as they looked for promising precedents for Mussolini's institutional experiments.[4] Both seemed the product of a romantic conservatism which looked back to a world of harmonious hierarchy (see Peter Burke, Chapter 1 in this volume) before the deplorable and divisive upheavals of the French Revolution so vaunted by the Left ever since. There is of course no reason why even passionate political commitment should not produce excellent and stimulating history. Mousnier's own determination to document his position has added enormously to our knowledge of seventeenth century French society and the sources for its study. It has not, however, produced a picture of a society notably more harmonious than what came later. The suspicion remains that the driving force behind the society of orders model is more political than scholarly.

A second doubt concerns the limited authority upon which the model has been constructed. What would Mousnier have done without Loyseau? He calls him, somewhat disingenuously, a typical jurist of a society of orders, but few others are ever cited. Without the resurrection conferred by Mousnier, it seems probable that Loyseau would have remained as obscure and isolated for posterity as he probably was for most of his contemporaries; and would chiefly be known, perhaps, as one of the many sources fertilising the conceptual genius of Montesquieu. Besides, (as Peter Burke points out in Chapter 1) Loyseau was scarcely himself a detached analyst.

---

[2] The early stages of this argument are reviewed in J.H.M. Salmon, 'Venality of office and popular sedition in seventeenth-century France: a review of a controversy', *Past and Present* 37 (1967): 21–43.

[3] *Les Hiérarchies*, p. 43.

[4] See e.g. F. Olivier-Martin, *L'Organisation corporative de la France d' ancien régime* (Paris, 1938).

He spoke for his own social group and its particular legal values, and it is not self-evident that he was articulating the wider consensus which Mousnier believes must underlie any system of social stratification. It seems that Loyseau was as much concerned to create as to describe the social structure found in his writings. To raise on such narrow and ambiguous foundations not only a model of seventeenth-century French society, but also one claimed as valid for most recorded human societies, is surely to impose on poor Loyseau's shoulders a burden far greater than they can possibly bear.

Especially since Loyseau was a lawyer, and writing largely for his own kind, to accept his precise and carefully expressed categorisations as readily as does Mousnier is to fall into the trap of what Peter Burke calls legalism. (Chapter 1 of this volume.) To an extent social realities must obviously be expressed in terms of laws and rules, but that does not mean that laws and rules always express social realities, or even the most important ones. Most people pass their lives in complete ignorance of, and indifference to, the vast bulk of laws that technically bind them. There is little to suggest that early modern Frenchmen were significantly more conscious of such matters than we are. That was precisely why it was so shocking when, in September 1788, the Parlement of Paris called for the forthcoming Estates General to meet according to the forms of 1614, which entailed three separately elected estates deliberating apart and voting by order.[5] None of this is to say that people had, or have, no sense of hierarchy: merely that it is superficial to try to identify that sense through legal or official formulations to which few enjoyed or sought access. Future historians of this country might as well try to identify our own perceptions by analysing the patterns of precedence set out in court circulars, or by the official categorisation of social groups into A, B, C and D. Their results would tell us little about how late twentieth-century British citizens actually perceived one another, let alone why. It might, indeed, be asked how far social distinctions are ever perceived at a general, rather than a personal level. William Reddy's notion of exchange asymmetry, seems designed to address this difficulty (among others) and to elaborate some objective means of weighing individual perceptions in social terms.[6]

The sort of group whose members are likely to look to rules and

---

[5] C. Lucas, 'Nobles, bourgeois, and the origins of the French Revolution', *Past and Present* 60 (1973): 84–126.

[6] See W. Reddy, *Money and Liberty in Modern Europe: a Critique of Historical Understanding* (Cambridge, 1987), ch. 3.

laws for identifying their social position is in fact the sort Loyseau belonged to: a profession. Self-recruiting, enjoying exclusive privileges, displaying considerable hereditary tendencies but ignoring purely economic qualifications, professions need to be publicly defined. They are archetypal orders: neither Gregory Freeze nor Joe Bergin, whose titles in this volume (Chapters 4 and 5) suggest that estates differ from professions, go on to define in clear theoretical terms what the differences might be. Unless valid distinctions of this sort can be found, it might be fair to argue that since most societies do incorporate professions, most are societies with orders. To go on to call them societies of orders, however, requires something more. It requires the professional model to obtain throughout their organisation, to the extent of being its determining principle. It is true that in medieval and early modern times many urban economic activities were also organised along professional lines in the form of trade guilds. To that extent the principle of orders operated more widely in these societies than in our own. But guild organisation was never universal, even in towns; and in the countryside, where the overwhelming majority of the population lived, it was practically unknown. Indeed, even those, like Michael Bush (see Chapter 8 in this volume), who accept the value of orders as a means of characterising pre-industrial societies admit that the peasantry were not defined by them. Values generated by, and appropriate to the professions, in other words, have limited use in describing or defining society as a whole.

And above all, they entirely omit the economic dimension. This is the most fundamental of all objections to the notion of societies of orders. No hierarchy can exist without reference to power differentials; and power differentials unrelated to wealth are quite inconceivable. While admitting that there often is a connection, Mousnier insists that there is no necessary connection. This seems a wilful refusal to face reality; but of course reluctance to confront the unwelcome is one of the main impulses driving those responsible for the concept of orders. Where was the sale of offices in Loyseau's scheme of things? Yet it was already the main motor of the system he described; while for Mousnier to allow wealth any determining role in early modern social stratification was to reopen the field to the sort of Marxist analysis he was determined to refute. Orders were intended to divert attention from something dangerously important – the economic structure of society. In so far as the idea has prospered among scholars, the diversion has been effective. Major works of great erudition, such as Jerome Blum's *End of the Old Order in Rural*

Europe have been fatally skewed by uncritical acceptance of the society of orders concept.[7] The translation of so many of Mousnier's works promoting the idea into English reflects the seriousness with which his ideas have been taken outside France.[8] And among students of the *ancien régime*, routine allusions are made to it as a society of orders often enough to suggest that this approach has won widespread acceptance.

Yet we might ask, as a final objection, what has it really clarified that we did not know already? Nobody has ever denied that pre-revolutionary French society, and that of much of Europe as well, was legally divided into orders, and that some enjoyed more prestige and privilege than others. Nobody has ever denied that the French Revolutionaries sought to destroy these structures, so that post-revolutionary society lacked a number of the *ancien régime*'s organising characteristics. It has always been generally recognised too that they disappeared throughout most of the rest of Europe over the following century. What used to be claimed by historians of France is that at the upper levels order was synonymous with class – at least in the case of the nobility. Michael Bush addresses just this question (see Chapter 3 in this volume) and concludes convincingly that nobility was an order not a class; thus generalising for Europe as a whole what 'revisionist' historians of the French Revolution have concluded for that country over the past generation.[9] But to demonstrate that orders were not classes is not to prove that there were no classes in societies with orders. To draw that conclusion, as Mousnier and his followers tend to do, leaves us, not with the least dangerous of models for pre-industrial societies, as Peter Burke claims (in Chapter 1 in this volume), but on the contrary with a very dangerous obfuscation of social realities. There is no harm in noting that social classification by orders was one feature of these societies, and indeed it would be wrong to fail to make the observation. But to elevate orders to an exclusive criterion, and thereby to refuse to recognise the importance of economic differences, is to set back rather than to promote our understanding of such societies.

These are the objections which have always made me sceptical of Mousnier's attempt to introduce a new typology of *ancien régime*

[7] J. Blum, *The End of the Old Order in Rural Europe* (Princeton, 1978).

[8] Most notably *Social Hierarchy* (London, 1973) and *The Institutions of France under the Absolute Monarchy 1598–1789*, 2 vols (Chicago, 1979).

[9] See T.C.W. Blanning, *The French Revolution: Aristocrats versus Bourgeois?* (London, 1987) for a convenient summary of these debates.

societies – not to mention ones earlier or later in time. In what ways do the contributions to this book persuade me to modify or abandon my scepticism?

First, I was impressed by the number of contributors who found social analysis in terms of orders useful. Peter Burke, Michael Bush, Joe Bergin, Gregory Freeze and Charles Timberlake clearly saw value in looking at early modern societies, at least, from this viewpoint. One should not reject such an informed consensus lightly. On the other hand, only Peter Burke explains why he finds it useful rather than accepting it without discussion; yet his reasons still seem open to the objections expressed earlier.

But if recognition of the social importance at certain times of orders, estates, or *sosloviia*, was consensual, so was acceptance that they can exist alongside classes. Whether Mousnier would accept this wholeheartedly seems open to doubt. He certainly recognises that transitions occur from one type of society to another, and that during those transitional phases elements of both types of society exist and compete side by side. He also recognises that there are intermediary types of stratification, as in England between the fifteenth and the twentieth centuries,[10] where elements of order and class mingle. But he insists that in most societies one or other type of stratification is dominant, and therefore characterises the society as a whole. There is little sign in this book of such a position being accepted. Peter Burke warns that any exclusive categorisation is likely to distort reality in some way (see Chapter 1), and most contributors seem implicitly to accept the common sense of such a warning. All this echoes some of the doubts expressed above, and to that extent confirms rather than alters my previous scepticism. It certainly offers little support for the extreme position favoured by Mousnier that it is inappropriate to speak of classes in early modern society.

And meanwhile further doubts have been added. Peter Burke notes that in a number of particulars the orders model does not fit even early modern Europe (see Chapter 1). The classic tripartite division into fighters, prayers and workers was not universal. In some countries with a division into estates there were four; while in Poland, where the nobility certainly looked like a classic order, there were no others, not even the clergy. And then there is the problematical case of England, raised in the conference discussions by Frank O'Gorman. He could see no evidence of anything resembling orders in English society; he could not even see any compelling need for people to

[10] Mousnier, *Les Hiérarchies*, ch. 4.

perceive themselves invariably as part of some permanent greater collectivity. In England such collectivities were mostly intermediate, like religious congregations, or transitory, like bodies of electors. Mousnier and his disciples are certainly well aware of the problem posed by England. His solution was to depict the last five centuries of English history as a time of slow transition from orders to classes. Jerome Blum simply accepts that it was an exception.[11] But as exceptions of one sort or another mount up they serve only to reinforce already existing doubts about the concept as a whole. If, as Michael Bush suggests (in Chapter 8 of this volume), the peasantry cannot be seen as an order in itself, for all the various rights peasants might have enjoyed, then the majority of society functioned largely with little reference to the structure of orders. And nobody has spoken of a bourgeois order, or even a middle *soslovie*, amid all the discussions of the middle classes. It is surely permissible to doubt the value of an organising principle which specifically takes in only a few per cent of society's members, the nobility and the clergy. It is true, of course, that everybody else fell into the biggest order of all, the third estate; but that category was so wide as to mean very little of importance until the last year of its existence.

The idea of societies of orders, therefore, receives little reinforcement from this book; whereas most of the doubts about it remain, or have been reinforced. Since early modern societies undoubtedly did look at themselves in terms of orders, it seems both useful and legitimate for historians to analyse them in these terms, among others. But it does not seem justifiable to regard orders as the predominant defining characteristic of such societies; much less a number of others, widely separated in time and space. The impression remains that whatever new insights may have been produced by Mousnier's attempt to change our approach to early modern social history, it has been an expensive diversion yielding dividends of limited value.

Are we, then, back to where we were before the detour began? Is class, after all, the criterion by which in the first instance all social structures should be analysed? And if it is, must we accept the corollary, derived from Marx, that conflict is inherent in the notion? Notions of class at least have the merit of being based firmly in the tangible realities of wealth. But, as several of the contributions to this volume point out, they are subject to just as many doubts and

11 Blum, op. cit., p. 11.

difficulties in their way as the attempt to define societies by orders. Are there, therefore, any intermediate or alternative positions less open to the criticisms that vitiate the others? There are; although the conference scarcely discussed them.

The most recent is William Reddy's idea of monetary exchange asymmetry[12] – not a matter of groups at all, but rather of individual perceptions. Despite Reddy's presence, not much attention is given in the book to the possibilities of conceiving social interaction as something independent of group definitions. He retains a place for class, meaning a relationship rather than a group, but makes no mention of order. Enjoying legal definition, unlike class, order is a term whose meaning is less easy to transmute. The problem for Reddy, as for all who seek to change the meaning of conventional vocabulary, is to persuade even those who recognise its inadequacy to abandon using it in the old way, and to accept the new one proposed. There is little sign so far that this latest attempt has provoked more than polite interest.

A similar fate befell an earlier attempt to restructure social vocabulary in history, launched in 1965, when Peter Laslett argued that pre-industrial England, at least, was a one-class society.[13] There were plenty of status groups (perhaps what Mousnier would call orders?) but if a class was a nation-wide 'number of people banded together in the exercise of collective power, political and economic' then there was only one in sixteenth- and seventeenth-century England. This was a notion of class without class conflict. Laslett did not rule out social antagonisms, even hatreds of the sort so vividly documented by Keith Snell (see Chapter 9 in this volume). But he argued that no other part of society was organised on class lines, and therefore equipped to pursue its interests against those of society's rulers. And although he made no claims for the applicability of this model outside England, its appropriateness is obvious if we do not allow ourselves to be dazzled by the idea of a society of orders. Revisionist historians of eighteenth- and early nineteenth-century France, in pointing to an educated amalgam of non-capitalist nobles and bourgeois, later to be termed the notables, as the key actor in the revolutionary crisis,[14] seem to imply the existence of a one-class society. A recent study of seventeenth-century Languedoc is more explicit. That province, and

---

[12] Reddy, op. cit., ch. 3.
[13] *The World we have Lost* (London, 1965), pp. 22–3.
[14] W. Doyle, *Origins of the French Revolution* (2nd edn, Oxford, 1988), pp. 24, 208, 212.

French society as a whole, argues William H. Beik,[15] was dominated by a privileged class of 'lords of manors but also of officers with ownership of delegated power'. No other part of society was capable of challenging this group's position, especially since it was hand-in-glove with the state. On his way to this conclusion, Beik explicitly rejects Mousnier's society of orders model.[16] In the conference discussions, Michael Bush dismissed the notion of a one-class society as fatuous, and certainly none of the other contributors thought it worth discussing. Yet it scarcely seems open to more objections than the other models discussed, and avoids some of them, such as the problem of fitting England in.

We should not, however, make the mistake of assuming that Beik was consciously accepting the Laslett model. He never mentions it, and in fact goes out of his way to deny any similarity between France and England in his period.[17] The closest he comes to any previous model of seventeenth-century French society is to that of Porchnev; and although he can see many of the ambiguities and contradictions of the latter's conclusions,[18] they share a basic Marxism. Are we, therefore, back where we began, before the start of Mousnier's great detour? In certain senses we are. But the question would perhaps be more fruitfully put another way. Would Mousnier have launched his great detour at all if he had been confronted by today's Marxists rather than Porchnev?

For Marxism, never a monolithic creed, is more various nowadays than ever as its adherents confront its repeated intellectual and practical failures. It no longer seems as dangerous. Yet its capacity to reformulate itself remains a constant intellectual stimulus, and some of the more recent reformulations might well have removed elements which Mousnier found so objectionable in Porchnev, and which non-Marxists generally have most reservation about. Above all there are signs that class conflict or class struggle is being abandoned as an explanatory argument, at least in the period at the centre of this conference's discussions. As noted above, one of the main points made by revisionist historians of the French Revolution during the past quarter century of debate has been how little evidence can be found of conflict between nobility and bourgeoisie before the French Revolution. Marxists at bay responded initially by trying to differen-

---

[15] W.H. Beik, *Absolutism and Society in Seventeenth Century France: State Power and Provincial Aristocracy in Languedoc* (Cambridge, 1985), p. 336.
[16] Ibid., pp. 6–9.
[17] Ibid., p. 339.
[18] Ibid., pp. 23–7.

tiate within the bourgeoisie,[19] but now they are beginning to accept that the search for class conflict in the period is a vain one. The boldest of recent theorists, George Comninel,[20] argues that Marx was wrong to think of the Revolution as the work of the rising bourgeoisie, accepting from revisionist empirical scholarship that 'no social boundary at all existed between the bourgeoisie and the nobility except for noble status itself, and that was readily acquired'.[21] In other words, 'if landed property and state office were the joint basis of class relations of exploitation in the *ancien régime*, the bourgeoisie and the nobility *together* made up its ruling class'.[22] The Revolution was a civil war within the ruling class,[23] rather than a class struggle: something Marx had profoundly misunderstood. There seems little in this that supporters of a one-class model for early modern society might wish to dispute.

Yet Comninel remains a Marxist. Indeed, his professed aim is to rescue Marxism, both from its critics and from its founder. In his final words he even commits himself to class struggle as the key to human history.[24] What seemingly it cannot be the key to is revolution. It can be invoked only to explain much slower, and much longer term change.

Most of the contributors to this book would appear to share that view. The time scale for social change, whether through class struggle or evolution without it, is a long one. Social transitions are not sudden. But if this is the consensus, it is only implicit, since the question of transitions is yet another issue scarcely discussed. Absorbed by structures, the book leaves development relatively neglected. Only Joe Bergin and Gregory Freeze address it. One of them notes how slowly transitions occur (see Chapter 5) even in an order as well defined as the clergy; the other observes how hard they are to promote, and how easily new forms can revert to more traditional usage (see Chapter 4). Yet sudden changes can occur. The most obvious is the French Revolution itself, with its abrupt, and final, abolition of orders. Although in time certain orders were able

---

[19] R. Robin, *La Société française en 1789: Semur en Auxois* (Paris, 1970).
[20] *Rethinking the French Revolution: Marxism and the Revisionist Challenge* (London, 1987).
[21] Ibid., p. 181.
[22] Ibid., p. 196.
[23] Ibid., p. 200.
[24] Ibid., p. 205.

to resurrect themselves in an amended form as professions,[25] most disappeared for ever in 1789 in France. Mousnier's explanation for this shadowed the classic Marxist one. Since mid–century a society of classes had been hatched within the society of orders. The latter became increasingly hollow, and in 1789 the realities broke through. The Revolution was not a conflict of classes, but a conflict of different types of society. If, however, this is as unacceptable as explaining the Revolution in terms of class conflict, what *was* the significance of the abolition of orders and privileges?

Initially it appears to have been a matter of self-definition, or rather re-definition, within the ruling class. If a representative assembly was to govern France in the future, all men of wealth and property, members of the ruling class, must have access to this new vehicle of power in equal measure. The medieval organisation of the Estates General precluded that, and hence the attack upon it. But this movement gave rise to a debate which soon transcended the initial question. Discussion of a specific political privilege rapidly broadened into an argument about privileges in general, which produced not only attacks, but also defences of a sort scarcely considered worth articulating before. Thus, the French Revolution became in effect a struggle to *prevent* a society of orders from coming into being.

That was the purpose of the anti-aristocratic ideology then launched upon the world, and it succeeded. The society of orders was a myth that never became a reality. But paradoxically the very process of prevention strengthened the myth, both for its friends and its enemies. We are still grappling with it, as this conference bears witness. Nor was it the only myth generated during the revolutionary process. Another was that the bourgeoisie had finally arrived in 1789 at a consciousness of its own strength as a class, and shaken off aristocratic hegemony. Most historians would nowadays accept that this is not what occurred. But Marx thought it was, and he made the bourgeois class, and its struggles with other classes, above and below, the centre of his theory of modern history.[26] The concept of class discussed at this conference depends heavily on these formulations. So does that of the bourgeoisie, which was only discussed tangentially. Never credible as an order, scarcely more so nowadays as a class, there is perhaps less to differentiate the bourgeoisie from the English middle

---

[25] M.P. Fitzsimmons, *The Parisian Order of Barristers and the French Revolution, 1789–1815* (Cambridge, Mass., 1987).

[26] See Comninel, op. cit., ch. 7, and F. Furet, *Marx et la révolution française* (Paris, 1986).

classes than John Seed implies (see Chapter 7 in this volume). More myths; and perhaps society can never begin to be understood without them. The task of social history is to test and refine them repeatedly in the light of empirical evidence.

CHAPTER THIRTEEN
Class and historical explanation

Huw Beynon

University of Manchester

My concern as a sociologist is that sociologists and historians should become more involved in common projects and in serious intellectual cooperation. This concern recognises the problems and difficulties inherent in the conjunction of the two disciplines. Several years ago I remember one colleague asking contemptuously, 'But what *is* history?', and dismissing the work of historians as too empiricist and theoretically naive. Equally, I am sure, historians have registered their disquiet over sociology and what may be seen as its theoretical pretentions. I sense, however, that there is now more solid support for a common accord between historians and sociologists than there has been in the past. In the 1980s several sociologists produced books which dealt directly with the idea of a historical sociology.[1] As social historians have opened up debates which have made use of sociological and social anthropological writings, so too have sociologists produced books with a wide historical sweep.[2] This mutuality of interest has been aided by the development of journals like *History Workshop* and *Historical Sociology*. There seems to be every likelihood that this collective work will continue, and this view is supported by a reading of the chapters in this book. Most would, I think, sit easily in the proceedings of a sociological conference dedicated to questions of inequality, conflict and order in modern societies. All this supports the view of Philip Abrams that 'in terms of their fundamental preconceptions, history and sociology are, and always have been, the same'.[3]

---

[1] See e.g. P. Abrams, *Historical Sociology* (Shepton Mallet, 1982) and G. McLennan, *Marxism and the Methodologies of History* (London, 1981).

[2] See e.g. M. Mann, *The Sources of Social Power* (Cambridge, 1986).

[3] P. Abrams, *Historical Sociology*, p. x.

Abrams's book *Historical Sociology* has been extremely influential and it is worth quoting his views further. For him

> Historical sociology is not . . . a matter of imposing grand schemes of revolutionary development on the relationship of the past to the present. Nor is it merely a matter of recognising the historical background to the present. It is the attempt to understand the relationship of personal activity and experience on the one hand and social organisation on the other as something that is continually constructed in time [and therefore] there is no necessary difference between the sociologist and the historian. . . . Sociology which takes itself seriously must be historical sociology.[4]

I have always felt this to be true, and I became firmly convinced of it during the research I carried out with colleagues on the Durham coalfield in the 1980s. We were helped to this view by a meeting which took place in the city of Durham. It was described in the following way by a local reporter:

> Two of Britain's wealthiest families were joined by marriage in Durham Cathedral yesterday. Lady Isabella Lambton, the 21 year old youngest of five daughters of Mr and Mrs Tony Lambton of Lambton Park, Burnmoor, married banker Mr Philip Naylor-Leyland. The bridegroom, a 26 year old former Household Cavalry Officer, will inherit £20 million from the late Earl Fitzwilliam, his mother's step-father. His inheritance includes 13,000 acres and two stately homes, one of them with 365 rooms. A total of 300 guests, including staff from the Lambton Estates in Northumberland and Durham went on to a champagne reception and buffet in Durham Castle's Great Hall. Lady Isabella wore a dress of white slipper satin. Her silk veil was set off with a circle of yellow roses and she carried a single rose instead of a bouquet. The four bridesmaids wore silver grey, full length dresses with white bonnets and carried posies of yellow roses. All the dress designs were inspired by the painting of the 18th century artist Thomas Lawrence and made by Belville Sassoon, of London. The page boys wore colourful period suits in red and blue velvet with matching bows on their shoes.[5]

The father of the bride was the former Earl of Durham, who had relinquished his title to advance his career in the Commons. It was he who resigned from Heath's government in 1973 after a call-girl scandal, and outfaced a rather sheepish Robin Day in his resignation interview. The family survived the scandal, retaining their powerful presence in the area, and the family motto 'The Day Will Come'. It has been one of the most powerful families in Britain for two centuries. It developed its wealth in the coal trades in the nineteenth century, and its members have played a significant role in party

[4] Ibid., pp. 16 – 17.
[5] *The Sunderland Echo*, 19 March 1980.

politics in the nineteenth century as Liberals, more recently in the Tory party. Generally the family has provided personnel for the upper circles of the British state.[6] In the context of our researches into the social structure of the Durham coalfield the example of the Lambtons served to illustrate well the enduring nature of wealth and political power, and this led us to accentuate the historical aspects of our research into class formation.[7] Here it serves as an introduction to the question of social class and historical change.

The use of social class as the basis for a general conceptual framework through which to analyse society and social change has been the subject of detailed debate and discussion for over a century. This debate has taken place both *within* the Marxist tradition and between it and other schools of thought. Often the lines of disagreement have been more apparent than real; occasionally the opposite has been the case.[8] In reflecting on this it is hard to resist the view that the idea of class is, at one and the same time, the most useful and the most problematic of concepts employed by historians and social scientists. Its attractiveness lies initially in its potential for identifying coherent groups of people via their economic position within society. Furthermore, if these groups are seen as being in conflict or competition with each other, class position can be seen as a significant key to an exploration of people's motives and political action. The problems arise in different ways. To begin with it is not clear how and upon what basis groups can be located in the economic structure of a society. Furthermore, whichever scheme is chosen there is likely to be ambiguity and marginality. In Reddy's words, 'once the microscope is brought into focus neat class boundaries dissolve.[9] In addition, and perhaps most importantly, it is arguable that people, however located, will behave and think in ways which are not determined by their class position. Again in Reddy's view, it is difficult 'to speak of socially distinct sets of individuals, united by some identifiable trait or traits, [and] having shared intentions'.[10]

This problem can be understood as one involving classification (by some objective sets of criteria) and of interpreting the subjective

---

[6] See Sir John Colville, *Those Lamptons: a Most Unusual Family* (London, 1988).

[7] H. Beynon and T. Austrin, *Masters and Servants: Class and Patronage in the Making of a Labour Organisation* (London, 1990).

[8] For an account which illustrates similarity see T. Skocpol, *States and Social Revolutions* (Cambridge, 1979); for a different view see E. Meiksins Wood, *The Retreat from Class: a New 'True' Socialism* (London, 1986).

[9] See W.M. Reddy, *Money and Liberty in Modern Europe: a Critique of Historical Understanding* (Cambridge, 1987), p. 9.

[10] Ibid., p. 8.

experiences and understandings of people in relation to the classificatory system chosen. The doubts and questions raised by Reddy are important ones. However, his conclusion that 'the whole notion of class as an explanatory principle in history is . . . brought into question' is, in my view, premature.[11]

In assessing these issues it is helpful to place them in historical context. Kolakowski has maintained that most of the significant issues and debates relevant to Marxist theory were fully discussed in the nineteenth century, and there is some support for this view.[12] Certainly the writings of Marx show a keen awareness of these problems, and while the judgement of recent authors that they are 'irrefutably ambiguous' on the question of linking the objective and subjective dimensions of class, may be over harsh, their contribution is helpful in drawing attention to the variety of different ways in which Marx addressed this central issue.[13]

On questions concerning the social basis of classes and class relationships, for example, Marx's writings occasionally establish the analysis with great clarity. Here class in capitalist society is related directly to property (or propertylessness) and the operation of the division of labour and the labour process produces a tendency toward polarisation and class conflict. In a much quoted passage he asserts:

> the owners merely of labour power, owners of capital and landowners whose respective source of income are wages, profit and ground-rent, in other words wage labourers, capitalists and landowners, constitute the three big classes in modern society based upon the capitalist mode of production.[14]

However, Marx observed that the social and technical division of labour had operated within these classes to produce an 'infinite fragmentation of interest and rank'.[15] Here, as all Marxologists inform us, 'the manuscript breaks off', leaving us with what has become known as 'the boundary problem'. It was this problem which was picked up by Weber in his detailed distillation of the variety of economic processes at work upon group formation in a market economy. As a result, the possibility emerged of Marx's 'three big classes' fragmenting into a greater number based not only upon position within the production process but through competition over

[11] Ibid., p. 9.
[12] L. Kolakowski, *Main Currents in Marxism* (Oxford, 1978), vols 1 and 2.
[13] G. Marshall, H. Newby, D. Rose and C. Vogler, *Social Class in Modern Britain* (London, 1988).
[14] K. Marx, *Capital* (Moscow, 1971), vol. 3, p. 885.
[15] Ibid., p. 886.

a range of marketable goods. Given this, Reddy's view that it is 'difficult to be precise about class boundaries and class membership' is undeniable (Woolf would call it a truism: see Chapter 10 in this volume); so too Reddy's observation that 'if one were to take singly a strict definition of "proletariat" and look across the globe today, we would find an awesome diversity of fates summed up in that word' (see Chapter 2 in this volume).

Certainly the chapters in this book all illustrate the fact that within any broadly defined class of people a great variation exists, in both terms of economic rewards and interests and in sets of ideas and beliefs. Michael Bush's account of the European peasantry (see Chapter 8) is particularly helpful in outlining both the diversity of fates associated with pre-capitalist social relations, and their multiplicity of causes. Patterns of land utilisation and landholding, taxation policies as well as kinship and demographic factors all contributed to the fates of peasants. It was for these and other reasons that Shanin referred to the peasantry as 'the awkward class'.[16] They too severely taxed Marx's own conceptual scheme and drew from him an assessment of class in terms of their relationships. In France he wrote of 'small-holding' peasants' forming 'a vast mass, the members of which live in similar conditions but without entering into manifold relations with each other'. From this he concluded generally:

> Insofar as millions of families live under economic conditions of existence that separate their mode of life, their interests and their culture from those of the other classes and put them in hostile opposition to the latter, they form a class. In so far as there is merely local interconnection among these small-holding peasants and the identity of interest begets no community, no national bond and no political organisation amongst them, they do not form a class.[17]

This element of community is, in different ways, seen as critical by Reddy and Snell – 'class is a community issue' – (see Chapters 2 and 9) and is taken up forcefully by Patrick Joyce (see Chapter 11). His account of industrial workers in the nineteenth century reveals the extent to which the working class was made up of fragmented groups, often locally isolated and divided rather than united by their economic position as wage labourers. While aspects of this account can be questioned, it shows clearly that it is particularly difficult to establish evidence for a single coherent working class in Victorian

[16] T. Shanin, *The Awkward Class* (London, 1973).
[17] K. Marx, *The Eighteenth Brumaire of Louis Bonaparte* (New York, 1963), pp. 123–4.

England. This (via discussion of the 'labour aristocracy' and the 'reserve army') has been recognised for some time. Joyce's chapter takes us a further step along the road of deconstruction, and uncovers another awkward class.

To this problem of the internal variation within a class (and the related question of subjective class identity) can be added a further set of problems relating to class boundaries. Again Bush's account of the peasantry (see Chapter 8) is suggestive. He raises questions about the experiences of free peasants in relation to those of serfs, and suggests circumstances in which the latter status would be preferable to the former thereby raising the possibility of a severe disjuncture between analytical categories and everyday experience. Similar ideas have influenced the discussion of slavery in the Americas. Here attention has been drawn to the variability of slavery as an institutional form, and the similarity and difference between the experience of slaves and free workers in the industrialising USA.[18] These issues, of course, affected perceptions of the workers themselves – in the USA and in Europe. Marx's notion of a 'wage slave' flowed from a popular discourse that was influenced, in part, by the fact that significant numbers of workers were involved in a tied relationship to their employers. Of these, the coal-miners of Scotland and northern England were the most significant group. These workers were employed as bonded servants until 1872. As the first General Secretary of the Durham Miners' Association put it in 1871: 'When you felt the full weight of the burden you longed to be free; you looked around but found no means of escape; you were lashed to the PLACE by English law, and while there, constantly scorched by the employers' scorpion whip'.[19] In this way, perhaps, Snell's observations (see Chapter 9) on the blurring of distinctions between peasant and agricultural labourers in the English and Welsh countryside could be extended to a group of workers whose centrality to the working class has become almost legendary.[20]

The miners in the eighteenth and nineteenth century were employed under arrangements similar to those experienced by agricultural labourers. Equally, and in spite of an over-enthusiastic interpretation of industrialisation as an *urban* process, they lived in villages which were most often situated apart from the towns and

[18] See e.g. R.W. Fogel and S.L. Engerman, *Time on the Cross* (Boston, 1974) and H.G. Gutman, *Slavery and the Numbers Game* (Urbana, 1975).

[19] Quoted in Beynon and Austrin, *Masters and Servants*.

[20] For a discussion see R. Harrison (ed.) *Independent Collier: The Coal Miner as Archetypal Proletarian Reconsidered* (Sussex, 1978).

cities. As such John Campbell in his biography of Nye Bevan draws close attention to the link between solidarity and local chauvinism among mine-workers and how in any assessment of Bevan it is important to understand that

> he was in a real sense a country boy. The mining communities are not truly urban but *valleys* with open hillside in between them . . . the mountain – more accurately the bare heather moors – came almost literally to his doorstep.[21]

These problems of establishing clear class categories based upon forms of labour and production are exacerbated when we consider the vexed question of the middle class. Seed's historical dilemma (see Chapter 7) is to identify a class whose name denotes not a role or activity but 'a space, a between . . . a group that fails or refuses to fit the dominant social division between rich and poor'. This difficulty has been compounded by the rise of large-scale organisations and a growing non-capitalist salariat to form 'one of the most intractable issues in contemporary sociology'.[22] Here the problem is partly one of definition (why 'middle' class?) and sociologists have suggested new terms to handle modern conditions – the service class being the most common. More significant is the question of class boundaries and the allocative process whereby people are placed in the class categories.

This particular problem, of course, is a general one and not peculiar to sociology and history. One of the features of modern states has been their concern with classifying and collecting data about their populations. Timberlake (see Chapter 6) points to the elaborate devices developed by the Tsarist state in its attempt to retain an established system of classification in the face of an enduring and dynamic division of labour.[23] The activities of the British state were different in kind but no less problematic. The 1851 census, for example, located the royal family in the professional class. This classification system became refined in the twentieth century into the widely used Registrar General's scale. While more comprehensive, this outline of categories was not without its problems and idiosyncrasies. Its underlying theoretical assumptions were those of the

---

[21] See J. Campbell, *Nye Bevan and the Mirage of British Socialism* (London, 1987), p. 7.

[22] N. Abercrombie and J. Urry, *Capital, Labour and the Middle Classes* (London, 1983).

[23] See E.O. Wright, *Class Crisis and the State* (London, 1979); and E.O. Wright, *Classes* (London, 1985); J. Goldthorpe, *Social Mobility and the Class Structure in Northern Britain* (Oxford, 1980); Marshall *et al.*, *Social Class in Modern Britain*.

eugenicists and their view of superior and inferior types. It has frequently been pointed out that the scale is based on a range of intuitive and a priori assumptions, and Nichols has observed how, in this scheme of things, capitalists and inmates of mental hospitals are brought together in the same class.[24] Against this background, sociologists and historians have attempted to develop more refined classificatory systems. In his assessment of historical researches into the middle class, Seed (see Chapter 7) points to the 'limited value of using occupation as an index of social position'. Much contemporary sociological research bears this out. Elaborate and sophisticated attempts at establishing scales which link occupation to class have indicated the problematic nature of this exercise. They have also pointed to the critical role played by the evaluative judgements of the researchers themselves.[25] Even given these problems, however, empirical sociological researchers would argue that while class categories (like all categories) contain internal variation, they remain a powerful explanatory tool in accounting for people's attitudes at work, voting preferences, educational performance and so on. To go beyond this, many would argue, requires more detailed, ethnographic evidence and qualitative investigations into people's lives.[26]

It is, of course, at this broad level of subjectivity that the argument becomes most complex. Classificatory systems are all inherently difficult to establish and historians and sociologists recognise this as a necessary evil. For Reddy (see Chapter 2) the classificatory problem is a stalking horse for a greater enemy; that is, the view that classes themselves become agents in history, being ushered on and off the stage by historians to explain (or explain away) particular events and developments. Here too (as with the 'infinite fragmentation of interest and rank') the problem, the challenge and the crisis is not a new one. Certainly in their own empirical analyses it is possible to discern an awareness of this issue in the minds of Marx and Engels. Marx's reference to the peasantry has already been noted. To this could be added Engel's account of the religious views of the English middle classes in the 1850s. Engels makes clear that the class interest of this particular group had become effectively masked by the depths of their religious beliefs and could not, as such, be used as an explanation of their behaviour. In this he concludes that 'religious views and their

---

[24] T. Nichols, 'Social class: official, sociological and Marxist definitions', in J. Irvine, I. Miles and J. Evans (eds) *Demystifying Social Statistics* (London, 1979).

[25] See e.g. D. Rose (ed.) *Social Stratification and Economic Change* (London, 1988).

[26] See G. Marshall, 'Some remarks on the study of working class consciousness', *Politics and Society* 12 (1983): 263 – 301.

further development into systems of dogmas' in many cases predominate in determining the form and the course of historical struggles.[27] As Abrams has astutely observed, the problem here (and elsewhere) is *not* that the analysis

> too closely explains all historical events and developments in terms of the relations of production, ownership and class, but that it makes such generous provision for the *mediation* of these influences by political, cultural and ideological factors that the causal connection between economic relationships and historical change becomes extremely difficult to trace.[28]

These accounts leave us with a paradox. In one reading Marx's observations on the peasantry reinforced by the reference to 'potatoes in a sack' leads to the sharp dichotomy he draws between true and false consciousness, between reality and illusion. It is this framework which allows the interests of classes to lurk undetected for decades before finally emerging at critical moments in the agency of class action. This is the Marxism of the Third International and it shares many assumptions with more liberal and empiricist researchers. This is the object of Reddy's initial scepticism with class analysis. However, these same observations can also lead to a theorisation of class which sees economic and political classes (and the arena of class struggle) as non-reducible categories, a view which is compatible with a radical interpretation of Weber. In the 1960s E.P. Thompson entered the contest over the theory of class with the publication of his momentous study *The Making of the English Working Class* and a series of essays eventually published as *The Poverty of Theory*. Reddy extends his criticism of class analysis to encompass the solution suggested by Thompson (see Chapter 2).

Thompson's writings are well known. He has made clear his dislike of formulations of class which derived from Stalinist and structuralist schools of Marxism. He has extended his displeasure to styles of sociological investigation which had hitherto been obsessed with problems of classification and had 'stopped the time machine'. His project was to rescue the experiences of working people 'from the enormous condescension of posterity', thereby addressing the central problem of linking day-to-day experience and the meaningful worlds of workers to analyses of class relationships.[29] In this he asserted:

---

[27] F. Engels, *Socialism, Utopian and Scientific* (London, 1892).

[28] P. Abrams, *Historical Sociology*, p. 49.

[29] E.P. Thompson, *The Making of the English Working Class* (London, 1968), p. 13.

we cannot deduce class from a static 'section' (since it is becoming over time) nor as a function of a mode of production, since class formation and class consciousness (while subject to determinate pressures) evaluate in an open-ended process of relationships – of struggle with other classes – over time.[30]

Class for Thompson was a 'junction concept', a means of handling the intersection between structure and action. Its open-endedness eschewed versions of true and false consciousness:

> Class consciousness is the way these experiences are handled in cultural terms . . . If the experience appears as determined, class consciousness does not. We can see a logic . . . but we cannot predict any law. Consciousness of class arises in the same way in different times and places, but never in just the same way.[31]

As such, it ushered in an investigation of the world of the worker as a central and necessary part of any class analysis. This view has greatly influenced social historians and sociologists and ironically (given Thompson's antipathy toward much sociological work) it has been instrumental in generating common approaches and questions between the two disciplines. The mark of Thompson's influence can be seen in this collection. Seed (see Chapter 7) writes of class as 'something more than a passive or static description based upon certain kinds of quantifiable information', and states that it is 'not a matter only of this or that aspect of a group – but a shifting totality of social relations'. He also points to the need to investigate the vocabulary of class used in popular discourse. This is important and is based upon the observation that, whatever the classification problems, people have used and continue to use a language which identifies other groups and classes in society. Often they have used the idea of class in imaginative and metaphysical ways. Snell (see Chapter 9) for example, recounts the term 'burglar class' as used in the fields of England and Wales in the nineteenth century. In contemporary society French car workers have described their managers as 'the grey suits' and British chemical workers refer to their superiors as 'the big books'.[32] Equally, Snell's emphasis on the 'phenomenology of class' fits well with studies which have attempted to relate the interpretative worlds of workers to an analysis of class relations. In his detailed study of Limerick, for example, McNabb examined the ways in

[30] E.P. Thompson, *The Poverty of Theory* (London, 1978), p. 299.
[31] E.P. Thompson, *The Making of the English Working Class*, p. 10.
[32] See R. Linhart, *The Assembly Line* (London, 1978); T. Nichols and H. Beynon, *Living with Capitalism* (London, 1978).

which 'the class structure is revealed in ordinary day to day life'. He observed how the cooperative organisation, Maintir na Tire, organised meetings in which the platform and the front-row seats were occupied by the farmers. In turn many farm labourers left because, in their view, the farmers 'wanted nobody to have a say but themselves'. In response the farmers were critical of the labourers arguing that 'they won't speak up when they're at a meeting, we do all their talking outside the door'. In his analysis McNabb demonstrates equally how 'the end to be achieved and towards which the society is organised . . . is the preservation of property'.[33] In this it is clear that the role of men as husbands and fathers is central to the social structure; and this points to some problems.

Many of the criticisms of Thompson are well known. His attack on the classifiers has made him vulnerable to the charge that his empirical material is too narrowly based to do justice to the title of his study.[34] Structuralists like Richard Johnson have criticised his culturalist approach for being too naively naturalistic and for having too little analysis of the dynamic of change in the eighteenth and nineteenth centuries.[35]

In his view, Thompson allows 'the economic' a place in his analysis but only 'through the category of experience': that is, economic relations existing in the feelings expressed by members of the class. Economic forces as a set of objectively present relations appear only in an attenuated form, *through* the cultural, *through* the 'inwardness of experience'. As such, argues Johnson, Thompson's solution makes it 'extremely difficult to employ economic categories in any very exact way', thereby robbing the historian of 'a powerful tool of analysis'. Johnson concludes with a restatement of the old problem:

> [Thompson's analysis] produces serious difficulties . . . when it is necessary to analyse moments in the history of classes when cultural and political fragmentations do actively prove, in political outcomes, to be more powerful than any sense of class unity. Do classes then not exist?

[33] P. McNabb 'Social structure', in J. Newman (ed.) *The Limerick Rural Survey 1958–1964* (Tipperary, 1964) p. 242.

[34] This criticism has been put in a forceful way by Perry Anderson: 'It comes as something of a shock, at the end of 900 pages, to realise that one has not been told such an elementary fact as the approximate size of the English working class, or its proportion within the population as a whole, at any date in the history of its "making".' See P. Anderson, *Arguments within English Marxism* (London, 1980), p. 33.

[35] Johnson, in particular, takes issue with Thompson's contention that, in his researches 'the material took command of one', seeing this as 'a tendency to prefer "experience" to "theory"'. See R. Johnson, 'Edward Thompson, Eugene Genovese and socialist-humanist history', *History Workshop* 6 (1978): 79 – 100.

One might consider the question for the 1850s and 1860s in Britain and, for the present, of the 'disappearance' of class in . . . the 1950s.[36]

From another standpoint Perry Anderson has vigorously explored the variety of uses made by Thompson of the key ideas of 'agency' and 'experience'. In this he noted the passage:

> experience walks in without knocking at the door, and announces deaths, crises of subsistence, trench warfare, unemployment, inflation, genocide. People starve: their survivors think in new ways about the market. People are imprisoned: in prison they meditate in new ways about the law.

To this, Anderson adds the comment: 'Thompson clearly assumes that the lessons taught will be the correct ones' and concludes that this leaves the analysis in a vulnerable state, for 'what ensures that a particular experience of distress or disaster will inspire a particular (cognitive or morally appropriate) conclusion?'[37]

Patrick Joyce's contribution to this volume (see Chapter 11) develops this debate further in the context of Victorian England. His analysis of the capital – labour relation leads him to conclude that a 'diverse and fragmented labour force' existed in Britain and that the economic position of workers 'emerges as so ambiguous and so fractured that the very idea of class may itself be questioned'. By this route, political parties and organised forms of popular culture are seen to have more bearing than economics on the uniformities of sentiment uniting workers. There is no doubt that the emphasis given by Joyce to political parties and their mode of organisation, as well as to the imaginative realm, is of great importance, although it is possible that he has overemphasised the influence of non–class elements in popular culture. Undoubtedly the miners are an important case and the continuity of their liberal affiliations is of great significance to an analysis of the working class in Victorian England. In this, of course, John Wilson is a critical figure and Joyce's interpretation of him is quite meagre. Certainly Wilson's own accounts of his life and his involvement with the Durham miners and the Liberal party provide evidence of the enormous tensions that built up between the accommodating role played by the Durham Miners' Association, and other powerful understandings present among coal–miners.[38] These disjunc-

---

[36] Ibid., p. 97.

[37] P. Anderson, *Arguments within English Marxism*, p. 28. The quotation from Thompson comes from *The Poverty of Theory*, p. 201.

[38] See J. Wilson, *A History of the Durham Miners 1870–1904* (Durham 1907) and J. Wilson, *Memories of a Labour Leader* (London, 1910).

tures often became most clear in periods of industrial dispute or at election times: in 1874, for example, when, in the run-up to the election, feelings were running high among the miners as a consequence of Londonderry's attitude to the 1872 Miners Act and towards trade unionism in general. Wilson describes how riots were broken up by police who took several miners prisoner. While standing on a waggon in an attempt to keep order, he was told by two young men that he should take no notice: 'Just watch and you'll see some fun'. It seems that they were right:

> The police were returning from the lockup after securing their prisoners when they were met by a shower of whin stones. They were a very dangerous missile having very sharp edges . . . The officers were taken at a disadvantage for the attack was well concerted and the stones were delivered with precision. The officers retreated and were chased to the lockup.[39]

He then recounts how the lockup was attacked, the prisoners released, and how on that night 'considerable damage was done'. Similar incidents (too regular to be dismissed as sporadic outbursts of militancy) can be worked into a pattern which relates to a tension between different understandings of politics and action in relation to specific organisations, notably the trade union and the state. Something of this tension comes through in the work songs and ballads of Durham's 'pitman poet' Tommy Armstrong. These contain the populist and nationalist references to which Joyce refers, but they also contain strongly worked ideas of class antagonism and that sense of moral outrage which have become associated with mining as an occupation. Mine officials (like Maiden Law Joe) are violent and condemned ('born without feelings or shame'). In 1885, the year of the major strike in the county, he wrote *Oakeys Strike*. This like his poem *South Medomsley Strike* is a powerful attack on the masters and their henchmen, the candymen (the bailiffs). In it Armstrong raises the question: 'What would I do if I had the power myself?' His answer is clear: 'I'd hang the twenty candymen and Johney that carries the bell'.[40]

These accounts endorse Joyce's view that historians and sociologists should look beyond economic factors for sources of explanation, and consider cultural and political activities in their own right. In embracing this non-reductionist perspective, however, it is important to

[39] See Wilson, *A History of the Durham Miners*.
[40] See H. Beynon, 'Introduction', to R. Forbes (ed.) *Polis and Candymen* (Durham, 1985).

keep open the question of the relationship between these various levels – between class and culture and politics. There is a danger that in cleansing the analysis, the baby is being jettisoned with the bath water. This is an important point to make at a time when the debate about class is clearly going through an episodic crisis.

Reddy's contribution to this collection is significant in this context for he takes the criticism of Thompson a step further via a strict interpretation of the view that class should be understood as a social relationship. In this Reddy focuses on Thompson's view that a 'structure', not even a 'category' but . . . something which in fact happens . . . in human relationships, . . . class entails the notion of a historical relationship . . . which evades analysis if we stop it dead at any given moment and atomise its structure'.[41] Clearly this formulation contains a strong element of polemic which was directed, significantly, at those who make use of the 'finest meshed sociological net'. The polemical element in Thompson's writings should always be kept in mind, and in this respect, the strictness of Reddy's approach may limit its helpfulness. It leads him to assert that, for Thompson, class must 'be seen, not as a group of individuals, but as a relationship', whereas at several points in his writings Thompson clearly writes of classes as groups. For example, he speaks of a class as 'a very loosely defined body of people who share the same congeries of interests, social experiences, traditions and value system, who have a disposition to behave as a class'.[42] This in many respects can be seen as a classic definition deriving from Marx's account of the French peasantry. It seems more pertinent to argue that the problem with Thompson is not that he sees class simply as a relationship, but that he tends, in developing his argument, to conflate what are, in fact, logically separate parts of the analysis. This problem is central to the critique developed by Johnson and, more recently, by Ira Katznelson.[43] Katznelson, for example, argues that Thompson 'moves much too quickly' between what might be termed 'levels of class'. Here Katznelson, like Johnson, argued for the need to identify structural aspects of class – associated with capitalist division of labour and labour process – as a preliminary part of a class analysis. This is not a simple process of classification (with all its recognised problems) but one which involves preliminary empirical and theoretical investi-

---

[41] Thompson, *The Making of the English Working Class*, p. 9.
[42] E.P. Thompson, 'The peculiarities of the English', in R. Miliband and J. Saville (eds) *The Socialist Register 1965* (London, 1965), p. 357.
[43] I. Katznelson and A.R. Zolberg, *Working Class Formation* (Princeton, 1986).

gations into the nature of a society, and its component economic sectors. To this a further element is added – that of subjective understanding and this too requires detailed, interpretative investigations which examine the fireside worlds referred to by Snell (see Chapter 9) as well as the worlds of work. The arena of class struggle, of organised and motivated groups operating with a common purpose, involves an additional investigation. Clearly it is possible to identify classes at each of these levels. What is not clear is the closeness of fit that will operate between them.

Katznelson's framework is clearly helpful. Some might say that it reworks an old problem and that the question of determinacy is still left unresolved. Of greater concern, perhaps, is the absence of a detailed discussion of class *composition* and the processes whereby different groups of people (men and women; black people and brown people) are brought into a framework of labouring for capital. Furthermore, the approach (formally stated) allows for a sophisticated analysis at the level of the economic structure, but perhaps a less developed one at the subjective level. In this the growing literature on issues relating to domination and power is important, as it develops ways of cutting through the social structure and involving the personal experiences and day-to-day lives of its people. In this, of course, the work of the French theorists Foucault and Bordieu is well known.[44] Equally useful is Stephen Lukes's analysis of power which develops debates within American political science. Lukes draws attention to three levels of power: he identifies the process whereby people make decisions that affect others; where a 'mobilisation of bias' occurs limiting the choices open to decision-makers; and where there is a general *shaping* of people's wants and desires.[45] In developing this analysis, Lukes borrows from Gramsci's acute awareness of the 'profound contrast in a social historical order'. In this vein Gramsci wrote of a situation where

> the social group in question may indeed have its own conception of the world, even if only embryonic; a conception which manifests itself in action, but occasionally and in flashes when the group is acting as an organic totality. But this same group has, for reasons of submission and intellectual subordination, adopted a conception which is not its own but is borrowed from another group; and it affirms this conception verbally and believes itself to be following it, because this is the conception it

---

[44] See e.g. P. Bordieu, *Distinctions: A Social Critique of the Judgement of Taste* (London, 1984); M. Foucault, *Discipline and Punish* (London, 1979).
[45] S. Lukes, *Power – A Radical View* (London, 1974). See also S. Lukes (ed.) *Power* (Oxford, 1986).

follows in 'normal times' – that is, when its conduct is not independent and autonomous, but submissive and subordinate.[46]

This idea of a contrast between normal and abnormal times is potentially very helpful. For Lukes, the 'supreme and insidious exercise of power' is deeply related to the process whereby people can 'see or imagine' no alternative to the established order of things or because they see it as natural and unchangeable or because they value it as divinely ordained or beneficial.[47]

This analysis is schematic and suggestive rather than conclusive, but it has been developed by John Gaventa and others in ways which represent quite significant steps in our understanding of historical and social processes. John Gaventa's study of Appalachian coal-miners begins with the question:

> Why, in a social relationship involving the domination of a non-elite by an elite, does challenge to that domination not occur? What is there in certain situations of social deprivation that prevents issues from arising, grievances from being voiced, or interests from being reorganised? Why, in an oppressed community where one might intuitively expect upheaval, does one instead find, or appear to find, quiescence? Under what conditions and against what obstacles does rebellion begin to emerge?[48]

He writes of the importance of looking at periods when the normal state of affairs is broken or when power of the elite weakens for

> if the non-elite begin to assert latent challenges then one is provided with the demonstration of a 'relevant counter-factual'. This would suggest that the power situation has not been based on consensus but on something else – such as control.

The worry with Lukes's analysis was always that, beneath the talk of levels, there lurked the idea of 'real' interests and the associated idea of 'false consciousness'. In his detailed empirical investigations (which rest upon the expressed desires and choices of the coal-miners, in normal and abnormal times), Gaventa successfully escapes this trap and produces a highly persuasive account of how groups of people behave and understand themselves as classes at one time but not another.[49]

[46] A. Gramsci, *Selections from the Prison Notebooks* (London, 1971), p. 24.

[47] Lukes, *Power – A Radical View*.

[48] J. Gaventa, *Power and Powerlessness: Quiescence and Rebellion in an Appalachian Valley* (Urbana, 1980), p. 3.

[49] For criticism of Lukes see T. Benton, 'Objective interests and the sociology of power', *Sociology* 15 (1981): 161 – 84; B. Hindess, 'Power, interests and the outcomes of struggles', *Sociology* 16 (1982): 498 – 516; S. Clegg, *Frameworks of Power* (London, 1989).

This reference to empirical evidence is a helpful reminder of the fact that while some questions of class analysis can be settled by logical discussion, ultimately the efficacy of the concept relates to its ability to render intelligible human experience and produce credible explanations of historical change. In this we are drawn toward an issue which, in an understated way, is present throughout these chapters, and to which the question of orders and classes is central. This is, of course, the transformation of societies through processes of industrialisation, modernisation and the development of capitalist forms of production and exchange. This process has been a central concern of sociology which has its roots in the historical writings of Durkheim, Marx and Weber. It is in the context of this transformation of society that issues of state and class have their origin. Here Durkheim's developed sense of pre-capitalist society operating within 'a strong and defined . . . common conscience' has exerted a strong influence, and there is a generally accepted rubric which associates capitalism with the rise of individualism, the separation of economic forces from the constraint of other legal and political constraints and the ascendance of classes (that is economically based groupings) over groups based upon status, honour and legal protection.

A clear example of this process is provided by Snell (see Chapter 9) when he writes of 'a rural society of complex ladder-like stratification . . . based upon a general and enduring moral economy' changing in the south of England to a more polarised society dominated by 'simpler conceptions of station and clear cut lines of hostile class division'. He draws attention to the particular factors which influenced this development, implicitly contrasting them with a different pattern of change in the agrarian societies of northern England. In this way the idea of variation is introduced into the discussion and it is worth examining this further. It was in the North, of course, that coal-mining developed with the operation of a detailed system of bonded labour. Under this system miners were provided with housing and coal by the employers, and the annual bond detailed their respective obligations. Attention has been drawn to the iniquities associated with this system and its influence upon trade union development. However, it is important to note the degree to which the aristocratic capitalists were strongly committed to the ideas of paternalism and to a view of society based upon status and obligation. This came out clearly at times of conflict between Lord Londonderry and newly established joint stock companies. In 1844, for example, after a terrible disaster in the Haswell mine, the Haswell Coal Company issued a public appeal for the relief of the families of the victims. To this Londonderry wrote of his 'extreme regret that the Company should appeal to the public'. In his view the mine-owners had a deep responsibility to the workers in their employ. It was in fact 'the bounden duty of all proprietors' to care for their work people in such circumstances, for

> as the collier or pitman devotes his labour and uses the risk of the mines for the benefit of his employer so is the latter in common duty, honesty and charity bound to provide for and protect those who are bereft of their protectors by any fatality that occurs.

It was, he concluded, the sacred duty of employers to 'support those left behind'.[50]

This view is reinforced by a reading of Timberlake's account of industrialisation in Tsarist Russia (see Chapter 6). Here we find a highly formalised system of orders being bent and amended to cope with an expanding division of labour as industrialists and bankers and others pressed for recognition within the *soslovie* system. It is possible to interpret this, as Timberlake does, as an emerging conflict between a society of orders and one based on classes. However, what is clear from his account is that the new class of capitalist (being propelled into the old society) were no automatic converts to ideas of liberalism, individuality and the free market-place. For them the operation of the system of ranks was no mere epiphenomenon over which class interests dominated. In this period individual businessmen (and Movozot is a good example) were both antagonistic to and deeply influenced by the assumptions and operations of the old estate system. It took the critical *event* of 1905 with all its attendant violence to create within the business community an understanding that the *soslovie* system was not the well-integrated ordered society that they had supposed, and that it could not shield Russia from the unrest that had been associated with capitalist development in western Europe.

If ideas relating to a world dominated by orders had influence among industrial employers, there is considerable evidence to suggest that similar processes were also present within the growing numbers of industrial workers. Much has been written about the dense occupational cultures of miners in Britain in the nineteenth century, and some play has been made of the way in which this group of workers defended its interests through the state. In Germany, for example Tenfelde has written of miners having a separate festive culture which derived from 'the singularity of mining as an occupa-

---

[50] See Beynon and Austrin, *Masters and Servants*.

tion [and] the unifying force of its special legal status'. These factors together with the pattern of settlement combined, he argued, to produce a distinct occupational culture celebrated through festivals which were 'saturated with practices derived from religion, communal and courtly festivals'.[51]

A similar pattern can be observed in the UK. In Britain, after all, the miners won the right to a checkweighman by Act of Parliament before they had established trade union bargaining rights. All this is very reminiscent of the corporate groups that Woolf writes of within the *ancien régime* (see Chapter 10). It suggests a complex pattern of change, in the transitional process from the old society to the new. Perhaps it is helpful to see this as an amalgam of different forms of social organisation, in which orders are renegotiated in the context of a class society. Corrigan has written of the various ways in which 'relics' of the feudal order were maintained as 'capitalist monuments'.[52] In this, of course, the most significant groupings would be those based upon sex and gender. The earlier discussion of property rights in western Ireland pointed to the ways in which the position of men was central to the reproduction of the social structure. There has been much recent research which argues in a similar vein, and feminist writers have discussed the processes whereby capitalism and patriarchy established themselves as mutually supporting systems. It would be quite conceivable to rework these discussions through the framework of orders and class.

These examples further question any simple, unilinear account of the process of industrialisation and the rise of capitalist societies. They also point to a variety of possible ways in which sociologists and historians can cooperate together, in studying a social process which is more complex than the 'combined and uneven' development of economic forces. It suggests ways in which pre-capitalist forms (and orders) are maintained and reproduced during the process of capital accumulation. In particular it poses questions about Marx's use of England as a classic case of proletarianisation, suggesting its inadequacy both in the context of Britain as a whole and as a model for explaining this process globally. A similar point could be made in relation to the process of capital formation and its relation to state power.

---

[51] See K. Tenfelde, 'Mining festivals in the nineteenth century', *Journal of Contemporary History* 13 (1977); and also, H. Beynon and T. Austrin, 'The iconography of the Durham Miners' Gala', *Historical Sociology*, 2 (1989): 66 – 82.

[52] See P. Corrigan, 'Feudal relics or capitalist monuments', *Sociological Review* n.s. 24 (1976).

There is clearly a need to understand class analysis in relation to a complex and variable pattern of historical change. In this, the question of whether all the critical features of this process are determined by, and are understandable through, the process of class formation is a moot point. Undoubtedly pre-capitalist relations such as those based around sex and gender are maintained to different degrees and give weight to the capitalist forms which are established. It is possible to see the labour process and the commodity markets operating in similar ways providing a context within which the fields of class relationships are established. Here the renewed interest in the writings of Polanyi (and his sense of economic relationships being 'embedded' in social relationships) is both helpful and illustrative of the ways in which a broad range of theoretical ideas is now being brought to bear on the enduring questions of order and change.[53] That, in this firmament, the debate over class rages anew is not surprising: for in this age-old concept is condensed a range of ideas and problems associated with understanding historical changes and contemporary society. It is, in its very nature, a contested and contestable concept and talk of its death is greatly exaggerated.

[53] See K. Polanyi, *The Great Transformation: The Political and Economic Origins of our Time* (Boston, 1944), and G. Dalton (ed.) *Primitive, Archaic and Modern Economies: Essays on Karl Polanyi* (Boston, 1971).

Suggestions for further reading

CHAPTER 1: THE LANGUAGE OF ORDERS IN EARLY MODERN EUROPE

R.M. Berdahl, *The Politics of the Prussian Nobility* (Princeton, 1988).

E.A.R. Brown, 'Georges Duby and the three orders', *Viator* 17 (1986).

G. Duby, *The Three Orders: Feudal Society Imagined* (Chicago, 1980).

E. Labrousse (ed.) *Ordres et classes* (Paris, 1973).

R. Mousnier, *Social Hierarchies: 1450 to the Present* (London, 1973).

R. Mousnier, *Problèmes de stratification sociale* (Paris, 1968).

O. Niccoli, *I sacerdoti, i guerrieri, i contadini: storia di un immagine della società* (Turin, 1979).

S. Ossowski, *Class Structure in the Social Consciousness* (London, 1963).

W.H. Sewell, 'Etat, corps and ordre: some notes on the social vocabulary of the French old regime', in H.-U. Wehler (ed.) *Sozialgeschichte Heute* (Göttingen, 1974).

CHAPTER 2: THE CONCEPT OF CLASS

W. Doyle, *Origins of the French Revolution* (Oxford, 1988, 2nd edn).

G. Eley and D. Blackbourn, *The Peculiarities of German History: Bourgeois Society and Politics in Nineteenth-Century Germany* (Oxford, 1984).

L. Hunt, *Politics, Culture and Class in the French Revolution* (Berkeley, 1984).

G. Stedman Jones, *Languages of Class: Studies in English Working Class History, 1832–1982* (Cambridge, 1983).

P. Joyce, *Work, Society, and Politics: the Culture of the Factory in Later Victorian England* (Brighton, 1980).

J. Rancière, *The Nights of Labor: the Workers' Dreams in Nineteenth-Century France*, trans. J. Drury (Philadelphia, 1989).

W. Schieder (ed.) *Liberalismus in der Gesellschaft des deutschen Vormärz* (Göttingen, 1983).

W.H. Sewell, jr, *Work and Revolution in France: the Language of Labor from the Old Regime to 1848* (Cambridge, 1983).

J.J. Sheehan, *German Liberalism in the Nineteenth Century* (Chicago, 1978).

E.P. Thompson, *The Making of the English Working Class* (London, 1963).

M. Walker, *German Home Towns: Community, State and General Estate, 1648–1871* (Ithaca, 1971).

CHAPTER 3: AN ANATOMY OF NOBILITY

Comparative studies

M.L. Bush, *Noble Privilege* (Manchester, 1983).

M.L. Bush, *Rich Noble, Poor Noble* (Manchester, 1988).

J.-P. Labatut, *Les Noblesses européennes de la fin du XVe siècle à la fin du XVIIIe siècle* (Paris, 1978).

J. Meyer, *Noblesses et pouvoirs dans l'Europe d'ancien régime* (Paris, 1973).

M.J. Sayer, *English Nobility, the Gentry, the Heralds and the Continental Context* (Norwich, 1979).

O. Subtelny, *Domination of Eastern Europe: Native Nobilities and Foreign Absolutism, 1500–1715* (Gloucester, 1986).

Collective studies

I. Banac and P. Bushkovitch (eds.) *The Nobility in Russia and Eastern Europe* (New Haven, 1983).

B. Köpeczi and E.H. Balázs, *Noblesse française, noblesse hongroise, XVIe–XIXe siècles* (Budapest/Paris, 1981).

Individual studies

M.L. Bush, *The English Aristocracy* (Manchester, 1984).

S. Becker, *Nobility and Privilege in Late Imperial Russia* (Dekalb, 1985).

R.M. Berdahl, *The Politics of the Prussian Nobility* (Princeton, 1988).

F.L. Carsten, *A History of the Prussian Junkers* (Aldershot, 1989).

A. Dominguez Ortiz, *Las clases privilegiadas en la España del antiguo régimen* (Madrid, 1973).

J.K. Fedorowicz (ed.) *A Republic of Nobles: Studies in Polish History to 1864* (Cambridge, 1982).

R. Forster, *Merchants, Landlords, Magistrates: the Depont Family in Eighteenth-Century France* (Baltimore, 1980).

S.A. Hansen, 'Changes in the wealth and the demographic characteristics of the Danish aristocracy, 1450–1720', *Third International Conference of Economic History*, IV (Munich, 1965), pp. 91ff.

B. Meehan-Waters, *Autocracy and Aristocracy: the Russian Service Elite of 1730* (New Jersey, 1982).

J. Meyer, 'Les nobles français au XVIIIe siècle', *Acta Poloniae Historica* 36 (1977).

J. Nicolas, *La Savoie au XVIIIe siècle: Noblesse et bourgeoisie* (Paris, 1977).

O. Odlozilik, 'The nobility of Bohemia, 1620–1740', *East European Quarterly* 7 (1973).

A. Rössler (ed.) *Deutscher Adel, 1555–1740* (Darmstadt, 1965)

A. Schalk, *From Valor to Pedigree: Ideas of Nobility in France in the Sixteenth and Seventeenth Centuries* (Princeton, 1986).

CHAPTER 4: BETWEEN ESTATE AND PROFESSION: THE CLERGY IN IMPERIAL RUSSIA

A. Andrews, *The System of Professions* (Chicago, 1988).

F. Boulard, *Essou ou déclin du clergé français* (Paris, 1950).

E. Bryner, *Der geistliche Stand in Rußland im 18. Jahrhundert* (Göttingen, 1982).

K.-W. Dham, *Beruf: Pfarrer. Empirische Aspekte* (Munich 1971).

P. Elliott, *The Sociology of the Professions* (London, 1972).

G.L. Freeze, 'The *soslovie* (estate) paradigm and Russian social history'; *American Historical Review* 91 (1986): 11 – 36.

G.L. Freeze, *The Parish Clergy in Nineteenth-Century Russia: Crisis, Reform, Counter-Reform* (Princeton, 1983).

G.L. Freeze, *The Russian Levites: Parish Clergy in the Eighteenth Century* (Cambridge, Mass., 1977).

J.H.M. Geekie, 'Church and politics in Russia, 1900 – 1917: a study of political behavior of the Russian Orthodox Church in the reign of Nicholas II' (PhD, East Anglia, 1976).

A. Haig, *The Victorian Clergy* (London, 1984).

R.A. Hanneman and E.T. Gargan, 'Recruitment to the clergy in nineteenth-century France', *Journal of Interdisciplinary History* 9 (1978): 275 – 96.

B. Heeney, *A Different Kind of Gentleman* (Hamden, Conn., 1976).

P. Huot-Pleuroux, *Le Recrutement sacerdotal dans le diocèse de Besançon de 1801 à 1960* (Paris, 1966).

M.S. Larson, *The Rise of Professionalism: a Sociological Analysis* (Berkeley, 1977).

D. Mannsaker, *Det norske presteskapt i det 19. Hundret* (Oslo, 1954).

A. Neher, *Die katholische und evangelische Geistlichkeit Württembergs 1817 – 1901* (Ravensburg, 1904).

R. Norrman, *Fran prästöverflöd till prästbrist. Prästrykryteringen i Uppsala Ärkestift 1786 – 1965* (Uppsala, 1970).

A. Russell, *The Clerical Profession* (London, 1980).

H. Werdermann, *Der evangelische Pfarrer in Geschichte und Gegenwart* (Leipzig, 1925).

N.D. Zol'nikova, *Soslovnye problemy vo vzaimootnosheniiakh Tserkvi i gosudarstva v Sibiri (XVIII v.)* (Novosibirsk, 1981).

CHAPTER 5: BETWEEN ESTATE AND PROFESSION: THE CATHOLIC PARISH CLERGY OF EARLY MODERN WESTERN EUROPE

O. Chadwick, *The Popes and the European Revolution* (Oxford, 1981).

Diccionario de Historia Ecclesiastica de España (Madrid 1972 – 5) 4 vols.

C. Hermann, *L'Église d'Espagne sous le patronage royal 1469 – 1834* (Madrid, 1988).

P.T. Hoffman, *Church and Community in the Diocese of Lyon 1500 – 1789* (New Haven, 1984).

D. Julia and D. McKee, 'Le Clergé paroissial dans le diocèse de Reims sous l'épiscopat de Charles-Maurice Le Tellier: origines et carrières', *Revue d'Histoire Moderne et Contemporaine* 29 (1982): 529 – 83.

J. Quéniart, *Les hommes, l'église et dieu dans la France du xviiie siècle* (Paris, 1978).

R. Rémond and J. Le Goff (eds) *Histoire de la France religieuse* (Paris, 1988), vol. ii.

C. Russo, *Società, chiesa e vita religiosa nell'ancien régime* (Naples, 1976).

T. Tackett, *Religion, Revolution and Regional Culture in Eighteenth-Century France* (Princeton, 1986).

R.G. Villoslada (ed.) *Historia de la iglesia en España* (Madrid, 1979), vol. iv.

CHAPTER 6: THE MIDDLE CLASSES IN LATE TSARIST RUSSIA

S. Becker, *Nobility and Privilege in Late Imperial Russia* (Dekalb, Ill., 1985).

E. Clowes, S. Kassow and J. West, (eds) *Between Tsar and People* (Princeton, 1990).

P. Gatrell, *The Tsarist Economy, 1850 – 1917* (London, 1986).

V.R. Leikina-Svirskaia, *Intelligentsiia v Rossii vo vtoroi polovine XIX veka* (Moskva, 1971).

V.R. Leikina-Svirskaia, *Russkaia intelligentsiia v 1900 – 1917 godakh* (Moscow, 1981).

T. Owen, *Capitalism and Politics in Russia: a Social History of the Moscow Merchants, 1855 – 1905* (Cambridge, 1981).

A. Rieber, *Merchants and Entrepreneurs in Imperial Russia* (Chapel Hill, NC, 1982).

J.A. Ruckman, *The Moscow Business Elite: a Social and Cultural Portrait of Two Generations, 1840 – 1905* (Dekalb, Ill., 1984).

L.E. Shepelev, *Otmenennye istoriei: chiny, zvaniia i tituly v Rossiiskoi imperii* (Leningrad, 1977).

C. Timberlake, 'Higher learning, the state, and the professions in late Tsarist Russia', in K. Jarausch (ed.) *The Transformation of Higher Learning, 1860 – 1930* (Chicago, 1983).

Ia. E. Vodarskii, *Naselenie Rossii za 400 let (XVI – nachalo XX vv)* (Moscow, 1973).

CHAPTER 7: FROM 'MIDDLING SORT' TO MIDDLE CLASS IN LATE EIGHTEENTH- AND EARLY NINETEENTH-CENTURY ENGLAND

J.A. Banks, *Prosperity and Parenthood: a Study of Family Planning among the Victorian Middle Classes* (London, 1954).

L. Davidoff and C. Hall, *Family Fortunes: Men and Women of the English Middle Class 1780 – 1850* (London, 1987).

J. Field, 'Wealth, styles of life and social tone amongst Portsmouth's middle class, 1800 – 1875', in R.J. Morris (ed.) *Class, Power and Social Structure in British Nineteenth-Century Towns* (Leicester, 1986).

J. Foster, *Class Struggle and the Industrial Revolution: Early Industrial Capitalism in Three English Towns* (London, 1974).

S. Gunn, 'The "failure" of the Victorian middle class: a critique', in J. Wolff and J. Seed (eds) *The Culture of Capital: Art, Power and the Nineteeth-Century Middle Class* (Manchester, 1988).

P. Joyce, *Work, Society and Politics: the Culture of the Factory in Later Victorian England* (Brighton, 1980).

H. Perkin, *The Origins of Modern English Society 1780 – 1880* (London, 1969).

W.D. Rubinstein, *Men of Property: the Very Wealthy in Britain since the Industrial Revolution* (London, 1981).

J. Seed, 'Theologies of power: Unitarianism and the social relations of religious discourse, 1800 – 50', in R.J. Morris (ed.) *Class, Power and Social Structure in British Nineteenth-Century Towns* (Leicester, 1986).

CHAPTER 8: TENANT RIGHT AND THE PEASANTRIES OF EUROPE UNDER THE OLD REGIME

Overviews

J. Blum, *The End of the Old Order in Rural Europe* (Princeton, 1978).

M.L. Bush, 'Seigneurial rights', in *Noble Privilege* (Manchester, 1983), ch. VI.

C. Lis and H. Soly, *Poverty and Capitalism in Pre-Industrial Europe* (Brighton, 1979).

S.J. Watts, *A Social History of Western Europe, 1450 – 1720: Tensions and Solidarities among Rural People* (London, 1984).

Free Peasantries

P. Goubert, *The French Peasantry in the Seventeenth Century* (Cambridge, 1986).

P.M. Jones, *The Peasantry in the French Revolution* (Cambridge, 1988).

D.W. Sabean, *Power in the Blood: Popular Culture and Village Discourse in Early Modern Germany* (Cambridge, 1984).

D.E. Vassberg, *Land and Society in Golden Age Castile* (Cambridge, 1984).

Serf Peasantries

W.W. Hagen, 'How mighty the Junkers? Peasant rents and seigneurial profits in sixteenth-century Brandenburg', *Past and Present* 108 (1985): 80 – 116.

W.W. Hagen, 'The Junkers' faithless servants: peasant insubordination and the breakdown of serfdom in Brandenburg-Prussia, 1763 – 1811', in R.J. Evans and W.R. Lee (eds) *The German Peasantry* (London, 1986).

H. Harnisch, 'Peasants and markets: the background to agrarian reforms in feudal Prussia east of the Elbe, 1760 – 1807', in R.J. Evans and W.R. Lee (eds) *The German Peasantry* (London, 1986).

S.L. Hoch, *Serfdom and Social Control in Russia* (Chicago, 1986).

A. Klima, 'Agrarian class structure and economic development in pre-industrial Bohemia', *Past and Present* 85 (1979): 49 – 67.

H.E. Melton, 'Serfdom and the peasant economy in Russia, 1780 – 1861' (PhD, Columbia University, 1984).

H. Rebel, *Peasant Classes: the Bureaucratisation of Property and Family Relations under Early Habsburg Absolutism, 1511 – 1636* (Princeton, 1983).

'Symposium on neo-serfdom', *Slavic Review* 34 (1975).

CHAPTER 9: DEFERENTIAL BITTERNESS: THE SOCIAL OUTLOOK OF THE RURAL PROLETARIAT IN EIGHTEENTH- AND NINETEENTH-CENTURY ENGLAND AND WALES

J. Arch, *The Autobiography of Joseph Arch* (London, 1898, 1966).

G. Edwards, *From Crow-Scaring to Westminster* (London, 1922).

F.E. Green, *The Tyranny of the Countryside* (London, 1913).

J.L. Hammond and B. Hammond, *The Village Labourer* (London, 1911, 1978).

E.J. Hobsbawm and G. Rudé, *Captain Swing* (London, 1969).

A. Howkins, *Poor Labouring Men: Rural Radicalism in Norfolk, 1870 – 1923* (London, 1985).

D.J.V. Jones, *Rebecca's Children: a Study of Rural Society, Crime, and protest* (Oxford, 1989).

H. Newby, *The Deferential Worker* (London, 1977).

K.D.M. Snell, *Annals of the Labouring Poor: Social Change and Agrarian England, 1660 – 1900* (Cambridge, 1985).

A. Somerville, *The Whistler at the Plough* (Manchester, 1852; repr. London, 1989).

G. Sturt, *Change in the Village* (London, 1912).

D. Williams, *The Rebecca Riots: a Study in Agrarian Discontent* (Cardiff, 1955).

CHAPTER 10: ORDER, CLASS AND THE URBAN POOR

Contemporary

F.M. Eden, *The State of the Poor* (London, 1797).

J.M. de Gérando, *The Visitor of the Poor* (London, 1833).

J.M. de Gérando, *De la Bienfaisance Publique* (Brussels, 1839).

J.L. Vives, *De Subventione Pauperum* (Bruges, 1526).

Secondary

C.C. Fairchilds, *Poverty and Charity in Aix-en-Provence, 1670 – 1789* (Baltimore, 1976).

J.A. Garraty, *Unemployment in History: Economic Thought and Public Policy* (New York, 1978).

J.P. Gutton, *La Société et les pauvres en Europe (XVIe – XVIIIe siècles)* (Paris, 1974).

O. Hufton, *The Poor of Eighteenth-Century France 1750 – 1789* (Oxford, 1974).

C. Jones, *Charity and Bienfaisance: the Treatment of the Poor in the Montpellier Region, 1740 – 1815* (Cambridge, 1982).

P. Joyce (ed.) *The Historical Meanings of Work* (Cambridge, 1987).

C. Lis and H. Soly, *Poverty and Capitalism in Pre-Industrial Europe* (Brighton, 1979).

L. Martz, *Poverty and Welfare in Habsburg Spain: the Example of Toledo* (Cambridge, 1983).

J.R. Poynter, *Society and Pauperism. English Ideas on Poor Relief 1795 – 1934* (London, 1969).

B.S. Pullan, *Rich and Poor in Renaissance Venice* (Oxford, 1971).

T. Riis (ed.) *Aspects of Poverty in Early Modern Europe*, vol. 1 (Florence, 1981), vol. 2 (Odense, 1986), vol. 3. (Odense, 1990).

P. Townsend (ed.) *The Concept of Poverty* (London, 1970).

K. Williams, *From Pauperism to Poverty* (London, 1981).

S. Woolf, *The Poor in Western Europe in the Eighteenth and Nineteenth Centuries* (London, 1986).

CHAPTER 11: A PEOPLE AND A CLASS: INDUSTRIAL WORKERS AND THE SOCIAL ORDER IN NINETEENTH-CENTURY ENGLAND

J. Bratton (ed.) *The Victorian Music Hall: Performance and Style* (Milton Keynes, 1987).

J. Foster, *Class Struggle and the Industrial Revolution* (London, 1974).

P.N. Furbank, *Unholy Pleasure: the Idea of Social Class* (London, 1985).

L. Hunt (ed.) *The New Cultural History* (Berkeley, 1989).

P. Joyce, *Work, Society and Politics: the Culture of the Factory in Later Victorian England* (Brighton, 1980).

P. Joyce, 'Work', in F.M.L. Thompson (ed.) *Cambridge Social History of Great Britain 1750 – 1950*, vol. II (Cambridge, 1990).

P. Joyce, *Visions of the People: Industrial England and the Question of Class c. 1848 – 1914* (Cambridge, 1991).

I. Katznelson and A.R. Zolberg (eds) *Working-Class Formation: Nineteenth-Century Patterns in Western Europe and the United States* (London, 1986).

W.M. Reddy, *Money and Liberty in Modern Europe: a Critique of Historial Understanding* (Cambridge, 1987).

G. Stedman Jones, *Language of Class* (Cambridge, 1983).

M. Vicinus, *The Industrial Muse* (London, 1974).

D.G. Wright, *Popular Radicalism: the Working-Class Experience 1780 – 1880* (London, 1988).

Notes on contributors

Joseph Bergin is a Senior Lecturer in Modern History at Manchester University. His publications include *Cardinal Richelieu: Power and the Pursuit of Wealth* (London, 1985) and *Cardinal de la Rochefoucauld: Leadership and Reform in the French Church* (London, 1987).

Huw Beynon is a Professor of Sociology at Manchester University. His publications include *Working for Ford* (London, 1973) and (with Theo Nichols) *Living with Capitalism: Class Relations and the Modern Factory* (London, 1977).

Peter Burke is a Reader in History at Cambridge University. His publications include *Popular Culture in Early Modern Europe* (London, 1978) and *The Historical Anthropology of Early Modern Italy* (Cambridge, 1987).

M.L. Bush is a Reader in History at Manchester University. His publications include *Noble Privilege* (Manchester, 1983) and *Rich Noble, Poor Noble* (Manchester, 1988).

William Doyle is a Professor of Modern History at Bristol University. His publications include *The Old European Order, 1660 – 1800* (Oxford, 1978) and *The Oxford History of the French Revolution* (Oxford, 1989).

Gregory L. Freeze is a Professor of Comparative History at Brandeis University, Massachusetts. His publications include *The Russian Levites: Parish Clergy in the Eighteenth Century* (London, 1977) and *The Parish Clergy in Nineteenth Century Russia: Crisis, Reform and Counter-Reform* (Princeton, 1983).

Patrick Joyce is a Lecturer in Modern History at Manchester University. His publications include *Work, Society and Politics: the Culture of the Factory in Later Victorian England* (Brighton, 1980) and *Visions of the People: Industrial England and the Question of Class, c. 1848-1914* (Cambridge, 1991)

William M. Reddy is a Professor of Modern History at Duke University, North Carolina. His publications include *The Rise of Market Culture: the Textile Trade in French Society, 1750 – 1900* (Cambridge, 1984) and *Money and Liberty in Western Europe* (Cambridge, 1987).

John Seed is a Senior Lecturer in History at the Roehampton Institute, London. His publications include (with Janet Wolff) *The Culture of Capital: Art, Power and the Nineteenth-Century Middle Class* (Manchester, 1988). He is Reviews Editor of *Social History*.

K.D.M. Snell is a Lecturer in Local History at Leicester University. His publications include *Annals of the Labouring Poor: Social Change and Agrarian England, 1660 – 1900* (Cambridge, 1985). He is Editor of *Rural History*.

Charles E. Timberlake is a Professor of Russian History at the University of Missouri. His publications include *Essays in Russian Liberalism* (Columbia, Missouri, 1972) and *Detente: A Documentary Record* (London, 1978).

Stuart Woolf is a Professor of Modern History at the European Institute, Florence and Essex University. His publications include *A History of Italy, 1700 – 1860: the Social Constraints of Political Change* (London, 1979) and *The Poor in Western Europe in the Eighteenth and Nineteenth Centuries* (London, 1986).

Index

GAS TURBINE COMBUSTION